Robert Lowell
Life and Art

Robert Lowell
Life and Art

Steven Gould Axelrod

Princeton University Press
Princeton, New Jersey

Copyright © 1978 by Princeton University Press
Published by Princeton University Press, Princeton, New Jersey
In the United Kindgom: Princeton University Press,
Guildford, Surrey

All Rights Reserved
Library of Congress Cataloging in Publication Data will be
found on the last printed page of this book

Publication of this book has been aided by a grant from
the Paul Mellon Fund of Princeton University Press

This book has been composed in VIP Palatino

Clothbound editions of Princeton University Press books
are printed on acid-free paper, and binding materials are
chosen for strength and durability.

Printed in the United States of America by Princeton
University Press, Princeton, New Jersey

"I scarcely know where to begin," Emily Dickinson once wrote, "but love is always a safe place." This book is for Rise, and for our son Jeremiah.

Contents

List of Illustrations

Acknowledgments

I am very grateful to Robert Lowell and to Anne Sexton, both of whom graciously answered my questions. I am pleased to be able to thank the other poets who generously helped me: Frank Bidart, Richard Eberhart, Isabella Gardner, James Laughlin, W. D. Snodgrass, and Allen Tate. My greatest debt in writing this book is to Richard Lehan, who after six years knows all too well "what I have worked through." Parts of my manuscript have also been read and criticized by Rise B. Axelrod, Calvin Bedient, B. Bernard Cohen, Edwin Fussell, Bruce Kawin, Lee Lemmon, Stephen Yenser, and my colleagues at Riverside, John Ganim and Marshall Van Deusen. All have saved me from more errors and infelicities than I like to contemplate. Jerome Mazzaro provided me with helpful advice at a crucial stage. I am more indebted to the entire body of Lowell criticism than my notes can possibly indicate.

Thanks are due to the following: Rodney Dennis and the staff of the Houghton Library at Harvard for allowing me to study the manuscripts and correspondence in the Robert Lowell Collection (helpfully catalogued by Patrick Miehe); Richard Ludwig of the Princeton University Library for providing me with correspondence from the Allen Tate Collection and for helping in other ways; Karl Gay and the staff of the Lockwood Memorial Library at Buffalo, Donald Gallup and the staff of the Bieneke Library at Yale, and Else Albrecht-Carrié of New Directions for allowing me to study manuscripts and correspondence in the William Carlos Williams Collections at Buffalo and Yale; Holly Hall and the staff of Washington University Library for allowing me to study materials in the Modern Poetry Collection; Walter W. Wright of the Baker Memorial

Acknowledgments

Library at Dartmouth for providing me with correspondence from the Richard Eberhart Collection; Thomas B. Greenslade and William T. Dameron of the Chalmers Memorial Library at Kenyon for providing me with Lowell photographs and materials; Mary Lee Cox of the St. Mark's School Library; Saundra Taylor of the Lilly Library at Indiana University; Jack Jackson of the Library of the Boston Athenaeum; R. Jackson Smith, photographer; Wilson Davis of the University of North Carolina, Greensboro; and the staffs of the UCLA Library, the Boston University Library, the Library of Congress, the Thomas Jefferson Library of the University of Missouri-St. Louis, the Huntington Library, and the Library of the University of California, Riverside.

I have benefited from the efficiency of my typist, Clara Dean; from the perspicacity of my wonderful research assistants, Joyce McLean and Denis Jones; and from the support of R. Miriam Brokaw, Marjorie Sherwood, and Judith May of Princeton University Press. I am also pleased to acknowledge financial support received from the Research Committee of the University of California, Riverside.

Thanks are due to the editors of *American Quarterly*, *Bucknell Review*, *Contemporary Literature*, and *Pacific Coast Philology* for allowing me to reprint portions of this book that first appeared in their journals.

Method of Citation

To avoid strewing numbers across my pages, I have placed all documentary references in single notes placed at the end of paragraphs. As often as possible, I have included my page references to Robert Lowell's volumes parenthetically in the text, with the following abbreviations:

LU   *Land of Unlikeness*. Cummington, Mass.: Cummington Press, 1944

LWC   *Lord Weary's Castle*. New York: Harcourt Brace, 1946

MK   *The Mills of the Kavanaughs*. New York: Harcourt Brace, 1951

LS   *Life Studies*. New York: Farrar, Straus & Cudahy, 1959

I   *Imitations*. New York: Farrar, Straus & Giroux, 1961

FUD   *For the Union Dead*. New York: Farrar, Straus & Giroux, 1964

OG   *The Old Glory*. 1964; rev. ed., New York: Farrar, Straus & Giroux, 1968

NO   *Near the Ocean*. New York: Farrar, Straus & Giroux, 1967

PB   *Prometheus Bound*. New York: Farrar, Straus & Giroux, 1969

N 1967-68   *Notebook 1967-68*. New York: Farrar, Straus & Giroux, 1969

N   *Notebook*. New York: Farrar, Straus & Giroux, 1970

H   *History*. New York: Farrar, Straus & Giroux, 1973

FLH   *For Lizzie and Harriet*. New York: Farrar, Straus & Giroux, 1973

D   *The Dolphin*. New York: Farrar, Straus & Giroux, 1973

DBD   *Day by Day*. New York: Farrar, Straus & Giroux, 1977

Robert Lowell
Life and Art

"What is the price of Experience do men buy it for a song
Or wisdom for a dance in the street? No it is bought with the price
Of all that a man hath. . . ."—*William Blake*

"One's cry of O Jerusalem becomes little by little a cry to something a little nearer and nearer until at last one cries out to a living name, a living place, a living thing, and in crying out confesses openly all the bitter secretions of experience."—*Wallace Stevens*

§ I §

Introduction: Lowell's Poetry
of Experience

The province of art is all life, all feeling, all
observation, all vision. . . . It is all experience.
—*James, "The Art of Fiction"*

"Risk was his métier," Lowell said of Ulysses, a symbol
of himself. Throughout his career, Lowell demonstrated an
astonishing willingness and ability to make his writing
new. "My books have changed," he once explained. "It
doesn't really matter whether one style is better than the
last. When it no longer serves, you must adventure." Despite this characteristic modesty, he was an ambitious
poet, and like other American poets before him—Whitman, Pound, Williams, Eliot—he spoke with different
voices. Each of his books embodies his struggle to find a
way to say the thing he had then to say. None succeeds
completely. The books, and the individual poems, are imperfect because not fully distinct from the indeterminacy of
the life that produced them. Lowell's "failure," if we want
to call it that, is an inextricable feature of his ambition, is
indeed part of what his poems are about: his attempt to
create a language in which he could more fully realize his
being.[1]

He thus stands firmly within the main line of American
poetry. Roy Harvey Pearce has observed that "American
poems record the discovery, rediscovery, and again and
again the rediscovery of the Fall into Existence—American
Existence." Lowell's poetry microcosmically recapitulates
that repeated rediscovery. Lowell once commented that
American literature looks like "a bravado of perpetual rev-

3

olution," and so indeed does his own poetic career. He successively appeared as the passionate young rhetorician-prophet of *Lord Weary's Castle* (1946); the Frost- or Browning-like storyteller of *The Mills of the Kavanaughs* (1951); the cold-eyed, witty memoirist of *Life Studies* (1959), narrating his family history with an art disguised as candor; the translator of *Imitations* (1961); the withered observer of *For the Union Dead* (1964); the playwright of *The Old Glory* (1964) and *Prometheus Bound* (1967); the Jeremiah of *Near the Ocean* (1966); the historian-on-the-run of *Notebook* (1970) and *History* (1973); the verse novelist-autobiographer of *The Dolphin* (1973), recounting his quest for an elusive creature of joy; and, finally, the aging and introspective diarist of *Day by Day* (1977). Yet for all its dynamism, his poetic oeuvre is unified. At its center is Lowell himself, discovering, altering, creating the conditions of his own existence.[2]

Although the style of Lowell's art changed radically over the years, its essentially experiential character remained constant. "The thread that strings it together," he remarked, "is my autobiography"; "what made the earlier poems valuable seems to be some recording of experience and that seems to be what makes the later ones." "Experience" does not mean only what "happened" to Lowell, for that formulation would place too much emphasis on an active but unilateral environment, and would reduce the experiencer's mind to the passive role of a transmitting lens. The mind itself is active, trembling to "caress the light" (*DBD*, 127). "Experience" more truly means the sum of the relations and interactions between psyche and environment. It grows from the Cartesian dualism of inner and outer, but through its interpenetrating energies abolishes the dualism. Just as experience mediates between self and world, partaking of both, so Lowell's poems mediate between himself and his world, and between his personal history and that of his readers. His poems are structures of experience. They both record his life and assume a life of

4

their own; and as they transform the poet's life into the autonomous life of art, they reenter his life by clarifying and completing it.[3]

In his first published essay, a review of Yvor Winters's *Maule's Curse* in the Kenyon College student journal *Hika*, Lowell revealed himself already to be centrally concerned with the relationship of art to experience. Just past his twenty-second birthday, he wrote that "literature can only dramatize life and world that is real to it. And literary reality must be judged on perception, consistency and moral seriousness." The crudities and cruelties of mortal life in this age, in any age, are difficult to bear, and artists and readers have therefore frequently conceived of art as a medium of escape, a "world elsewhere," a "beautiful illusion." Clearly, this conception of art never had the slightest interest for Lowell. From the beginning, he viewed art and life as being closely connected. In the *Hika* review he wrote, "When we ask [Winters] 'Is interpreted experience art?,' his answer is 'No, but what art is made from.' " Lowell soon came to ask the very same question of himself; his poetry is the history of his ever more sophisticated attempts at an answer.[4]

In choosing poems from his early, privately printed book *Land of Unlikeness* to reprint two years later in his first commercial book *Lord Weary's Castle*, Lowell chose the poems that he felt were "more experienced," "more concrete." A decade later, in *Life Studies*, he rejected the impersonal and metrically regular mode of *Lord Weary's Castle* entirely because he found he "couldn't get [his] experience into tight metrical forms." In changing his style and subject matter, he turned away from the canons of Modernist formalism, precisely because Modernist esthetics, from Hulme, Eliot, and Pound on, tended to view the poem as a world of its own, lacking reference to the poet and culture that produced it. Lowell came to see that—at least for himself and perhaps for others—the relationship of art to human experience was too elemental for an "Impersonal theory of poetry," as Eliot called his own early theory, to do anything but block up the springs of inspiration. Lowell explained to Frederick Seidel in 1960 that "writing seems divorced from culture somehow. It's become too much something specialized that can't handle much experience. It's become a craft, purely a craft, and there must be some breakthrough back into life." *Life Studies*, a book about "direct experience and not symbols," was just such a breakthrough. All of Lowell's subsequent work centered around his quest for the craft and inspiration to bring even more experience into his art, and his related quest to account for the place art makes in experience.[5]

Although art and experience continued to retain an important thin edge of distinctness for Lowell—art was experience that had been "worked up," imagined into form—the two came to have an increasingly complex interrelationship in his thought. His life made his writing possible, and the ability to write saved his life and gave it meaning. As much as Emerson, Lowell believed that "the man is only half himself, the other half is his expression"; as much as Henry James, he believed that art *"makes* life." He argued that for the American writer, "the arts should be 'all out'—you're in it, you're all out in it. . . . The artist finds new life in his art and almost sheds his other life." Over and over again his later poems return to the interrelatedness of "one life, one writing" (*FUD*, 68). One of the loveliest expressions of this idea occurs at the conclusion of *The Dolphin*, in which Lowell accepts responsibility for his book as he accepts responsibility for his life:

> My eyes have seen what my hand did.
>
> (D, 78)

The hand has written that which the eyes have previously seen, that which the I has experienced. But also, the eyes have seen, the I has experienced and acknowledges, the hand as it writes.[6]

Lowell did not write poems in hopes of achieving immortal fame, "grass on the minor slopes of Parnassus" (*H*, 194). His "open book," he suggests in *History*, amounts to no more than an "open coffin," doomed like his corporeal self to perish in time, though more slowly. Poetry had an entirely different value for Lowell, an existential value: it proved its maker was "alive" (*H*, 194). Thus he viewed himself as engaged in the quintessential labor of the American poet. For the difference between American and other writers, he once argued, is that in America "the artist's existence becomes his art. He is reborn in it, and he hardly exists without it."[7]

Believing that "the artist's existence becomes his art," Lowell made himself into the classic figure of the American poet, a Whitman for our time, though a more tragic one, as befits our time. Like Whitman's, his conception of poetry closely resembles that of Ralph Waldo Emerson. Emerson has been variously termed "the central figure in American poetry" (Hyatt Waggoner), a "hovering presence" in the work of virtually every American writer (Richard Poirier), and "our prophet" (Harold Bloom). More to the point, Lowell himself called Emerson "the beginning of American literature" and a "master." Therefore, a brief consideration of Emerson's ideas about poetry may help us to view Lowell's poetry in a clearer light—the light of his literary inheritance.[8]

In his key essay "The Poet" (1844), Emerson formulated a theory of poetry that in part acknowledged tendencies already manifest in American culture and in part organized those tendencies as a main tradition for future American writing. Emerson's conception of poetry was founded on the doctrine of experience. He argued that "skill and command of language" cannot by themselves produce a real poem. Rather, poetry results from the passionate, living articulation of life, of the mind's experience of itself and its

7

Introduction

world. The poet, for Emerson, is a teller of news, for he "was present and privy to the appearance which he describes." False poets write "from the fancy, at a safe distance from their own experience," while the true poet "traverses the whole scale of experience" and gives that experience expression. Thus true poetry is neither a vehicle of escape from life nor a mere exhibition of craft, but rather an opportunity for the poet to "tell us how it was with him." By defining "imagination" as "a very high sort of seeing, which does not come by study, but by the intellect being where and what it sees," Emerson sought to blur categorical distinctions between mind and world, ideal and real, word and deed, art and life. The poem, indeed, inhabits the place where each of these linked pairs meets. Such a poetry, though based on the individual life, ultimately proves not solipsistic but on the contrary "representative," for it democratically assumes that humanity's essential perceptions are common. It possesses (as Lowell said of Emerson's own writing) the quality of "specific generality." Although Lowell's metaphysics differed from Emerson's, he wrote out of a neo-Emersonian conviction that poetry is "neither transport nor a technique" but rather a verbal manifesting of experience that itself takes its place within experience. Robert Lowell, like Emerson, lived in his art, at the place where deed meets word, or in his own terms, where "what really happened" connects with the "good line."[9]

Lowell's esthetic places his art at the center of American literary tradition. In his seminal essay on this topic, "The Cult of Experience in American Writing," Philip Rahv termed the affirmation of individual experience the "basic theme and unifying principle" of American writing. Rooted in Puritan antinomianism, fostered by Jeffersonian democratic idealism, and formulated most eloquently by Emerson, this theme preoccupies the American literary mind. Whether the protagonist is Hester Prynne or Isabel Archer breaking out of conventionality through intense

8

personal suffering; Huck Finn or Jake Barnes trusting his own senses in opposition to society's conventional unwisdom and a friend's illusory book learning; Ishmael going to sea, Thoreau going to Walden, or Ike McCaslin going to the woods; Henry Adams perceiving his life as a perpetual quest for self-education; Lambert Strether learning painfully to live, and even more important, to *see*; Ellison's Invisible Man deciding to live out his own absurdity rather than die for the absurdity of others; or Augie March playing Columbus of the near at hand—the principle is always the same, the growth of consciousness and the deepened sense of personal identity resulting from immersion in firsthand experience. The greatest nineteenth-century poets, too, refused to "take things at second or third hand," as Whitman put it. We accompany Whitman creating his identity on the open road or in the populous city, and Dickinson creating hers in her house and garden. In the twentieth century, however, the Modernist notion of impersonal objectivity tended temporarily to obscure this interest in personal experience. In most of the poems of high Modernism, there is no *self* among the objects; or, as critics of *The Waste Land* have begun to show, the self is there all right, but under cover of the objects, as if in frightened awe of itself. Yet though the self is hidden, the world remains extraordinarily present in these poems. And our need to live in that world and have the world live in us remains the crucial theme, whether in the form of Pound vaunting (and later proving) his ability to "know at first hand," Stevens asserting that "the greatest poverty is not to live in a physical world," Moore insisting on real toads in her imaginary gardens, Crane voyaging through "the world dimensional," or Williams evoking the everyday objects upon which "so much depends." American literature, with Emerson as its prophet, understands the individual's existence-in-the-world as both the overwhelming problem and the source of redemption.[10]

Thus, in the radically experiential and existential qual-

Introduction

ities of his poetry, Lowell continues the central quest of the
American imagination. But his accomplishment is even
more significant than that. He has made himself an Emersonian "reconciler" for our time. For despite the wholeness
advocated by Emerson and exemplified in good measure
by Whitman, experience in American literature has tended
to fragment itself. Early in this century Van Wyck Brooks
lambasted American culture for failing to achieve an organic conception of life. Rather, Brooks argued, American
literature drifts chaotically between two extremes—the extremes, simply put, of understanding experience intellectually and understanding it through the emotions. Brooks
applied to these extremes his celebrated labels "highbrow"
and "lowbrow," and termed the failure of our writers to
synthesize the two "a deadlock in the American mind."
This kind of dualism may have originated, as Edwin Fussell has suggested, in America's divided loyalties between
Old World and Western Frontier; or it may have originated
in class difference. Whatever its source, some version of
the highbrow-lowbrow dualism has been discerned by
most students of American literature. Philip Rahv, for
example, argued that American literature composes itself
into a debate between "palefaces" and "redskins." The
"palefaces" (Henry James, T. S. Eliot, and Allen Tate
would belong to this party) produce a patrician art which is
intellectual, symbolic, cosmopolitan, disciplined, cultured.
The "redskins" (Walt Whitman and William Carlos Williams would tend to belong here) produce a plebeian art
which is emotional, naturalistic, nativist, energetic, in
some sense *un*cultured. Seen from individual critical perspectives, this dichotomy, or a closely related one, has
been variously termed "genteel" and "barbaric" (Santayana), "genteel" and "Indian" (Lawrence), "mythic"
and "Adamic" (Pearce), and, in an appropriation of Emerson's terms, "the party of memory" and "the party of
hope" (R.W.B. Lewis). All such formulations attest to a
basic bifurcation in American literature between writers

who experience primarily with the head and those who experience primarily with the blood. This dualism appears within Lowell's poetic career as well, as he felt himself caught between two competing kinds of poetry whose extreme forms he called (echoing Lévi-Strauss) "cooked" and "raw." The two strongest individual influences on his artistic development were first the "paleface" Tate, and then the "redskin" Williams. But like the very greatest of American poets, Lowell tried to diminish this split, to repair the "broken circuit" of American culture. His goal was not the middlebrow's bland insensitivity to *any* kind of experience, but rather the unified central vision of what Emerson termed "the complete man" among partial men.[11]

To borrow one of his own metaphors, Lowell's poetry "clutches only life," for it is based on his belief that "art and the life blood of experience can't live without each other." In the following chapters of this book, I document his major poetic changes, which grew out of his deepening sense of the relationship between art and experience. In his youthful period, under the direct tutelage of Allen Tate and the pervasive influence of T. S. Eliot, Lowell fit his personal experience into impersonal mythic patterns. He conceived of his life as being in service to the poetic idea, as needing to be depersonalized and transformed into art. He constructed verbal icons out of his experience, the most ambitious and powerful of these being "The Quaker Graveyard in Nantucket." In his second, "revolutionary" phase, he learned, under the approving eye of William Carlos Williams, to bring his undisguised personal experience to the forefront of his poetry. Exercising a brilliantly original art, he produced an album of "photographs" of experience, his Confessional masterpiece *Life Studies*. In the third, long period of his maturity, Lowell

11

continued to explore the domain along the boundary where life meets art. He now conceived of experience as being more inward than in his *Life Studies* stage: not isolable events from the past but a fusion of immediate impressions with consciousness itself. Experience in this sense, as T. S. Eliot wrote long ago, is indefinable except that it is "more real than anything else." In the great poems of this period—"For the Union Dead," the "Near the Ocean" sequence, and *The Dolphin*—Lowell revealed the truth of a human heart and mind, his own.[12]

Lowell's poetry of experience presents both danger and opportunity. The very word "experience"—signifying a trial, a putting to the test, an experiment, in Lowell's phrase a "working through"—implies risk. There is point in the fact that "peril" lies half-hidden within it. Yet the peril is redeemed by the reward: a poetry that unites the values of artistic creation with more universal human values. Lowell's poems plunge into, and thereby affirm for himself and for us all, the infinite possibilities for human life in the actual world. They embody a complex process of clarifying and thus culminating his experience; and then, since poems are themselves real, they take their rightful place within experience, leaving author and reader alike altered. Lowell once said of Thoreau that the most wonderful and necessary thing about his life was the courageous hand that wrote it down. The words apply equally to himself.[13]

Lowell described himself composing in this way:

I lie on a bed staring, crossing out, writing in, crossing out what was written in, again and again, through days and weeks. Heavenly hours of absorption and idleness . . . intuition, intelligence, pursuing my ear that knows not what it says. In time, the fragmentary and scattered limbs become by a wild extended figure of speech, something living . . . a person.

His "all out" commitment to an art that is ultimately inseparable from himself distinguishes him from both Estheticism, which expressed its distaste for life in the idea of *l'art pour l'art*, and Modernism, with its more complex ideas of detached, impersonal, self-reflexive art structures. Instead Lowell went back to his roots, wedding his art both to American tradition and to personal experience. In his poetry, the price of experience, though heavy, does not include the loss of innocence. Rather, innocence becomes modified by the self's new knowledge, transformed into a more complete way of knowing and feeling, which might be termed a state of tragic innocence. Lowell allows his mind to open fully to what it has encountered and undergone, for he knows that existence teems with latent and discoverable meanings. His poetry is a continual process of finding those meanings in the act of creation. [14]

❦ II ❧
Myths of Experience

Starting Out: Learning from Tate

Upon an ebony plaque
Engrave a word.
In grief and rage cut
ANGUISH.
—I. A. Richards,
"For a Miniature of Robert Lowell"

In his 1950 introduction to the *Oxford Book of American Verse*, F. O. Matthiessen speculated that Amy Lowell, had she lived long enough to know him, might have thought Robert an exception to her judgment that "I'm the only member of my family who is worth a damn." For Robert Lowell himself, the whole family—including his Puritan ancestors, great-granduncle James Russell, cousin Amy, and most especially his parents—was a dead weight to be cast off in its entirety. The anguish of his childhood, which is barely hinted at in his prose memoir "91 Revere Street," convinced him that no one in the Lowell family was worth a damn, not even, perhaps, himself. Born March 1, 1917 in Boston, the only child of Commander Robert Traill Spence Lowell (USN) and Charlotte Winslow Lowell, Robert Traill Spence Lowell Jr. had a childhood that was on its surface conventional and respectable. At the age of eight he entered Boston's exclusive Brimmer School, and at thirteen he began "six uncomfortable years" at St. Mark's Boarding School in Southborough, an institution whose function (he later said) was to prepare rich boys for Harvard and eventual careers as bankers, lawyers, or directors of industry. Ford Madox Ford observed that Lowell had been brought up to be president of Harvard.[1]

Yet as Lowell suggests in "91 Revere Street," he passed

his childhood in alternating moods of rage and gloom. His father was ineffectual and distant, his mother suffocatingly domineering, and the family life filled with bitter argument. John Crowe Ransom referred to Lowell's "storm of difficulties with his parents" and explained: "He was high-strung and headstrong; they had the social position of their families, but, not having the means to live in the style expected of them, were generally in straits, and bickering. It was a bad hurt for a boy who would have revered all his elders if they were not unworthy." Lowell's youth, then, possessed an outer husk of slightly shabby gentility and conformity, and an inner reality of "incredible tensions" (in the phrase of one family friend). This paradox produced in him a triptych of interrelated motives that informed his adult life and his art: the thirst for experience, the need to rebel, and the search for an adequate father.[2]

The motto of St. Mark's is the unexceptionable Ignation advice to "Do What You Do." In a speech lampooning his old school which Lowell wrote after graduating, he remembered his fellow St. Markers all intently doing what they were doing (which was mainly athletics), and characterized them as "neither efficient nor humane nor cultured." He rebelled against the institution and the milieu it represented by performing relatively poorly in his classes (except literature and history) and by behaving in such a manner as to earn the nickname "Cal," after Caligula. His few contributions to the St. Mark's literary magazine *The Vindex* reveal this Caligula side of his personality in conflict with a more conventional youthful idealism. The idealism shows in a poem on the Virgin Mary and essays on Velasquez and Dante; the Caligula-ism, the urge to murder, shows in an essay entitled "War: A Justification":

> What is the solution to this problem of overpopulation? Some believe that it is birth-control; but this obviously cannot be. Why should Germany be limited to a population of seventy million . . . ? There is but one answer.

15

The most progressive and advanced peoples should have the most territory, the largest population, and the greatest wealth. . . . The benefits of war are so great that [its] temporary misfortunes and horrors, important as they are, can be forgotten. . . . War is the fairest test of which we know.[3]

Lowell at this time developed his interest in poetry, at least partly as a way to escape from or channel his youthful rage. He was fortunate in having Richard Eberhart as one of his English teachers at St. Mark's. Then just beginning his career as a published poet, Eberhart was intellectually stimulating in the classroom and unpretentious in personal contact (after graduation Lowell nicknamed him "Cousin Ghormley"). Eberhart liked young Lowell, believing his "extravagances of nature" to be a sign of artistic sensibility. Encouraged by Eberhart's interest, Lowell began to write poetry of two distinct kinds: elaborate, formal poems, heavily influenced by Latin models; and free verse, inspired by some examples he had found in Louis Untermeyer's anthology of modern poetry. Thus the two poles of his later art appeared at the very outset: poetry conceived as conventionally formed object and poetry conceived as organically formed self-expression. But the poems Lowell wrote in free verse seemed unauthorized by his reading of the classics and by the proprieties of his upbringing, and he kept them hidden. Instead he concentrated on long poems about Jonah and the Crusades, and on formal lyrics with titles like "Madonna," "Jericho," "Death," "When Life Has Gone," "The End of the World," "Easter: an Ode," "Phocion," "Man and Existence," and "Departed." These somber, religious, rigidly metrical works are the ones he presented to Eberhart and published in his school magazine. Eberhart says that these early poems, about sixty in all, "showed that his mind was heavy and that it was essentially religious." Indeed, one of the most important poetic influences on Lowell at this time was his namesake, the Rev. Robert Traill Spence Lowell, a nineteenth-century Episcopalian minister, former headmaster of St. Mark's, and author of mediocre inspirational verse. Young Lowell sang of "bright angels dropping from the sky," much as the reverend had once sung of the "angel's symphony" "out of highest heaven dropping." Lowell's youthful style and subject matter are indicated by "Madonna," his first published poem (in *The Vindex*):

> Celestial were her robes;
> Her hands were made divine;
> But the Virgin's face was silvery bright,
> Like the holy light
> Which from God's throne
> Is said to shine,
> Giving the angels sight.
>
> .   .   .   .
>
> Her song will never cloy;
> She will not mar the quietness
> Which in eternal Paradise
> Is through the silence ringing.

His long process of artistic revolt and discovery had not yet begun.[4]

Lowell entered Harvard fired with the ambition of becoming a poet. He had avidly read Wordsworth's *The Prelude* and Amy Lowell's biography of Keats, and was enraptured by "the picture both give of the young poet forming into a genius, their energy, their rapid growth and above all their neverending determination to succeed." He fully intended to form into a genius himself, as he confided to Eberhart: "I have come to realize more and more the spiritual side of being a poet. It is difficult to express what I wish to say, but what I mean is the actuality of living the life, of breathing the same air as Shakespeare, and of coordinating all this with the actualities of the world." "O art," he exclaimed in a poem, "I am a beggar at thy shrine."[5]

17

Myths of Experience

At Harvard, Lowell's poetry did indeed grow more accomplished, at least at first. But his personal life was slowly dissolving into chaos. He has described his increasingly acrimonious family situation most fully in a sequence of poems in *History* (pp. 112-114); and Eberhart has made it the subject of his verse play called *The Mad Musician*. Eberhart portrays Lowell inveighing against St. Mark's as "that washed old school where none was free," against his Harvard professors as "unbloods of no compendious experience," and against his loveless parents: "My father I loathe, my mother I cannot endure." "Striking right and left," Eberhart's Lowell most of all detests himself:

My fury and my rage [are] fruitful conquests
Of my own impotence and self-deception,
In which I know myself mean, low, worthless, ragged.

Lowell's fury led him to increasingly erratic behavior, and ultimately to an act of violent rebellion. In an angry quarrel over his plans to leave school and marry a young woman five years his senior named Anne Dick, he struck his father, knocking him to the floor. Throughout his poetic career Lowell returned obsessively to this incident, and to his feelings of anguished remorse over it—from Cain and Abel jottings in his undergraduate notebooks, to "Rebellion" in *Lord Weary's Castle*, "Middle Age" in *For the Union Dead*, "Charles River" in *Notebook*, and "Robert T. S. Lowell" in *Day by Day*. The incident is described most nakedly in the sequence ending in "Daddy" in *History*:

I knocked my father down. He sat on the carpet—
my mother calling from the top of the carpeted stairs,
their glass door locking behind me, no cover . . .
. . . .
There was rebellion, Father, and the door was
    slammed.
Front doors were safe with glass then . . . you fell
    backward

18

on your heirloom-clock, the phases of the moon,
the highboy quaking to its toes. My Father . . .
I haven't lost heart to say *I knocked you down* . . .

.   .   .   .

I hit my father. My apology
scratched the surface of his invisible
coronary . . . never to be effaced.

(*H*, 112-114)[6]

Lowell's family anguish in 1935 and 1936 was accompanied by increasing intellectual and artistic frustration at Harvard. Indeed, these two sides of his life were closely connected. Reacting to the dullness, tension, and instability of his home, Lowell sought the exaltation and purpose of a life in art; reacting to his loneliness, he sought fame; and reacting to his own ineffective and rejected father, he sought a "guide," an artistic "master," a spiritual father. In I. A. Richards's poem "For a Miniature of Robert Lowell," the two key words that serve to define him are "ANGUISH" and "SEARCHES." Lowell's search began in earnest at Harvard—for his proper mode of artistic expression, and for a teacher or "father" to lead him to that mode and applaud his eventual successes within it.

Lowell's quest for a poetic father eventually centered on two men, Allen Tate and William Carlos Williams, each associated with a particular style of artistic expression, one "formal" and the other "free." Lowell has several times listed the poets who most strongly affected him. He told Stanley Kunitz: "The poets who most directly influenced me were Allen Tate, Elizabeth Bishop and William Carlos Williams." In a later, unpublished essay he wrote that he had been "explicitly influenced by Ransom, Tate, Williams, Jarrell, Eliot and Yeats." The two poets who appear on every such list are Tate and Williams. They satisfied Lowell's artistic need and filled his emotional void. His life came to depend upon them. In the years leading up to *Lord Weary's Castle*, Tate was a "kind guide," the person Lowell felt "closest to." Lowell once even dared to address him as "Father Tate," to the older poet's vast discomfort. Later Lowell would come to regard Williams as his "master," and would write of him, "Whom would I love more?"[7]

The story of Lowell's artistic development is to some degree the story of his shifting allegiances to these two poets. As a student at St. Mark's and Harvard, he felt attracted to both the traditional, formalist poems praised in his textbooks and to the more avant-garde style of free verse. In effect, he was torn between the "paleface" notion of art as a discipline and the "redskin" notion of art as a liberating opportunity for self-expression. Because he found little encouragement for his own attempts to write free verse, however, he eventually abandoned them and concentrated his energies on writing in a more traditional, artificial style modeled on that of Tate. Lowell's early poems, collected in *Lord Weary's Castle*, are written in this mode, and they are far from negligible achievements. But he was to develop his mature style, in *Life Studies* and the volumes following it, only by going back to Williams, absorbing some of Williams's simplicity, observation, and intuitiveness into his own poetry. "I had good guides when I began," Lowell has written. "They have gone on with me; by now the echoes are so innumerable that I almost lack the fineness of ear to distinguish them" (N, 263). Lowell's great poetry combines a Williams-like humanness with a Tate-like craftsmanship. He eventually learned to synthesize these two major influences, bringing the one to bear on the other, thereby discovering his own authentic voice. But in his youthful search for a guide, he felt that the two poets were mutually exclusive and competitive. He thought he had to choose between them.

In his freshman year at Harvard (1935-1936), Lowell made his first attempt to find a poetic father. The object was Robert Frost, who delivered the Norton Lectures that year; and the attempt failed utterly. "Hit hard" by the power of Frost's lectures and admiring the "human and seen richness" of Frost's poetry, Lowell paid a call on the great poet. He hoped that Frost could tell him how to bring his own poems alive. Even more importantly, he hoped for encouragement and approval, he hoped Frost would like his poetry. He brought Frost the epic on the Crusades that he had been working on since his days at St. Mark's, an extended pastiche drawn from Michaud's *History of the Crusades*. He thought Frost would "like to see that," but Frost didn't, commenting after reading a few lines, "It goes on rather a bit, doesn't it?" Frost then recited Collins's short poem "How Sleep the Brave" and remarked, "That's not a great poem, but it's not too long." Lowell later recalled Frost as being "very kindly about it" but there can be little doubt that the encounter had been a painful rebuff. Frost, Lowell came to think, "had no interest, not only in younger poets, but in any poet living besides Frost, and he was a terribly vain man." Lowell had learned something valuable from Frost—about his own diffuseness and lack of individual "voice"—but he had failed in his quest for a warmly personal relationship with a poet he could respect and model himself upon.[8]

Rejected by Frost and rejecting his Harvard professors whom he found "outworn and backward-looking," Lowell turned for guidance to books. Exposed at Harvard to Edith Sitwell's criticism and "metrical treatises by obscure English professors in the eighteen-nineties," he began making elaborate metrical experiments, writing "Spenserian stanzas on Job and Jonah surrounded by recently seen Nantucket scenery." This poetry, he later said, "was grand, ungrammatical and had a timeless, hackneyed quality." But then came a culture shock. He met fellow-student James Laughlin, several years his senior and already founder of the *New Directions* annual. Lowell was understandably unsettled by Laughlin's own poems, which were written according to a meter he had devised in which all lines used a uniform number of typewriter spaces. Within this strange artificial structure, however, Laughlin's language was breezily colloquial, striking Lowell's ear as unpoetic. Further, Laughlin introduced Lowell to the poetry of William Carlos Williams, which was even more unsettling, even more fascinating. Lowell was "dizzied" by Williams's complex, irreducible art: "It was as though some homemade ship, part Spanish galleon, part paddle-wheels, kitchen pots and elastic bands and worked by hand, had anchored to a filling station." Lowell had read other new poets besides Williams, but none had given him "such a shock of failure." He immediately abandoned his Sitwellian metrical experiments and began again to concentrate on free verse, this time "trying to write like William Carlos Williams." But once more, his efforts received no encouragement. The editor of the *Harvard Advocate*, a conservative follower of Frost, turned down his candidacy. The *Advocate*'s later description of the event suggests the polite cruelty with which the young would-be poet's aspirations were met: "When Robert Lowell was . . . at Harvard and a candidate for the *Advocate*'s literary board, he was asked to tack down a carpet in the sanctum and when he was finished, told that he needn't come around any more." It was at this moment that Lowell's proliferating rejections at Harvard combined with the increasing tensions of his home life to produce the violence of his assault on his father. His art and life had exploded into wordless rage. Stunned, his parents considered institutionalizing him.[9]

Fortunately, he made his way to Allen Tate instead. Lowell had recently met Ford Madox Ford at a cocktail party, and Ford urged him to go south if he wanted to be a poet. This advice was supported by the psychiatrist his parents had sent him to—who, as luck would have it, was Dr. Merrill Moore, a poet of Tate's "Fugitive Group" then in private practice in Boston. Lowell agreed to visit Ford at Benfolly, the shabby antebellum mansion belonging to

Starting Out: Learning from Tate

Tate and his wife Caroline Gordon at Clarksville, Tennessee, outside Nashville. Having heard of Tate but never having acutally read any of his poems, Lowell hastily crammed and then set out, in a mood close to desperation. As he recalls in his essay "Visiting the Tates," he arrived at Benfolly in April 1937, his head full of "Miltonic ambitions," his suitcase "heavy with bad poetry":

> I was brought to earth by my bumper mashing the Tates' frail agrarian mail box post. Getting out to disguise the damage, I turned my back on their peeling, pillared house. I had crashed the civilization of the South.

This visit was a turning point in his career and his life. In Tate he found the teacher or father he had been seeking. "Like a torn cat," Lowell states, "I was taken in when I needed help, and in a sense I have never left."[10]

Tate that afternoon was enthusiastic and magisterial about poetry and flatteringly interested in Lowell, whom he treated as part of a legend, a member of an Abolitionist, poetry-writing family whose own views and aspirations deserved to be taken seriously. Tate thought of Lowell as "an idealist New Englander, a Puritan," the heir to a three-hundred-year-long history of heroism and tragedy which had wound down to "moral decadence and depravity." It was a role Lowell found instantly congenial. Warmed by his visit, he soon returned to spend the entire summer, camping out in a translucent green umbrella tent on the Tates' lawn, surrounded by meandering barnyard stock which occasionally scratched or leaned on the tent. Lowell conversed eagerly with Tate and Tate's friends, accompanied him and Ford to a writers' conference at Olivet College in July (where he met another fledgling poet, Theodore Roethke), and intoned his Miltonic verse at every opportunity. Ford, the original object of his visit, was made uncomfortable by the "ardent and eccentric" undergraduate, and refused to speak to him. But Tate liked Lowell immensely. Autocratic, extravagant, and generous,

Tate thought he recognized in his young visitor a potential poet much like himself, and he immediately formed "great hopes" for him.[11]

Tate both affirmed Lowell's aspirations to be a writer and gave those aspirations direction. He settled Lowell's inner debate between free and formal expression by firmly advocating the latter. For Tate was a committed formalist. Strongly influenced by the traditionalism of Eliot and Pound, he went far beyond them in his desire to breathe new life into conventional forms and intricate meters. He told his new protégé that "a good poem had nothing to do with exalted feelings of being moved by the spirit. It was simply a piece of craftsmanship, an intelligible or *cognitive* object." Sandburg was slipshod, and even Williams, though the best of the vers librists, was "secondary and minor." (Tate was later to mock in print Williams's "rhetorical Rousseauism.") And so, as Lowell has explained: "I became converted to formalism and changed my style from brilliant free verse, all in two months."[12]

Nevertheless, the formalism to which Tate "converted" Lowell was not that of the dry academic treatises he had encountered at Harvard, devoid of interest in experience or feeling. On the contrary, Tate provided him with both a theory and practice founded on the doctrine of experience. In *Reactionary Essays on Poetry and Ideas*, published the year before Lowell's arrival at Benfolly, Tate had argued that poetry "is the art of apprehending and concentrating our experience in the mysterious limitations of form." Tate conceived of poetry as a kind of conflict between experience and form, a conflict that both combatants could win. For in the successful poem, experience emerges from its struggle with form stronger than before, precisely because it has now consented to be bound by form. Within the form of the poem, experience has been "concentrated" and "apprehended"; that is, it has been converted from chaos into "knowledge"—not knowledge for the intellect merely, but "knowledge carried to the heart." Tate's poetic theory, like that of T. S. Eliot on which it was based, advocated a poetry that is paradoxically impersonal *and* experiential. In "Tradition and the Individual Talent," Eliot had proclaimed that "the more perfect the artist, the more completely separate in him will be the man who suffers and mind which creates"; yet he also acknowledged that the created poem depends for its existence upon that private experience which, in the manner of a "transforming catalyst," it has transmuted and intensified into universality. For Eliot and for Tate, the poet's task was to amalgamate his fragmentary and disparate experiences into the autonomous unity of the poem. The great poet, wrote Tate in *Reactionary Essays*, puts himself "at the center of [his] experience" of past and present, in order to give us "knowledge, not of the new programs, but of ourselves."[13]

When Lowell came to call, Tate had on hand his own recently published *The Mediterranean and Other Poems* (1936) to illustrate his theory. Herein was exemplified the terrific clash between experience and craft which resulted in the "intelligible or cognitive object" called a poem. In "The Mediterranean," for example, Tate depersonalizes his real experience of a day's outing on the French Riviera by contrasting the event with Aeneas' more heroic arrival on the Italian shore in *The Aeneid*. The poem is not personal memoir but an *experienced* revelation of *impersonal* ideas—the ideas of lost heroism, cultural decline, and modern-day solipsism. Tate's transformation of private event into universal, artistic truth takes place under great formal pressure; his heroic quatrains strain, at times past the breaking point, against rhyme pattern and iambic pentameter. Thus Tate introduced Lowell to a poetry that retains marks of the poet's "real struggle with form and content"—a struggle, as Lowell later said, that "centered on making the old metrical forms usable again to express the depths of one's experience." Lowell had come to Tate suspecting that "crafts were repeatable skills and belonged to the pedestrian boredom of manual training classes," but Tate showed him that poetic craft could be a dangerous and consuming enterprise: a desperate quest for form and meaning, a continual skirting of confusion, a "wrestling" with every line "until one's eyes pop out of one's head." Lowell soon found that out of all this "splutter and shambling" came Tate's "killing eloquence," as he smashed through "the tortured joy of composition to strike the impossible bull's-eye."[14]

That kind of poetry perfectly suited Lowell's own needs. The harsh struggle with traditional form satisfied his need for violent rebellion against authority and his equally deep need to acknowledge authority. The ambivalent relationship to experience—seizing upon what Tate termed "inward meaning of experience" while concentrating and depersonalizing that experience—satisfied Lowell's need to express his own experience and the equally felt imperative to escape from or master it. Finally, Tate's description of the poetic act itself as a kind of disciplined ecstasy satisfied Lowell's own yearnings for intensity and meaning in his life. Converted within two months not so much to "formalism" per se as to Tate's own "tortured joy of composition," Lowell dedicated himself for the next decade to learning a style which was not just influenced by Tate's, but in fact synonymous with it. The process of learning was a slow and painful one.[15]

In the fall of 1937, exhilarated by the recognition he had received from Tate, Lowell decided, against his parents' wishes, to leave Harvard. He enrolled instead at the then-inconspicuous Kenyon College in order to study with John Crowe Ransom, whom he had met during the summer at Benfolly. Ransom, Tate's elder and the dean of the Fugitive group of poets, was himself new to Kenyon that fall, having been hired away from Vanderbilt University. He brought to Kenyon two of his best students (Randall Jarrell and Peter Taylor) and the dynamic ideas and presence that were soon to transform the school into a center of literary activity and a home for the New Criticism. By October, Lowell was attending classes, and sharing a book-cluttered bedroom with Randall Jarrell in Ransom's house. The next year he moved, with Peter Taylor, into a long, gabled upstairs room in a dormitory cottage called "Douglass House," where he composed poems on the same oak table Taylor used to write some of his now well-known early stories. The move to Gambier, Ohio, Lowell was later to feel, "was a happy decision for me."[16]

Lowell thought his "life was changed, how much I'll never know, when I followed Ransom to Kenyon." Studying at the small Episcopal college, he was no longer the morbid, raging youth of six months before, though he was still "a-bristle and untamed." He later remembered himself as becoming "loud humored, dirty and frayed—I needed to be encouraged to comb my hair, tie my shoes and say goodbye when leaving a house," a deliberate rejection, perhaps, of the rigid civilities that obtained in his parents' home in Beacon Hill. Peter Taylor recalls him as "the most slovenly and ragged-looking of us all," and remembers walking down country roads with him, "talking every step of the way about ourselves or about our writing." John Ransom found him high-spirited and "a little bit overpowering"—his "way of reading literature was to devour it." At Kenyon, Lowell threw all his immense energies into his literary studies, and into teaching himself to write.[17]

Yet he did not learn to write at Kenyon. The quality of his poetry in fact declined during his three years there, and by the end of his stay he had stopped writing poetry altogether. Away from Tate, he could find no poetic master whose work could serve as a guide. Ransom, though his conversation was instructive, was no model. His graceful, smooth small poems were foreign to Lowell's sensibility.

Lowell recalled that Ransom "would say to me, 'You're a forceful poet but your poems are weighty,' and I knew that my poems would always be weighty next to his." Nor was Jarrell a suitable model. He was only three years older than Lowell and was himself learning to write during this period. A further difficulty for Lowell arose from the historical and New Critical study of poetry he encountered in his classes. This approach encouraged him to regard poetry as purely a craft, rather than as the poet's imaginative expression of the people, events, feelings, and ideas that he has experienced and that matter to him. Lowell's study only dried up the springs of his creativity, even as it increased his technical knowledge of poetry. "For the poet without direction," he was later to write, "poetry is a way of not saying what he has to say" (N, 263). That seems to describe precisely his situation at Kenyon.[18]

Lowell's classes at Kenyon were the least significant aspect of his stay there. A classics major, he dutifully attended classes in classical and modern literature, languages, and philosophy, and performed brilliantly in his written work. Indeed, he performed well enough to graduate in 1940 summa cum laude, Phi Beta Kappa, and class valedictorian. Yet he found even the best of his teachers, John Crowe Ransom, to be "humdrum" in the classroom. And his classmates, who were mostly interested in sports, beer, girls, and successful careers, he thought deplorable. In an essay published in the college journal *Hika* in November 1939, he argued against a radical student's plan to alter Kenyon's system of compulsory classes and prescribed assignments, yet his "defense" of the status quo reveals a sense of alienation nearly as thorough as that which he had felt at St. Mark's. Lowell argued that because the average Kenyon student found his studies only "a matter of intermittent interest" and thought of his college degree as having "commercial value" only, real educational reform was impractical. And so, he concluded, the situation at Kenyon must continue to be one in which "the bewildered student discovers that he is practicing what is useless and painful." Lowell's tone in such writing, resembling that of Tate's Agrarian manifestoes, was curiously elitist and radical at once. He was even more outspoken in his valedictory address, titled "From Parnassus to Pittsburgh," in which he contrasted the "whitewashed illusion" of Kenyon as an "Episcopal Valhalla" with its pernicious social reality:

> Incongruous learning, a rotation of polite daisy-picking and brutal cramming, is the precious, or at worst, purple pabulum of transcendental moonshine. Green with sweltering summer and breathless with a solemn, valetudinary fragrance, Gambier advertizes the sociable splendors of a landscape where students drink beer and skim books.

Lowell's basic criticism of Kenyon was that its ersatz intellectual idealism merely disguised its actual subservience to the values of industrial capitalism. The "ignorance and irresponsibility" of the Kenyon education, he edgily hectored his classmates, "are auguries of the opulence of your fathers."[19]

Official Kenyon produced in Lowell only an ambivalent and confused rage, paralleling the rage he felt toward other centers of misused authority: his family, the national government, and the nation's economic system. Yet unofficial Kenyon had a more beneficial effect. "It was not the classes," Lowell said later, "but the conversations that mattered," conversations especially with Ransom and Jarrell. Ransom, about fifty, was a brilliant thinker and talker, and more exciting to Lowell in his book-lined den than in the classroom. "He talked metaphysics if he could, and poetry if he could, and gossip if he could. The strands were indistinguishable." Often Ransom would argue with Jarrell, then a graduate instructor of about twenty-four, puzzling and attractive, who was soon to become Lowell's best friend. Lowell wrote in a letter to Eberhart that Jarrell was a modern—"a complete abstraction who believes in Shelley, machines, 'ambiguities,' and intelligence tests." Ransom, and Lowell himself, of course believed in none of those. Jarrell was also "upsettingly brilliant." He knew "everything"—Marx, Auden, Empson, Kafka, the ideologies and news of the day—"everything, except Ransom's provincial world of Greek, Latin, Aristotle and England." Like Ransom, Jarrell thought dialectically and loved literary disputation. Lowell later remembered them seated on a love seat in Ransom's den, arguing about Shakespeare's sonnets, "each expounding to the other's deaf ears his own inspired and irreconcilable interpretation." Out of such arguments, out of the passionate intelligence of both men, Lowell gleaned his education.[20]

Another source of learning was his reading of contemporary literary critics. Criticism was in a period of revival, and Kenyon was one of its centers. The latest essays of the major poet-critics, T. S. Eliot, R. P. Blackmur, Yvor Winters, William Empson, and of course Ransom and Tate, seemed as exciting to Lowell as new imaginative works. Yvor Winters was especially influential in shaping his ideas about poetry. Although loosely associated with the New Critical movement, Winters thoughtfully challenged some portions of its orthodoxy. Lowell had first read Winters during his summer with Tate. Winters shared Tate's taste for seventeenth-century Metaphysical poetry and for Emily Dickinson and Hart Crane; and his method of close criticism meshed with the emphasis on verbal richness evident in the writings of Tate and other New Critics. Yet Winters also functioned as a useful antidote to the ideology of Benfolly and Kenyon. He viewed poetry as a "moral discipline," a view rather different from the more esthetic perspectives of Tate and the New Critics. He advocated a poetry of rational thought and feeling, and brought the stylistic dislocation and obscurity of Eliot and Tate into sharp question. When Lowell came upon Winters arguing (in *Primitivism and Decadence*) that Williams's "By the road to the contagious hospital" was "far more solidly written" than Eliot's "Gerontion," he could barely believe his eyes. Yet Lowell was impressed by Winters's arguments, and dutifully jotted down in his notebook titles of the poems by Williams, Marianne Moore, and Wallace Stevens that he had praised. Reviewing Winters's *Maule's Curse* (1938) in *Hika*, Lowell termed this study of nineteenth-century American writers "morally and aesthetically . . . of first-rate importance." Although he dissented from the dogmatism of Winters's negative abstractions concerning Emerson and James, he for the most part admired the essay. "Mr. Winters," Lowell wrote, "has united the principles of humanist and aesthete, the thunders of ethics with the specialization of the craftsman. That unstinted, one can walk in the other's shadow, is obviously impossible; but as irrational colleagues they form a compelling apparatus of criticism." Winters's insistence on the moral dimension of literature and his related view that a poem must be judged as to its veracity were new additions to Lowell's thought. Although Lowell was not ready to forgo obscurity and intensity in his own poetry, Winters's moralism accorded with his own ethical bent and made a lasting impression on his poetic practice.[21]

Another source of Lowell's education was his independent reading of great works of poetry. At Kenyon, he began the habit, maintained for several years after graduation, of copying favorite poems into his notebooks. He did not regard these poems as objects for his critical scrutiny; with one or two exceptions, he appended no commentary at all to them. Rather, he inscribed them into his notebooks for inspiration and as stylistic models for his own creative efforts. As might be expected, his choice of poems reflected the taste of the critics he most respected—Eliot, Blackmur, Winters, Empson, Ransom, and Tate. Thus, the large majority of the poems he copied derived from the late sixteenth and seventeenth century; most of the rest were from the twentieth. Lowell's modernism was that fostered by Eliot's essay on "The Metaphysical Poets." In the words of Tate's *Reactionary Essays*, "it is the modernism that re-establishes our own roots in the age of Donne."[22]

At one time or another between 1939 and 1943 Lowell copied into his notebooks seven poems by Donne, ten by Herbert, six by Milton, and a smaller number by Herrick, Shakespeare, Marvell, Crashaw, Jonson, Carew, Raleigh, Marlowe, and Daniel. (A complete list of the poems copied is given in Appendix A.) Of more modern poets, Lowell's favorites were Emily Dickinson and Wallace Stevens. These choices were conditioned by brilliant essays by Tate, Blackmur, and Winters in praise of Dickinson, and by Winters's sympathetic reading of Stevens in *The Anatomy of Nonsense*. Lowell copied five of Dickinson's poems: "Because I could not stop for death" (which both Tate and Winters had singled out for praise), "If you were coming in the fall," "I found the words to every thought," "A thought went up my mind today," and "The last night that she lived." He also copied five of Stevens's poems: "Le Monocle de Mon Oncle," "On the Manner of Addressing Clouds," "Of Heaven Considered as a Tomb," "The Death of a Soldier," and, on three separate occasions, passages from "Sunday Morning." All of these poems appeared on Winters's list of Stevens's six best poems in *Anatomy of Nonsense*, though Lowell's inscriptions of "Sunday Morning" and "Monocle" seem to antedate Winters's book. Lowell also copied into his notebooks three poems by Hart Crane—"Repose of Rivers," "Voyages II," "For the Marriage of Faustus and Helen II"—the three which Winters in *Primitivism and Decadence* had listed as his best. Other poems Lowell wrote out were by Hopkins, Yeats, Thomas, Ransom, Tate, Eliot ("Ash Wednesday"), Bridges, Mac-Neice, Shapiro, and Blackmur.[23]

As a student, Lowell fervently devoted himself to reading poetry and forming a critical intelligence about the poetry he read. Yet despite his effort and intellectual brilliance, his own writing remained sterile. In Lowell's first year at Kenyon, Ransom accepted two of his poems called "The Cities' Summer Death" and "The Dandelion Girls" for publication in the newly founded *Kenyon Review*, but then refused to take any more. Nor could Lowell get his increasingly obscure poems published elsewhere. Toward the end of his education at Kenyon, he abandoned his efforts at serious publication and allowed six of his clotted and abstract poems to be printed in the college magazine *Hika*. Lowell's poetic failure during this time resulted largely from a failure to wed his art to his experience. After years of academic study, he had little of his own to say, but an exaggerated interest in stylistic complication. In classroom essays on art, he often affirmed that "literature can only dramatize life and world that is real to it" and that "art must be true to life." Yet in actual practice he ignored these truisms. He sought instead something like the "watertight, pure expression" he thought he observed in the poetry of Dylan Thomas. In an autobiographical aside in a student essay on Pope, Lowell asserted: "Surely a young writer could not do better than to ignore his heart and learn his craft, to exclude the callow turbulence of youth and concentrate on elegance." Ignoring his own heart, escaping from the profound (not callow) turbulence and reality which he knew resided there, but which he felt incapable or afraid of translating into the energy and reality of poetry, Lowell wrote "poems" which were neither "true to life" nor well-crafted.[24]

For example, for a number of years in the late 1930s and early 1940s he devoted himself to writing and rewriting a mock epic (seemingly modeled on Byron's "The Vision of Judgment") called "Great Britain's Trial." In this never-published poem, which lifelessly lampoons Great Britain for its conventionality, materialism, and anti-German foreign policy, John Bull stands trial for his sins, along with his co-defendant Custom, his "ox-eyed queen." Other prominent characters include Mammon and Armageddon, along with Satan who is a character witness for John Bull's

33

defense. When Ransom was shown this poem he pro-
nounced it "oppressive." Another poem that consumed
Lowell's interest for several years was variously called
"The American Jew's Prayer," "Prayer of the Jews for the
Land of their Adoption" and "An American Jew's Prayer
for Israel." Like "Great Britain's Trial," this poem bears no
relation to Lowell's (or anyone's) experience. It is an exercise. It draws upon stereotyped political attitudes to supply the pretext for what is really an experiment in metrics
and poetic rhetoric. Indeed, the poem's refrain is merely a
restatement of Thomas Nashe's refrain in "Litany in Time
of Plague": "I am sick, I must die. Lord, have mercy on
us!" It is no coincidence that William Empson and Yvor
Winters had both praised Nashe's use of the refrain in
critical essays. [25]

The eight poems Lowell published in the *Kenyon Review*
and *Hika* between December 1938 and February 1940 dem-
onstrate the rhetorical excess and intellectual and emotional deficiency that mark all his poetry of this period.
Consider, for example, the last poem he published in *Hika*,
four months before he graduated in June 1940.

Sublime Feriam Sidera Vertice
In compensation for blind circumstance,
Nature charged brute devotions to the soul,
   A patriot patrol,
To underwrite human designs, that man's
Least Action seem to take a righteous role.

Finding instead satanic partnership,
Nature put out a fall, an Ark, a Flood,
   Like as a common good
Christ Jesus and his golden rule . . . the ship
Of state has learned Christ how to sail on blood.

Great Commonwealth, sail on and on and roll
On blood, on my free blood; my heart misgave,
   Confessed itself a slave,

And Hegel proved State an invested soul,
Oh mortmain, patron and gaoler of the grave.

This poem tells us certain things. Lowell has read Horace:
the title, which may be translated "With my head raised so
high then shall I strike the stars," derives from the dedicatory Ode in which Horace expresses hopes for a career in
poetry. Lowell has also read Hobbes and Hegel, whose
terms he applies to his own strong but undefined feelings
about the growing bloodshed of World War II. And his
sensibility remains, as Richard Eberhart found it at St.
Mark's, religious. Yet the poem, despite its learning and
complexity, does not succeed. It clothes certain attitudes
about history and current events in verbal wit and complicated stanza form, but these attitudes fail to be tested in
the way Tate said all ideas must be tested in poetry: by experience, by direct apprehension. The poem is abstract and
lifeless, and Lowell knew it. He published no more poetry
for three years. Later he recalled: "I just stopped, and really sort of gave it up. I seemed to have reached a great im-
passe. The kind of poem I thought was interesting and
would work on became so cluttered and overdone that it
wasn't really poetry."[26]

Two months before graduating from Kenyon College,
Lowell married an aspiring novelist named Jean Stafford,
whom he had met during the summer of 1937 while accompanying Ford and Ransom to a writers' conference at
the University of Colorado. Lowell also converted to his
new wife's religion, Roman Catholicism. Following graduation, he taught briefly at Kenyon, did a year of graduate
study in English at Louisiana State University under
Cleanth Brooks and Robert Penn Warren, and worked as
an editorial assistant at the Catholic publishing house of
Sheed and Ward in New York. Still he wrote little and published nothing. Then late in 1942, he returned for an ex-

tended stay with Allen Tate, who then was living at Monteagle, Tennessee, a few miles from the University of the South at Sewanee. Living with Tate, Lowell began to write again. In an adjoining room, Jean Stafford worked on the novel that was to become the best-selling *Boston Adventure* (1944), and Tate's wife Caroline Gordon worked on her book *The Woman on the Porch* (1944). Tate and Lowell, sharing a study, both began writing prose as well. Tate worked on a sequel to his novel *The Fathers*, and Lowell on a biography of Jonathan Edwards. Finding themselves blocked in their writing, however, they then undertook to edit jointly an anthology of sixteenth- and seventeenth-century poems. Moved by the "formal, difficult poems" they both preferred, and by the warmth of their personal association, the poets grew inspired. They abandoned the anthology and in a "burst of creative activity" started to write poems themselves. Tate, able to write poetry for the first time since *The Mediterranean*, composed "Jubilio," "Ode to Our Young Pro-Consuls of the Air," "Winter Mask" and "Seasons of the Soul" (all published in *The Winter Sea*, 1944) and translated (with advice from Lowell) the Latin poem *Pervigilium Veneris* (published in 1943 as *The Vigil of Venus*). Lowell, for his part, started work on the poems that were to establish him as the leading poet of his generation.[27]

During this stay with Tate, Lowell wrote (or in a few cases rewrote) the twenty-one poems of *Land of Unlikeness* (published in a limited edition in 1944). The best of these poems (about half) were then revised and included two years later in his landmark volume *Lord Weary's Castle*. In addition, Lowell's notebooks indicate that he began work in Monteagle on a number of poems which made their first book appearance in *Lord Weary's Castle*, including "As a Plane Tree by the Water," "Where the Rainbow Ends," and the book's best known and probably greatest poem, "The Quaker Graveyard in Nantucket."

Tate's personal presence seemed to animate Lowell's dormant creativity, and his poems served as Lowell's chief models. Lowell's avowals that Tate "was the closest direct influence" and that his "own poetry was closest to Tate's" if anything understate the case. More recently he said, "In the beginning [Tate] was not only an influence but often *the* (my) style of writing; not writing like Tate meant not echoing specific phrases." When Randall Jarrell read over the manuscript of *Lord Weary's Castle* he had to caution Lowell to delete the more blatant "Allen" effects. In assessing Lowell's debt to Tate, we may fairly say that it was threefold. Tate gave Lowell a style, a theme, and something greater than either of these—a vision of a life totally committed to art, and an assurance that he too could achieve such a life.[28]

In general terms the closeness of Lowell's early style to that of his mentor is evident. Like Tate's, Lowell's poems are verbally dense, complex, ironic, ambiguous. And also like Tate, Lowell "was all for the high discipline, for putting on the full armor of the past"—that is, for containing his energetic language within the strict confines of traditional meters and stanza forms, the more demanding the better. More specific similarities appear when passages by each poet are put side by side for comparison. Here, by way of illustration, is the way each poet begins an elegy:

> Row after row with strict impunity
> The headstones yield their names to the element,
> The wind whirrs without recollection;
> In the riven troughs the splayed leaves
> Pile up, of nature the casual sacrament
> To the seasonal eternity of death;
> Then driven by the fierce scrutiny
> Of heaven to their election in the vast breath,
> They sough the rumour of mortality.
>
>> (Tate, "Ode to the Confederate Dead")

> A brackish reach of shoal off Madaket,—
> The sea was still breaking violently and night
> Had steamed into our North Atlantic Fleet,

When the drowned sailor clutched the drag-net. Light
Flashed from his matted head and marble feet,
He grappled at the net
With the coiled, hurdling muscles of his thighs:
The corpse was bloodless, a botch of reds and whites,
Its open, staring eyes
Were lustreless dead-lights
Or cabin-windows on a stranded hulk
Heavy with sand. We weight the body, close
Its eyes and heave it seaward whence it came,
Where the heel-headed dogfish barks its nose
On Ahab's void and forehead; and the name
Is blocked in yellow chalk.
　　　(Lowell, "The Quaker Graveyard in Nantucket")

Metrically, the passages are comparable. Each uses a highly interwoven rhyme scheme; each is written in an iambic pentameter capable of absorbing a large amount of metrical variation (though Lowell differs from Tate in interspersing several trimeter lines which recall Milton's "Lycidas"). The insistent quality of the rhymes, the irregularity of the meter, and the rather spectacular use of such devices as consonance, assonance, and internal rhyme, all combine to give the verse a rough-hewn, hand-made intensity. Semantically, the passages are comparable as well. Each describes a landscape that yields a symbolic significance. Tate's deserted graveyard, whirring wind, and splayed leaves objectify the speaker's sense of futility and emptiness which is the poem's major theme. In a similar way, Lowell's brackish shoal and violent sea symbolize the violent disorder of the age, which is his poem's theme.[29]

The symbolic quality of both passages relates to a verbal trait both poets share, a characteristic that is the hallmark of Tate's style throughout his career and of Lowell's style at least in Lord Weary's Castle. This trait is the jarring combination of the abstract with the concrete, generalization with sensation. It is Tate's *"ideas* tested by experience, by *direct apprehension"* put into practice. Thus in Tate's poem, the leaves in the wind "sough" or moan the "rumour of mortality." The leaves' "sough," a direct apprehension, is yoked to "mortality," an idea. This yoking is reinforced by a similar linkage within the word "rumour," which in root meaning is sensuous (lament or howl) and in common usage is abstract (talk or opinion widely disseminated with no discernible source). Other examples of Tate's yokings might include the phrases "seasonal eternity" and "fierce scrutiny" and the use of the abstract, theological vocabulary of "sacrament," "election" and "vast breath" for the physical phenomenon of leaves being lifted by the wind. Stylistically, Tate emulates Donne and Dickinson, whom he praised for their metaphysical ability to *perceive abstraction* and *think sensation.* And Lowell emulates Tate. His "dogfish barks its nose on Ahab's void and forehead." "Void," the abstraction of empty space and perhaps philosophical nihilism, is given a physical property by its syntactical parallel with "forehead" and its capacity of being nosed by a fish. Indeed, in using the word "void," Lowell may merely, as Richard Ellmann and Robert O'Clair suggest, be displacing the indicated concrete referent, "heart," with an abstraction—much as Tate displaces the leaves' literal "howl" with the abstract "rumour of mortality." A great deal of Lowell's poetic effect is achieved through just this kind of systematic verbal displacement. He describes night as having "steamed" into the fleet, rather than the reverse. He substitutes (as Jarrell remarked on the manuscript) the abstraction of "light flashed" for the sensuous fact of the whiteness of the corpse's flesh. Tate and Lowell share the quality of verbal "tension" which Tate defined and praised in his essay "Tension in Poetry": a forcing of the extremes of a range of diction into a momentary unity within the limits of the poem. The syntax of both poets is distorted and surprising, reflecting the continual pressure of idea and sensation within the crucible of poetic form.

Yet Lowell's style is not *quite* the same as Tate's. Tate's poetry tends toward the idea, while Lowell's tends toward the sensation. In the passages quoted, Tate loads his lines with Latinate abstractions while Lowell loads his with sensual phenomena and kinetic energy: the sea is "breaking violently," the preternaturally active corpse "clutched" and "grappled at" the net, its muscles "coiled, hurdling," its eyes "open, staring." If Tate's poetry is ideas tested by direct apprehension, Lowell's poetry is direct apprehension tested by ideas.[30]

In the years following *Lord Weary's Castle*, Lowell moved away from the intricate metrical forms, the artificially charged language, and the depersonalization of raw experience, all of which he had learned from Tate. Yet Tate's influence endured. Even in his free verse Lowell retained vestiges of rhyme and iambic meter. He also retained the practice of verbal dislocation and surprise, of colliding the abstract with the concrete. This practice can be discerned, for example, in the celebrated conclusion of "For the Union Dead": "a savage servility/slides by on grease" (*FUD*, 72). It also underlies the stylistic "unrealism" of *Notebook* and later poems.

Another area of Tate's influence on Lowell is thematic. Tate has two overriding and closely related themes. First, he seeks to portray and remedy the modern-day dissociation of sensibility that separates intellect from emotion, and human beings from their universe. The "Ode to the Confederate Dead," Tate explained, concerns the "cutoff-ness" of the modern intellectual. Second, his poetry expresses a "love of past things" and a hatred of the rootless "secularization" and "mechanical order" of the present. This latter theme is intensified by his ever-present sense of *severance* from the past—it is one of the things he, as a modern intellectual, feels cut off from. These two themes, isolation and history, dominate Lowell's own poetry as well. From *Life Studies* through "For the Union Dead," "Waking Early Sunday Morning," and "George III," Lowell remains preoccupied with emotional dislocation·in a mechanistic and inhumane age; and with a complex sense of connection to and disconnection from the past. Although he moved to the left politically, he always remained a cultural conservative, a regionalist, and a Puritan moralist: Allen Tate's northern disciple. His poetry consistently assaults the modern age, in which technology and industrial capitalism work to obliterate human values. "Mechanical time is replacing organic time," Lowell once complained. "I wish to turn the clock back with every breath I take, but I hope I have the courage to occasionally cry out against those who wrongly rule us." R. K. Meiners, in his interesting book *Everything to be Endured*, sums up Tate's and Lowell's shared idea as the present-day loss of the traditional religious-humanistic view of human beings and culture. It is a loss both poets regard with anger and dread.[31]

Finally, Tate taught Lowell what it means to be a poet. It means (for Tate and Lowell, and perhaps for all American poets) to put the whole self, the whole of one's imagination and skill and energy, into the act of artistic creation. Tate showed Lowell that craft and inspiration could be one—that craft could be inspired, that inspiration could be heightened by being subjected to the demands of craft. He guided Lowell toward a poetry that "would take a man's full weight and that would bear his complete intelligence, passion and subtlety." Lowell learned from his mentor to think of poetry as being all-important, all-consuming, a putting together of all the genius and skill the poet possesses. Specifics of style and theme are less important than this sense of the sheer "all out" quality of the American poet's endeavor. Lowell learned at Monteagle to devote his life, as Tate himself did, to his art.[32]

41

Toward *Lord Weary's Castle*

Prison and personality were your fate.
—*Karl Shapiro*, "The Conscientious Objector"

In the fall of 1943 Lowell left Allen Tate's house to stand trial and go to prison. It was a characteristic act of rebellion. To his parents' horror, he had written a letter to President Roosevelt refusing induction into the armed forces: "I cannot participate in this war, not because I think wars are contrary to my religion, but because I believe that the conduct of this war is a betrayal of my country." Like Tate and many of his other literary friends, Lowell bitterly opposed America's demand for unconditional German surrender, which he thought would "imperil our national existence and human freedom" by leaving the Soviet Union in a position of unchallenged power. Underlying this stand was a basic hostility to the United States itself. Writing as early as 1938 (in the *Harvard Advocate*), Lowell had derided the United States as "this massive and mannerless democracy." His reading at Kenyon College and at Tate's house of such writers as Christopher Dawson, Jean de Ménasce, Etienne Gilson, Arnold Toynbee, Wyndham Lewis, Eliot, Pound, and Tate—all of them on the right and many of them leaders in the Christian revival—only increased his sense of disaffiliation with his country. Thus the characteristic politics of the Pound Era, which tended in Eliot's version to royalism and Catholicism, in Tate's version to Agrarianism and Catholicism, and in Pound's version to Mussolini, channeled Lowell's lifelong feelings of alienation and rage into an act of social defiance. For "telling off the state and President" (*LS*, 85), he was sentenced to a short term in federal prison. His first volume of poetry, *Land of Unlikeness*, which was completed in Monteagle before his incarceration and published soon after his release, was a similar act of defiance, of rage. Like his decision to go to jail, *Land of Unlikeness* makes manifest what Jerome Mazzaro has termed Lowell's "early politics of apocalypse." The "land of unlikeness" referred to in the title is that "massive and mannerless democracy," the United States of America, land of our fathers, land of his very own father who had served with distinction in his nation's navy during the First World War.[33]

Land of Unlikeness appeared in July 1944 under the imprint of the Cummington Press, which had published works of Tate and other well-known poets. The book was accompanied by an introduction by Tate praising Lowell for his "intricate meters and stanzas" and for his dissimilarity from "the democratic poets who enthusiastically greet the advent of the slave-society." Reviews by such prestigious critics as Conrad Aiken, R. P. Blackmur, Elizabeth Drew, and Lowell's friend Randall Jarrell were generally respectful. Yet the book was a creature of its moment, timely as a "manic statement" of cultural rebellion (*LS*, 85), but premature as artistic expression. After its publication Lowell came to fault the book for "too much twisting and disgust." Alternately brilliant and botched, *Land of Unlikeness* asks to be taken not as a finished work of art, but as a work in progress, a manuscript for *Lord Weary's Castle*. About half the poems in *Land of Unlikeness*, the brilliant ones, were improved and included in the later volume: "In Memory of Arthur Winslow," "Salem," "Concord," "Napoleon Crosses the Beresina," "Dea Roma," "The Crucifix," "Christmas Eve in Time of War" (retitled "Christmas Eve Under Hooker's Statue"), "The Drunken Fisherman," "Children of Light," Part I of "Scenes from the Historic Comedy" (retitled "The Slough of Despond"), and parts of "The Park Street Cemetery" and "Cistercians in Germany" (combined into "At the Indian Killer's Grave"). The egregious poems, two of which had initially appeared in *Hika*, were not included in *Lord Weary's Castle*.[34]

In his introduction, Tate distinguished between two types of poems in *Land of Unlikeness*, those consisting of intellectualized Christian symbolism and those which are "richer in immediate experience." Revising toward *Lord Weary's Castle*, Lowell deleted the first type of poem and kept the second. *Land of Unlikeness* is interesting chiefly for the way it shows him struggling to articulate his themes. He was still hampered by the abstract, abstruse rhetoric of his *Hika* days, a rhetoric that obscured his sense of his own experience, dulled his imagination, and prevented him from closing with his subjects. Lowell's comment about "Cistercians in Germany," one of the poems omitted from the revised volume, is instructive: "The 'Cistercians' wasn't very close to me, but the last lines seemed felt; I dropped the Cistercians and put a Boston graveyard in." Thus was "At the Indian Killer's Grave" born. By deleting what was merely bombastic and by concentrating on what was really felt, Lowell found his authentic voice. *Land of Unlikeness*, therefore, shows Lowell on the road from *Hika*, with its "abstraction" and "fierceness," to *Lord Weary's Castle*, whose chief value, he has said, is that it is a heart-felt "recording of experience."[35]

Lowell has three related themes in *Land of Unlikeness*: history, current events, and God. In one form or another, these subjects continued to haunt and nourish him throughout his career, but in *Land of Unlikeness* they are handled ineffectively. Despite its superficial historicity, for example, the book displays little real sense of the past. It uses history only as evidence to support an essentially antihistorical myth of apocalypse. Rather than explore recorded events as occurrences pregnant with living meaning, Lowell exhibits historical attitudes, and attitudes which are confused at that. In "Salem" he praises the New England colonists who "fought the British lion to his knees," yet in "Park Street Cemetery" he angrily terms those same colonists "Puritan Dracos." Depending upon which poem one reads, the Puritans are either heroic rebels against secular authority or knavish secular authoritarians themselves; they have been betrayed by the modern debacle or they are responsible for it. Praise and blame seem to reside in separate and untouching compartments of Lowell's mind. In his later work he learned to let his contradictory feelings work upon and modify each other, and developed an ironic, complex consciousness capable of connecting with the ambiguities of history. But the rigid contradictions in *Land of Unlikeness* serve only to cancel each other out. The logical inconsistencies result from Lowell's basically nonhistorical motive in writing: to denigrate the hated agnostic present. Relatively uninterested in the past as it really was, he came to it with a closed mind and forced its particulars to yield to his interpretation of them.

In the same way, Lowell's early poems on World War II, almost none of which are included in *Lord Weary's Castle*, merely use that event as a part of his larger apocalyptic vision. As Hugh Staples says, "the events taking place around him are merely reflections of the greater conflict. . . . Military disasters are rehearsals for the impending Day of Judgment." The young poet converts the war into a retelling of the Cain and Abel myth, with America playing the part of Cain. With the exception of "Cistercians in Germany," which attacks the Nazi regime (but only for persecuting the Cistercians, and for this America is made to share the blame), the many war poems in *Land of Unlikeness* all attack the United States with a vehemence that reminds one of Tate's contemporaneous antiwar satires and Pound's war broadcasts:

> So, child, unclasp your fists,
> And clap for Freedom and Democracy;
> No matter, child, if the Ark Royal lists
>   Into the sea;
> Soon the Leviathan
> Will spout American.
>
> ("The Boston Nativity")

Yet for all Lowell's anger at America's role in the war, and especially its use of saturation bombing, he focuses hardly at all on the human casualties. Even the diatribe "The Bomber" is coldly abstract:

> Bomber like a god
> You nosed about the clouds
> And warred on the wormy sod;
> And your thunderbolts fast as light
> Blitzed a wake of shrouds.

Lowell uses contemporary events as he uses history, as elements in a religious myth. The human beings involved, the whole human conflict itself, is of small importance. Cut off from the events and people around him, Lowell is reduced to an abstraction in which "the Ship / Of State is asking Christ to walk on blood" ("Leviathan").[36]

Lowell's religious myth is the key to understanding *Land of Unlikeness*, and to understanding its comparative failure. He himself later said that in writing these poems he was "much more interested in being a Catholic than in being a writer." This may exaggerate the case, but it does contain some truth. In writing these poems, he was obsessed with his Augustinian idea of the modern world as a "land of unlikeness" (*regio dissimilitudinis*), a land in which human beings have lost their likeness to God and therefore have become alienated from themselves as well. This estrangement, Lowell believed, was ultimately responsible for the collapse of civilization, embodied in the mass destruction of World War II. He sought to persuade his readers that secular history, itself only an aspect of God's larger design, was now at its preordained end.[37]

Superficially Lowell's religious perspective may seem close to that of T. S. Eliot, who did indeed influence him. In the only prose essays he published in 1943 and 1944, Lowell dwelt upon *sanctity* as a feature of Hopkins's poetry and Eliot's *Four Quartets*. In the essay on Eliot, he called *Four Quartets* "a quasi-autobiographical experience of the *union with God*, or rather its imperfect approximation in

this life." Lowell had just such motives himself in writing
Land of Unlikeness:

> It there no way to cast my hook
> Out of this dynamited brook?
>
> .   .   .   .
>
> On water the Man-fisher walks.
>
> ("The Drunken Fisherman")

Yet whereas *Four Quartets* values time as well as timeless-
ness, the turning wheel *and* the still point, Lowell's poems
are designed to refute time entirely. They deny the importance of human events except as part of a cosmic, age-
less pattern. They deny that history has any existence as a
nonrecurring, nonsymbolic, nonteleological movement
through time. For Eliot, history was valuable because it
provides access to religious experience: "history is a pattern of timeless moments." But for Lowell, history itself
had a religious significance: willful estrangement from
God. *Land of Unlikeness* does not give meaning to human
history, it seeks to abolish human history.[38]

Moreover, whereas Eliot's habitual feelings of repugnance are matched and overmatched in *Four Quartets* by
his feelings of religious love, in *Land of Unlikeness* love
seems possible as an idea but not as something actually
felt. Lowell's Christ occasionally puts in a brief appearance
at the end of poems, walking on water or peering through
the trellis, but he is as estranged as all the other characters
in the book. An intellectual abstraction only, he evokes no
emotions. In *Land of Unlikeness* there are ideas and doc-
trines, but no people and no minute particulars. There is
anger and revolt, but no sense of the heart's fullness. R. P.
Blackmur wrote in his review of the book:

> Dante loved his living Florence and the Florence to come
> and loved much that he was compelled to envisage in
> hell, and he wrote throughout in loving meters. In Low-

ell's *Land of Unlikeness* there is nothing loved unless it be its repellence; and there is not a loving meter in the book.[39]

Two years later, Lowell was back in print with the volume he later came to think of as his "first" book, *Lord Weary's Castle*. In the best poems of this volume, he made good on the promise implicit in *Land of Unlikeness*. Treating exactly the same themes as before, he plunged into the multiplicity and miscellaneousness of experience, opening himself to his experience as certain flowers open to the daylight. Much more than *Land of Unlikeness*, in which the atmosphere is airless, *Lord Weary's Castle* has the "exploratory," "human" quality Lowell later came to prize in poetry. Rather than demonstrating an already thought-out intellectual position, the poems make themselves vulnerable to the world, to the poet's wide range of intellectual, emotional, and imaginative responses to his world. It is this openness that distinguishes the best poems of *Lord Weary's Castle* and that connects them to Lowell's later work. The intelligence and experience that have gone into them are bone-deep.[40]

Containing ten poems carried over from *Land of Unlikeness* (often heavily rewritten), and thirty-two new poems, *Lord Weary's Castle* was greeted by critics and readers as a major literary event—the arrival of an important, possibly great, new poetic talent. The book was prominently reviewed in the literary weeklies and quarterlies, and received the Pulitzer Prize for poetry. It even occasioned one of the few opinions held in common by the aging lions of American poetry, T. S. Eliot and William Carlos Williams. T. S. Eliot wrote approvingly to Lowell's publisher in 1946 that he found the young poet "up to form." Williams thought that Lowell's "style should have been repugnant to me—but it wasn't. The American virus was in his veins. But his rhymed couplets, incongruous as they seemed, had a naive quality about them that attracted me. . . . I was intrigued." Donald Hall, speaking for the group of poets a half-generation younger than Lowell, remembers that "it took us some years to scratch out, in our own poems, the sounds of *Lord Weary's Castle*." Lowell's exact contemporaries also took note. In his review of the volume John Berryman wrote, "What is clear just now is that we have before us . . . a talent whose ceiling is invisible." Peter Viereck predicted that Lowell could become "the great American poet of the 1950s, for he seems the best qualified to restore to our literature its sense of the tragic and the lofty." And Randall Jarrell wrote the most enthusiastic (and perhaps most brilliant) review of his career:

> When I reviewed Mr. Lowell's first book I finished by saying, "Some of the best poems of the next years ought to be written by him." The appearance of *Lord Weary's Castle* makes me feel less like Adams or Leverrier than like a rain-maker who predicts rain and gets a flood which drowns everyone in the country. One or two of these poems, I think, will be read as long as men remember English.[41]

Although he did not mention it, the difference between *Land of Unlikeness* and *Lord Weary's Castle* may in part be ascribed to Randall Jarrell himself. Having taken up residence in New York, Lowell's Kenyon companion was by now established as a published poet (his second book, *Little Friend, Little Friend*, appeared in 1945) and as regular poetry reviewer for the *Partisan Review*. Lowell, who was also now living in New York, sought him out for critical advice on his poetry, and Jarrell gladly took on the chore. He was more than just Lowell's most beloved friend—a "poor modern-minded exile from the forests of Grimm," a "noble, difficult, and beautiful soul." He was also "a critic of genius," with a knack for "helping friends in subtle precarious moments." This was just such a moment. Mrs. Jarrell was later to observe that the two poets' "temperaments were opposite" but their "intelligences were complementary." Jarrell carefully went over the manuscript of *Lord Weary's Castle*, providing Lowell with a heavy marginal annotation which explained and evaluated individual poems, lines, and words with marvelous subtlety and rightness. Although Jarrell never suggested particular changes (except occasionally in the matter of punctuation), Lowell systematically altered lines and words disapproved by his friend, thereby strengthening his poems immensely.[42]

Apart from this general technical improvement, Jarrell's annotation had two important effects on *Lord Weary's Castle*. On the surface, he made the volume resemble Allen Tate's poetry less. He had by this time broken with Tate for obscure reasons (perhaps having to do with Tate's reservations concerning his poetic talent), and he discouraged Lowell from obtrusively imitating the stylistic idiosyncrasies, strident politics, and unrelieved pessimism of Tate's poems of the 1940s. In a deeper sense, however, Jarrell reinforced the Tate-like essence of Lowell's poetry. Like Tate, he insisted that Lowell test his ideas by experience. In his review of *Land of Unlikeness*, he had echoed Tate's introduction in discriminating between two types of Lowell poems: the poems based on "knowledge," in which the "propositions flower out of facts," and the less effective "satires of present-day politics" which seemed merely "harsh and arbitrary . . . exercises." By the time Lowell presented Jarrell with his manuscript of *Lord Weary's Castle* the satires had already been deleted; but even in the remaining poems of knowledge, Jarrell demanded that the propositions flower out of "facts," that ideas be firmly grounded in particular details, and that the details be accurately and convincingly described. In sum, Jarrell helped to save Lowell from imitation, doctrinaire thinking, and obliviousness to brute reality. In a retrospective essay on modern American poetry published several years before his death in 1965, Jarrell was to appraise Lowell's poetry in this way:

In his poetry fact is a live stumbling block that we fall
over and feel to the bone. But it is life that he makes into
poems. . . . The awful depths, the plain absurdities of his
own actual existence in the prosperous, developed, dis-
astrous world he and we inhabit are there in the poems.

By his skillful editing of the *Lord Weary's Castle* manuscript,
Jarrell himself helped guide Lowell toward the respect for
facts that allowed him to make life into poems.[43]

Lord Weary's Castle

In *Lord Weary's Castle* Lowell transformed life into art
through the medium of myth. Myth was the first of his
modes of ordering his experience, a mode he was later, in
Life Studies, to reject. In *Lord Weary's Castle*, however, the
mythic method served him well, within certain limitations.
Although they were later to come to seem intolerably confining, these limitations were for now welcome. They
excluded from his poetry precisely the material Lowell at
this time was unable or unwilling to involve in his art: the
material of autobiography. Yet despite its hostility to the
purely personal, the myth of *Lord Weary's Castle* does admit
a wide range of experience—of religion, history, literature,
contemporary events, culture—all the communal experience that might be seen as archetypal. In the two years between *Land of Unlikeness* and *Lord Weary's Castle*, Lowell's
mythic rhetoric had developed into a mythic imagination.
If, as Randall Jarrell commented, the Catholicism of *Land of
Unlikeness* tended to turn poems into "Onward, Christian
Soldiers," the Catholicism of *Lord Weary's Castle* is a
method of organizing and illuminating shared contemporary experience. It provides the poetry with a tragic perspective which encompasses and makes meaningful the
modern situation, without violating the reader's sense of
reality which may issue from quite a different perspective.
(Indeed it enriches that sense.) In the words of Jarrell, who

51

undoubtedly bore some responsibility for the increased sophistication of Lowell's use of myth, the "imaginative Catholicism" of *Lord Weary's Castle* "represents effective realities of human behavior and desire, regardless of whether it is true, false, or absurd; and, as everyone must realize, it is possible to tell part of the truth about the world in terms that are false, limited, and fantastic—else how should we have told it?"[44]

Following the practice of both Tate and Jarrell, Lowell carefully selected and arranged his poems to produce a rough sequence revealing a central theme. The theme of *Lord Weary's Castle* is the potential of Christian salvation in a modern nightmare landscape of war and sin. The crucial word in the volume, appearing in both first and last poems, is "exile." Lowell feels exiled from the contemporary world because of his faith; and in another sense he feels exiled *in* the contemporary world, like a Jew in Babylon, removed from Zion, his spiritual home. The focus of the book is on the two factors involved in the poet's exile: his own Christian humanism and the inhuman, doomed Godlessness of the world around him.

In the manner of Yeats's "The Second Coming," Eliot's "The Waste Land," and other guides to the twentieth century, *Lord Weary's Castle* adumbrates a myth of apocalypse. Its epigraph, from the Secret of the Mass for St. Stephen Protomartyr, suggests the possibility of individual redemption; while its title, from an old English ballad, points to the certainty of cosmic cataclysm. In the ballad of *Lamkin*, Lord Weary refuses payment to his castle mason Lamkin, whereupon Lamkin enters the castle and kills Weary's family. John Berryman explained that in Lowell's allegory, Lord Weary's Castle—the modern world—is a "house of ingratitude, failure of obligation, crime and punishment," and Lamkin (which Lowell spells "Lambkin") "is the Lord who enters with sharp sword the faithless house he built." On the manuscript of his title page, Lowell penciled in, "Death comes when the house is built." Years later, he said of the war's influence on *Lord Weary's Castle*, "the world seemed apocalyptic at that time and heroically so. I thought that civilization was going to break down" (adding, with irony, "instead I did").[45]

In the more fully realized poems of *Lord Weary's Castle*, Lowell's apocalyptic Christian myth is not the subject, but rather a way of ordering the various violent and desperate experiences that *are* the subject. Which are these more fully realized poems? In 1947 Lowell wrote to Louis Untermeyer, who had requested advice concerning selections for a new edition of his anthology, that he thought the best poems were "Where the Rainbow Ends," "The Death of the Sheriff," "Between the Porch and the Altar," "The Quaker Graveyard in Nantucket," and "At the Indian Killer's Grave." (Untermeyer ultimately included none of these in the anthology.) Twenty-nine years later, after Lowell had developed his doctrine of experiential poetry and thus lost "sympathy" with *Lord Weary's Castle*, he chose an expanded group for inclusion in his *Selected Poems*: "The Exile's Return," "The Holy Innocents," "Colloquy in Black Rock," "The Quaker Graveyard in Nantucket," "Death from Cancer" (part one of "In Memory of Arthur Winslow"), "Mary Winslow," "The Drunken Fisherman," "Between the Porch and the Altar," "The Ghost," "In the Cage," "At the Indian Killer's Grave," "Mr. Edwards and the Spider," "After the Surprising Conversions," "Noli Me Tangere" (part one of "The Death of the Sheriff"), and "Where the Rainbow Ends." I myself believe that "Quaker Graveyard," "Concord," "At the Indian Killer's Grave," and "Where the Rainbow Ends" are among the best of the volume's poems, and best exemplify its mode of depersonalized experience. These poems avoid the falsification and embarrassed obscurantism of the few poems in *Lord Weary's Castle* that attempt to record deeply personal events—"Rebellion," "Between the Porch and the Altar," "In the Cage"—and they also avoid the rhetorical abstraction of the book's weaker impersonal poems.

These superior works of Lowell's early imagination repay detailed examination. Like his later great poems, they absorb the complexities of the age and of the consciousness that experiences the age complexly. Outwardly impersonal, they nevertheless ring with "personal vibrance": the voice at their center, intense and "all out," is Robert Lowell's own.[46]

Lowell establishes the basic political and religious purview of his roughened sequence in the first eight poems, which range from the largely political depiction of American military victory in "The Exile's Return" to the purely religious evocation of Pentecostal experience in "Colloquy in Black Rock" (which was originally to be called "Pentecost" and is evidently a variation on part four of Eliot's "Little Gidding"). "The Quaker Graveyard in Nantucket" interweaves these religio-political concerns and gives them supreme expression. It is the longest and in my view most completely artful poem in the volume.

Although essentially religious and political, "The Quaker Graveyard" takes the outward form of an elegy for Lowell's cousin and childhood friend Warren Winslow, whose naval vessel sank after an accidental explosion during World War II. The poem's many affinities to Milton's "Lycidas," as Hugh Staples was first to show, firmly place it "in the great tradition of the English elegy," in which lament soon leads to "a larger consideration of contemporary and universal issues." The overriding issues of "The Quaker Graveyard" revolve around the human race's misuse of its "dominion over . . . the whole earth" and the consequences of that misuse. The poem does not provide us with a clear point of view on the issues it raises. Rather, like a poem by Tate, it is a field of conflict between opposing forces within the poet's psyche, and by extension within the collective psyche of our civilization. "The Quaker Graveyard" brings into high tension irreconcilable dualities of human experience: life and death, cruelty and suffering, rebellion and submission, violence and love, sin and salvation. An elegy for a drowned sailor, and at a deeper level an elegy for the poet himself, the poem is at bottom an elegy for all people as they encounter the dark contradictions of their nature and fate.[47]

"The Quaker Graveyard" contains numerous literary echoes, ranging from Melville to Hopkins and from Jonathan Edwards to *Catholic Art and Culture*. Lowell, as an Eliotesque inheritor of Western civilization, receives the seemingly opposed strands of its literary tradition into his own sensibility, as a way of universalizing his own inner oppositions. The poem becomes, as Lowell wrote of *Four Quartets*, "something of a community product," while remaining based in quite personal feelings. Lowell's imagination conflates his literary experience with his actual experience—a description by Thoreau of a sailor's drowning with a similar drowning Lowell had personally witnessed; *Moby-Dick* with World War II. "The Quaker Graveyard" actually began as several separate poems: a fragment describing the drowning of a coast guardsman, and a pair of philosophical poems called "To Herman Melville" and "Words with Ahab." As "The Quaker Graveyard" came into being, these personal and literary motifs merged with each other and with a third motif, perhaps Lowell's most characteristic: the death of a relative. This merger of personal, familial, and literary materials is another aspect of his refusal to make false distinctions between life and art: both reverberate in the consciousness as part of an experiential whole. Lowell seized upon the whole of his experience in order to create a poem riven with the conflicts which were for him the "inward meaning" of that experience.[48]

Part one describes the burial at sea of a sailor who is fictionally but not literally Winslow (in actuality his body was not recovered). Lowell took many of his descriptive details, as Staples and Mazzaro have shown, from Thoreau's *Cape Cod*: the sea "still breaking violently," the sailor's "matted head and marble feet," his "coiled" but "bloodless" body, and his "open, staring eyes" which resemble "lustreless dead-lights / Or cabin windows on a stranded hulk / Heavy with sand." Writing of T. S. Eliot at the same time he was composing "Quaker Graveyard," Lowell commented that "quotations" make passages "appear impersonal" and in addition provide "a richer and more inspired texture than the poet could sustain on his own." Yet Lowell significantly rearranges Thoreau's details, in order to integrate them into his *own* inspiration. He contrasts details suggesting kinesthesis (the sailor's "coiled, hurdling muscles") with features suggesting statuary ("marble feet") or a still-life ("a botch of reds and whites"), thereby highlighting the pathos of the sailor's movement from the energy of life to the stasis of death. The body which seemed actively to "clutch" and "grapple" is revealed to be passively "stranded," "heavy"; the "light" which "flashed" from his head darkens into the "lustreless dead-lights" of his eyes. Although partly fictional and partly expressed in borrowed language, the passage is in a sense highly personal. Lowell brilliantly transforms his borrowed details into a new entity that contains his own deep response to the pathos of mortality.[49]

The emotional effect is strengthened by a change of tone in the lines that follow this description. Here the speaker enters the poem in his own person (one of only three times he does so), joining Whitman-like in the group that heaves the sailor's body into the sea. The speaker reports that the sailor's name "is blocked in yellow chalk" (I.15-16). This touch of objective reportage (again Whitman-like) saves part one from the danger of excessive interiority. Most of the preceding details (as we saw in the comparison of this passage with Tate's "Confederate Ode") serve the Symbolist function of communicating the poet's emotion. For all of the power of Lowell's lines, the poem threatens to become too hermetic and monotonously intense. In early drafts Lowell had indeed tried to maintain subjective intensity by writing that the name was "scribbled with red chalk," but Jarrell objected that this was "unrealistic" and Lowell substituted the more documentary "blocked in yellow." With the addition of this factual, and hence moving, detail of the impersonal certification of death, "The Quaker Graveyard" opens to the real world. Because the poem is realistic in detail, the increasing bleakness of its moral vision is all the more convincing. Lowell terms the sailor's dead body a "portent," recalling John Brown's body in Melville's poem. If Brown's death portended the chaos of war, the sailor's war-death portends a condition even more extreme: a war with nature itself. The sailors "pitch" the dead body "at" the sea, but their gesture of defiance (like Ahab's in *Moby-Dick*) is doomed. The physical universe is a "hell-bent deity" against whose immutable laws human beings are "powerless." Lowell's earlier contrast of life and death is deepened in these final lines: no "Orphean lute" can challenge the finality of the guns' repeated "hoarse salute." Through its meticulous portrayal of an individual death, part one of "The Quaker Graveyard" enables us to experience fully the fact of Death's dominion.[50]

Removing us from the scene of the drowning, the five middle parts of the poem address an extended meditation to the dead sailor upon the historical and metaphysical meanings suggested by his death. In part two, the elements themselves are distempered by the death. The seabirds "tremble" momentously (just as the speaker of "Lycidas" trembles at the thought of Atropos and as all Hell trembles at the appearance of Death in *Paradise Lost*). For in the death of this archetypal "Sailor" we foresee the coming death of the human race. Lowell associates the Sailor with both the "Pequod" and "the hurt beast / Bobbing by Ahab's whaleboats" (II.5,17-18). To Lowell, modern war is as demonic as Ahab's rebellion against God, and the Sailor has played a role equivalent to both whaler and whale—Godless killer and suffering victim. The poet has begun to bring to life his eschatological theory of American history, with the help of Melville's metaphor. Lowell later said, "There are two great symbolic figures that stand behind American ambition and culture. One is Milton's Lucifer and the other is Captain Ahab: these two sublime ambitions that are doomed and ready, for their idealism, to face any amount of violence." The image of Ahab killing whales in "The Quaker Graveyard" stands for three contemporary evils (which are really one): the murder of nature for selfish ends (capitalism), the murder of young men like Winslow (war), and the murder of Jesus Christ (secularism). In Lowell's Weberian view, the hideous capitalism, war, and atheism of the present age derive inevitably from America's Calvinist-Quaker beginnings. The doomed Sailor—a representative of us all—has been the victim of his own sinfulness, the victim of his participation in his own deeply sinning culture.[51]

These meanings are extended in part three. Lowell for the only time in the poem shows personal warmth toward the Sailor by addressing him as "my cousin." Further, he endows the whale-killing Quakers with a certain colloquial attractiveness in allowing them to speak in their own foolish—humanly foolish—voices. But this emotional sympathy contrasts with the poem's increasingly negative moral judgment. Lowell makes God's anger at the human race explicit, in language that perhaps strangely derives from the great Puritan divine Jonathan Edwards. (It is useful to remember that Jarrell thought Lowell temperamentally the ideal follower of Calvin.) In "The Future Punishment of the Wicked," Edwards asked his congregation, "What art thou in the hands of the great God, who . . . when fixed time shall come, will shake all to pieces?" That time now come round at last, Lowell describes warships rocked "in the hand / Of the great God" (III.10-11). Edwards warned sinners that when God loosed his "black clouds of wrath" upon them they would be "weak as water" and "swallowed up and lost." Lowell's God makes good that threat: the Quaker sailors drown, even as they insanely deny having been "swallowed . . . up quick"

(III.24). The nineteenth-century Quakers, who are analogous to and symbolic of twentieth-century Americans, have "lost" eternally by murdering the sperm-whale, "IS, the whited monster" (III.12,18). This image of "IS," mediated by Melville's Moby Dick, refers to Christ himself—the "IS" of Gerard Manley Hopkins and (typologically) the "I AM THAT I AM" of *Exodus*. The Quakers have murdered their connection to holiness, and "what it cost them" is salvation itself. Milton's Lycidas, who drowned like Lowell's Sailor and Quakers, was yet "mounted high through the dear might of him that walks the waves." But we in our rebellion against God have forfeited that hope: "This is the end of running on the waves" (IV.17).[52]

In parts four and five the poem makes another of its shifts of movement. No longer content as accuser, indicting "you" and "them," the speaker now implicates himself in the bloody pageant of human sin, using the pronouns "we" and "our" (IV.18, V.18). Within the austerely impersonal framework of "The Quaker Graveyard," Lowell has arrived at a theme which could not be more personal: his own mixed motives of rebellion and remorseful quest for an authority able to forgive that rebellion. Lowell's way of understanding this theme is theological rather than psychological. "The Quaker Graveyard" is "Skunk Hour" seen through a thick glass of culture: an unspecified speaker using the pronoun "we" instead of Robert Lowell speaking as "I myself."

In order to achieve an air of anonymity for what is at base a confession of loathesome self-knowledge and guarded hope, Lowell takes his images from the impersonal source of *Moby-Dick* (chapters 61 and 135). In Lowell's version of the *Moby-Dick* myth, the white whale dies like Christ on the cross, "spouting out blood and water"—harpooned, crucified (IV.8). By repeating the murder of Christ through ceaseless violence, the human race (including now the speaker) has brought Apocalypse upon itself. Using the kind of paradox that earned him an early reputation for blasphemy, Lowell describes the sacrifice of the Christ-symbolizing whale in stomach-churning detail which suggests the whale's grossness and indeed "corruption" (V.2). (Remember that even earlier he thought of it as a "whited *monster*.") Lowell rebels even against reverence, should it smack of smugness. Only the hacked-apart, fish-eaten, nauseous carcass of an all-too-fleshly whale can earn this speaker's reverence; but earn reverence it does. The bloodied whale merges with Jesus Christ and Christ's prototype Jonah, as the speaker cries at last, "Hide, / Our steel, Jonas Messias, in Thy side" (V.17-18). As one of the Christ-killers, the speaker pleads to Christ for salvation—for himself and for the whole ship of fools. This direct address to Christ is really the first hopeful note in the poem, the first sign that salvation might still be possible.

Following this emotional high point the poem shifts tone once more. The Passion yields to mystical trance. Part six, called "Our Lady of Walsingham," presents an alternative to the modern catastrophe of unbelief depicted so vividly in the preceding parts. This alternative is contemplative Christianity, leading to union with God. In verse that is stately and harmonious (in contrast to the baroque style of the previous parts), Lowell imagines the Sailor visiting the shrine of the Virgin Mary at Walsingham, England. This description is, as Lowell's prefatory note explains, "an adaptation of several paragraphs from E. I. Watkin's *Catholic Art and Culture*." In his book Watkin contrasts Our Lady's supernatural expression of God ("that expressionless countenance expresses what is beyond expression") to the destructive logical positivism governing modern life. Borrowing from Watkin, Lowell's "Our Lady of Walsingham" describes the condition Eliot achieves in the triumphant conclusion to *Four Quartets*: "A condition of complete simplicity / (Costing not less than everything)." Yet does Lowell's mystical condition cost him "not less than everything"? One of his discerning critics, Marjorie Perloff, finds the Christianity of the passage smug. I believe that, far from smug, it is wracked by a sense of failure. The speaker sees (and invites the Sailor to see also) the face that expresses God, but the face proves "expressionless" to human beings. In his prepublication commentary, Randall Jarrell wrote on the margin of these lines: "This is as frightening as anything could be, after the beautiful beginning." That remark seems to me to get to the center of Lowell's religious vision here: it is colored by a sense of the extreme improbability and even, perhaps, the undesirability of faith. Unlike his source Watkin, who makes the Virgin's "inner beauty" his major point, Lowell depicts a face that is simply charmless, "heavy," inimical. Ironically, this image of divinity is less humanly attractive than the image of the drowned Sailor, his body flashing with light, or of Christ the bloodied "monster," hiding our steel spears in his side. The shifting dialectic of "The Quaker Graveyard" cannot be reduced to the logic of pious doctrine. Although part six of the poem presents the only existent alternative to human chaos, it is not an alternative Lowell can endorse with whole heart.[53]

The last part of the poem returns us to the specific Nantucket landscape. Since we left the scene at the beginning of the poem the elements have become even more disordered: the wind (instead of the oak) is "creaking," the oak (instead of the sea) "splatters," the sea (instead of the bombs of war) is "exploding." Standing by the Sailor's cenotaph, the speaker ceases his monologue addressed to the Sailor and addresses the Atlantic itself. He recapitulates some of the poem's key images of natural process and stasis ("trembling" in air, "bobbing" on water, sailors made "blue" by drowning) and then renders a final judgment on the fact that human beings die. The judgment is pitiless. "It's well," he tells the Atlantic, "you are fouled with blue sailors" (VII.6-7). Nonetheless, this Edwards-like justification of the angry God is almost immediately

countered by defiant feelings of sympathy for the suffering
sinners. The·speaker reproaches the time

> When the Lord God formed man from the sea's slime
> And breathed into his face the breath of life,
> And blue-lung'd combers lumbered to the kill.
>
> (VII.14-16)

Here Lowell returns to the poem's dominating image of
the mortal being whose fate it is to be preyed upon by
sharks (the "dog-fish" of part one, the "combers" here), or
shark-like fish (the "flukes" of part five). The speaker's
submission to God turns to rebellion; his merciless judgment on humankind turns to sorrow. These tensions are
silenced in the ambiguous purity of the poem's concluding
Orphic statement:

> The Lord survives the rainbow of His will.

The rainbow of God's will, of course, is his covenant with
Noah that "the waters shall no more become a flood to de-
stroy all flesh" (Genesis 9:15). By stating that God survives
this covenant Lowell seems to suggest that the Apocalypse
is at hand. The Biblical flood, a destruction of the wicked,
is now to be followed by a new destruction of the wicked,
augured or embodied by the fire of world war. Humankind
will divide itself into "downward fish" (the damned) and
"upward angel" (the saved); and the latter, who have entered into God through the death of Christ, will survive
eternally as God himself survives.

Lowell thus resolves his meditation on the horror of
mortality by insisting on the possibility of salvation. But is
this vindication of God truly a "final affirmation," as many
of Lowell's critics have believed? Doctrinally it is, but emotionally it is not, for the God who survives has been portrayed as remorselessly cruel. The human violence casti-
gated in the first parts of the poem seems to have its source
in Lowell's "Great God," who drowns sailors, who has
created the human race to be wasted by "blue lung'd comb-

ers." "The Quaker Graveyard" is a Christian poem without being a Godly poem. At its deepest level, it is a dialectic between those who inflict violence (which Lowell has called "*the* hellfire") and those who suffer violence. In the moral hierarchy of the poem, Jesus, who has taken all suffering to himself, stands at the top; the human race, which repeatedly plays the role of both Christ-killer and Man of Sorrows himself, stands ambiguously at the middle; and God, the vengeful authority-figure in whom "non est species, neque decor" (there is neither beauty nor gracefulness), in some ways stands at bottom (VI.16). Lowell's Jeremiad against God's sinning children modulates into an exposure of the cruel Father. Ultimately the poem is a protest against fate itself, against the force (whatever one chooses to call it) that has doomed the human race to suffer and cause suffering.[54]

In "The Quaker Graveyard in Nantucket" Lowell constructed a verbal structure to contain the profound antinomies of his own being: reverence and rebellion, condemnation and forgiveness, guilt and innocence, love of life and half-wish for oblivion. The poem's verbal texture itself is antinomic. The flood of double meanings—sailors drowned "quick," news "fabled" of God, the "end of the whaleroad," a whale "sick as a dog"—justify Jarrell's marginal comment that the poem "beats Empson at his own game." Lowell's ironies do not degenerate into mere rhetorical cleverness, however, because they are attached to hard worldly realities which he takes pains to insist upon: the ugly-beautiful physicality of the Sailor's dead body (I), the all-too-human sins of the Quakers (III), the grossness of the mutilated whale (V). Further, the poem contains hints of a unifying vision capable of stilling its conflicts. The verbal parallels which make the drowned sailor and butchered whale-Savior both "coiled" (I.7, V.11), the sea-gulls and Our Lady both heavy-lidded (II.12, VI.14), and the whale and the sea both "hurt" (II.17, IV.12) may suggest that human being / Divinity / nature share in a unitary wholeness.

Yet it would be wrong to emphasize this underlying potential for integration, for "The Quaker Graveyard" on its face remains a brutal clash of opposites. The poem grows out of the rending psychic divisions attendant upon the poet's knowledge of death and sin. Lowell's two uses of the first-person pronoun in the latter half of the poem reveal his divided nature in terms of Christian metaphor. In the first he identifies himself (and all people) with Jesus Christ: "We are poured out like water," like the water which poured from the side of Christ (IV.18). In the second he identifies himself (and all people) with the murderous centurion: "Hide, / Our steel, Jonas Messias, in Thy side" (V.18). This inner conflict is not logically resolved in the poem but imaginatively undergone. The poem has no "answer." It is a way of more fully experiencing questions that are central to human existence.[55]

The volume's first segment of eight religious and political poems is followed by a sub-sequence of four familial elegies (*LWC*, 18-25)—touching Christian analogues to the elegies that commence the "Life Studies" sequence (*LS*, 59-78). These familial poems are followed by another sub-sequence of four poems, which concern the New England past (*LWC*, 26-29). Lowell seems to have considered calling these poems (or perhaps only some of them) "The Blood of Abel; a New England Sequence." Although he rejected this title, it accurately reveals his underlying notion that the history of colonial (Puritan) and modern (Protestant-capitalist) New England in some sense parallels Cain's murder of Abel. Lowell's use of this Biblical metaphor is complicated by the fact that it enacts one of his own deepest contradictions: his sense of himself as both sinner and sinned-against. Intellectually, Lowell may abhor Cain's violent rebellion, which he identifies as Satanic (*LWC*, 28), but emotionally he identifies himself *with* Cain.

As an illustration, he originally thought to call "Rebellion"—the story of his own violent attack on his father—"The Seed of Cain" or "The Blood of Abel." Lowell thus brings to his poems on New England history a deep division within his own mind. This kind of inner division can result in great, ambiguous poetry, if contrary is allowed to work upon contrary, as occurs in "The Quaker Graveyard."

Two of the four poems in Lowell's New England sequence, however, fail to acknowledge their sources in emotional ambiguity and so fail as poetry, however impressive they may be as rhetoric. These poems are "Salem" and "Children of Light" (both virtually unchanged from *Land of Unlikeness*). The first poem glorifies New England's rebellious past while the second bitterly denounces it. Equally vehement, the poems hold diametrically opposite views of New England's history (and, inferentially, of violent rebellion). The poems fail because they are false to history and, even more, because they are false to Lowell's feelings.

"Concord," conversely, advances a view of the past that does justice to the inner complexity of both past and poet. In place of the unbridled castigation of the *Land of Unlikeness* version of this poem (in which Emerson is vilified because he "washed out the blood-clots on my Master's robe" and even because he "forgot the fathers' flintlock guns"), the present "Concord" develops a vocabulary of mixed blame and praise. The past is presented neither as a heroic contrast to present evil (as in "Salem") nor as the sole source for present evil (as in "Children of Light"), but as part of a historical continuum ambiguously composed of both good and evil. Although it ultimately moves to even more important themes, "Concord" begins as an indictment of America's severance from its own history. "Ten thousand Fords are idle here in search / Of a tradition" (*LWC*, 27). These "Fords" are not only the parked autos but their Mammonish owners as well, who share Henry Ford's prejudice against history as "bunk." They are engaged in a search which (like the cars' engines) is "idle": hastily inspected landmarks cannot provide a sense of vital continuity, a Jamesian "sense of the past." Walden's perch have been "fished-out"; even in mid-nineteenth century, Thoreau tells us, the pond was "not very fertile in fish," but now it is entirely barren, a fitting symbol of American tradition. Yet if the past is severed from us as a cultural resource, it is continuous with us as a harbinger of the present moral malaise. Concord's Unitarian Church, now as in the days when Emerson attended it each Sunday, "rings out the hanging Jesus": "rings out" not so much in the sense of "proclaiming" as in the sense of "registering departure." New England's faded Protestantism has made Christianity impotent to counter modern "Mammon's unbridled industry."

Although Lowell sees the new thinkers of Concord, led by Emerson and Thoreau, as unwitting moral villains, he is also eager to praise their moral heroism. Remembering Thoreau's categorical refusal in *Walden* to carry firearms ("there is a finer way of studying ornithology than this"), and his lifelong sympathy with American Indians ("every circumstance touching the Indian [was] important in his eyes" said Emerson), Lowell writes: "Thoreau / Named all the birds without a gun to probe / Through darkness to the painted man and bow." He thus portrays Thoreau as an innocent Adam, capable of passing Emerson's test of ideal nobility in "Forbearance": "Hast thou named all the birds without a gun?" Pacifist and Indian-lover, Thoreau is Lowell's foil to American violence and racism. These latter traits are epitomized in "Concord" by King Philip's War, a war of extermination waged by Cotton Mather's Puritans against the Indians. Lowell views American history (perhaps reflecting his own inner conflict) as a symbolic opposition of the pacifism and genius of Thoreau and the genocidal violence of Puritanism and Mammon. Tragically, he sees the violence as predominant. The echo of the Indian king's "scream" of death has "girdled this imperfect globe" up to the present moment, in which civilian populations perish in the "jellied fire" of American World War II bombing raids (*LWC*, 68).

Lowell means "Concord" to stand in ironic though complementary relation to Emerson's "Concord Hymn," one of his favorite poems. He begins his poem by repeating Emerson's reference to "the ruined bridge"; but even here we feel that this bridge is ruined by more than Time and the dark stream. Its "ruin" is moral as well. By the conclusion, Lowell's position is clear. He once said of Emerson's Concord poem that it "becomes more internal as it goes on and you find Emerson's old themes . . . flashing in one historic moment." So it is with his own Concord poem. In place of Emerson's "shot heard round the world," a line Lowell called "ironic and urbane," he substitutes the Indian's unironic, unurbane, horrifying scream of death. Faithful to the opaque ambiguities of history, Lowell in "Concord" achieves moral lucidity.*[56]

"Rebellion," the last poem of Lowell's New England group, fails—though in a more interesting way than "Salem" and "Children of Light." "Rebellion" seeks to masquerade personal confession as historical and mythic statement, a disguise that serves only to confuse the poem. Lowell's adolescent assault on his father is inflated into an obscure parable of patricide and damnation, heavy with overtones from *Job* ("Behemoth and Leviathan") and American history (the "flintlock" which is said to break the

* Although Lowell obviously intended his final two lines as a modern revision of Emerson's celebrated "Concord Hymn" phrase, they also parody lines by his great-granduncle, James Russell Lowell, a poet he once dismissed as "pedestalled for oblivion." One of J. R. Lowell's Concord poems asks rhetorically, "What earthquake rifts would shoot and run / World-wide from that short April fray?" This poem, "Lines Suggested by the Graves of Two English Soldiers on Concord Battleground," and another entitled "Ode Read at the One Hundredth Anniversary of the Fight at Concord Bridge" are the kind of overblown patriotic poems that "Concord" is intended to deflate.

father's skull). Unable to account for personal feelings and events on their own terms, Lowell interprets the incident variously as an expression of divine wrath against the ruling class or as a damnable act of American violence. (In rewriting the poem for *History* he dropped both the allegory and the exaggeration.) This severe discomfiture with the materials of autobiography is characteristic of *Lord Weary's Castle*. In "In the Cage," for example, Lowell transforms himself and his fellow short-term convicts into hardened "lifers." (The *History* version of this poem changes "the lifers" to "we short-termers.") In "Winter in Dunbarton" he labels his grandfather's gravestone "father's stone." In the first published version of the childhood reminiscence "Buttercups," in *Partisan Review*, he impersonally refers to his subjects as "you" instead of "we." And the manuscript versions of "Rebellion" are addressed by a Cain-figure to the "Brother" he has murdered. In writing *Lord Weary's Castle*, Lowell resisted the autobiographical mode while evidencing a drive to do *something* with autobiographical experience. Paradoxically, the great impersonal poems in the volume ultimately are more personal than the quasi-autobiographical poems, because they are truer to their author's uncensored consciousness. Lowell's mastery of the art of autobiography, so necessary to the fulfillment of his particular genius, was still to be achieved.

The New England poems are followed by several religious poems, a large group of war poems (from "The North Sea Undertaker's Complaint" through "1790") which seem to me among the least realized poems in the book, and an even larger miscellany of adaptations, monologues, narratives, and Empson-flavored Jeremiads. (One, "The Crucifix," was called in manuscript "Empson.") Although this second half of *Lord Weary's Castle* lacks the inspired intensity of the beginning poems, it does contain two high points: another group of retrospective New England poems ("Mr. Edwards and the Spider," "After the Surprising Conversions," and the brilliant and disturbing

"At the Indian Killer's Grave") and a concluding prophecy, "Where the Rainbow Ends."

This second group of New England poems exhibits Lowell's new-found awareness of the complexities within culture and himself. The two monologues, adapted from Jonathan Edwards' own writings, brilliantly convey the rhetorical excess of the Great Awakening ("Mr. Edwards and the Spider") and the societal breakdown which follows from that excess ("After the Surprising Conversions"). In the spirit of philosopher Ernst Cassirer, who wrote in 1944 that "history is not knowledge of external facts or events; it is a form of self-knowledge," Lowell portrays Edwards and his "undone" parishioners as precursive symbols of the apocalyptic drama of sin and destruction now at hand in post-Puritan America. But the Edwards poems point to a self-knowledge even more personal than that. Edwards, the arch-Puritan, in a sense the architect of all our woe, is viewed (as Dallas Wiebe first noted) with surprising sympathy. Lowell gives us an Edwards of inherent genius (exemplified by his eloquent observation of nature in the first stanza of "Mr. Edwards") as well as an Edwards of violence (exemplified by the rhetoric that drives Josiah [Joseph] Hawley to his death in the poem's last stanza). Lowell recognizes in Edwards, his ideological enemy, a human brother.[57]

"At the Indian Killer's Grave," like "Concord," recalls the slaughter of Indians in King Philip's War (*LWC*, 54-57). This war, caused by the colonists' territorial expansionism, was the bloodiest of all the wars between the newcomers and native Americans. The colonists' eventual victory over the forces of King Philip in 1676, marking the end of the Indians as a national entity in New England, serves Lowell as a symbol of American violence, idealism, and ambition. The theme of "At the Indian Killer's Grave," therefore, has enduring significance. In the poem's epigraph, Lowell changes Hawthorne's past tense to present, to suggest that we *all* "are veterans of King Philip's War, who burned villages and slaughtered young and old, with pious fierceness"—a slaughter of innocents that recurs in the present day.[58]

Lowell's public poem has personal dimensions as well. On a subjective level, the national violence he finds so abhorrent has an analogue in his very own personality. More objectively, the poem may be viewed as yet another of his family poems. Almost in the manner of Hawthorne's Pyncheons, Lowell has been given blood to drink: the leader of the colonists' military forces was Josiah Winslow, commander-in-chief and governor of Plymouth Colony, and Lowell's direct ancestor on his mother's side. (The "John and Mary Winslow" whose cenotaph is in the graveyard are other Lowell ancestors, Josiah's uncle and aunt [II.19].) Winslow and his men burned villages of men, women, and children, and caused the virtual annihilation of the Narragansetts. In "At the Indian Killer's Grave," then, Lowell confronts national guilt that ramifies deep in his own psyche.

As the poem begins, the speaker stands in the blackened graveyard of the Indian killers, briefly imagining them in Jehoshaphat, disgraced and awaiting judgment. Unlike the elegies to which it is principally indebted—Gray's "Elegy in a Country Churchyard," Longfellow's "The Jewish Cemetery at Newport," several *Symboliste* graveyard poems, and Tate's "Ode to the Confederate Dead"— Lowell's poem reveals not the virtues of its subjects but their sins, their damnation. This garden of the dead is "rotten to the root" (I.9), and its fruit is likewise rotten. The Puritans' modern-day descendants, whose smog "confounds with" the dust of the pilgrims and whose subway "racks / The Pilgrim Fathers' relics," are equally "disgraced" (I-III). Like Lowell's later poem "For the Union Dead," "At the Indian Killer's Grave" pictures modern civilization desecrating the memory of the past while unconsciously repeating its brutalities. Remembering that King Philip's head was exhibited at Plymouth for many years after his death, Lowell in the third verse-paragraph has the head of Philip deliver judgment on New England past and present. The judgment is of earthly defeat ("this people . . . will pass") and eternal damnation ("Your election . . . Flutters and claws in the dead hand of time").

In the final verse-paragraph the speaker turns in revulsion from this past and future. Historical meditation resolves into personal religious confession. Speaking for the first time in the first person,* Lowell recalls Hawthorne's retelling of the Cadmus myth, in which the dragon's teeth sprout into "a multitude of polished brass helmets." (Lowell's mother read this fable to him as a child and it became "history to [him] and just as much fact as the earth, the water, and the sky.") In "At the Indian Killer's Grave" he conflates Cadmus with the fallen Adam, and war with original sin:

> Who was the man who sowed the dragon's teeth,
> That fabulous or fancied patriarch
> Who sowed so ill for his descent?
>
> (V.2-4)

The way to escape this ancestral curse on human destiny, here as everywhere in *Lord Weary's Castle*, is through union with Christ. Lowell's speaker rejects merely "verbal" Paradises and the "garden rotten to its root" for the Garden:

> John, Matthew, Luke and Mark,
> Gospel me to the Garden, let me come
> Where Mary twists the warlock with her flowers—
> Her soul a bridal chamber fresh with flowers

---

* In his revision of the poem for Faber's *Robert Lowell's Poems: A Selection* in 1974, Lowell deleted the third verse-paragraph, and changed the pronoun in the opening lines of the fourth from "you" to "we" and "us." As in most of his latter-day revisions, Lowell sought by such changes (however unsuccessfully in this case) to make the poetry more personal. In the Farrar, Straus, and Giroux *Selected Poems* of 1976, he restored his original version.

And her whole body an ecstatic womb,
As through the trellis peers the sudden Bridegroom.
(X.6-11)

This conclusion, powerfully combining natural and erotic imagery, imagines salvation as incest. Incest,the other side of parricide, is a great and often hidden theme in much of Lowell's work. Christ the Bridegroom penetrates to the ecstatic womb of Mary. If the Bridegroom is also a figure for the poet, as Jonathan Raban suggests perhaps on the authority of Lowell himself, then the poet's union with Christ occurs in the bridal chamber of the mother. In this conclusion Lowell replaces a world grown black with age with a new world "fresh with flowers," replaces violence with love, and recovers his spiritual innocence through sexual experience. Neither murderer nor victim now, the rebel has gained access to the seat of authority, and has found it or made it the seat of love.[59]

Although in some ways similar to "The Quaker Graveyard in Nantucket," "At the Indian Killer's Grave" comes to a very different close. In "The Quaker Graveyard" Mary has "no comeliness / At all or charm," and this cold, repellent, impossible vision of salvation yields to the more attractive vision of agonizing death as "blue lung'd combers" lumber to the kill. "At the Indian's Killer's Grave" has a more humanist and humanitarian cast. Even in its condemnation of sin, one senses pity for the sinners, for the very fact of sin: "the clouds / Weep on the just and unjust as they will" (II.11-12), "Who sowed so ill for his descent?" (V.2). The poem's answer to sin, its vision of divine grace in the final lines, takes the humanized form of erotic metaphor (though it is clouded by incest). There is a greater acceptance of humanness in this poem than in the book's earlier poems, which writhe with rage. Lowell has achieved a spirit of charity that extends even so far as to himself. In "At the Indian Killer's Grave," Lowell exchanges the flames of destruction for the light of salvation—a salvation possible because it is not inimical to the essentially human.

An identical insight informs the volume's last poem, "Where the Rainbow Ends" (*LWC*, 69). This clear response to both "The Exile's Return" and "The Quaker Graveyard" begins where those poems finish, in a condition near spiritual despair:

> The scythers, Time and Death,
> Helmed locusts, move upon the tree of breath;
> The wild ingrafted olive and the root
> Are withered.

The conclusion of "Where the Rainbow Ends," however, points to a new spiritual place, where the "rainbow of God's will" may end in peace rather than destruction, where the exile may find succor, where the withered olive may be restored:

> I kneel and the wings beat
> My cheek. What can the dove of Jesus give
> You now but wisdom, exile? Stand and live,
> The dove has brought an olive branch to eat.

Upon reading this poem, Jarrell wrote to Lowell: "This . . . has the most hopeful ending I can remember in a poem of yours, and is a sweet and hopeful sign, an olive-leaf." Eloquently expressive of Lowell's anguish, *Lord Weary's Castle* at the last delivers him from that anguish. In a pattern characteristic of his later books, *Lord Weary's Castle* moves through death to life, through pain to wisdom, affirming finally, after bitter testing, the value of experience and the necessity of survival.[60]

"Stand and live, / The dove has brought an olive branch to eat": in *Lord Weary's Castle* Lowell finds salvation within human experience. In his next stage of development, a short but agonizing step ahead, he will find salvation to *be* human experience.

Drift

By thirty, O the case was plain:
We'd never be so good again.
—*I. A. Richards*, "For the 50th
Birthday of Robert Lowell"

In the years following the publication of *Lord Weary's Castle*, an "astonished" Lowell gained the kind of notice he had longed for from the beginning. He was, said *Time*, "the year's most rewarded poet." In addition to the Pulitzer Prize, he received grants from the American Academy-National Institute of Arts and Letters and the Guggenheim Foundation, and was asked to serve as Poetry Consultant to the Library of Congress and as a member of the first Bollingen Prize Committee. (He voted with the majority to give the prize to Pound.) In 1947 he was the subject of flattering articles in *Current Biography*, the *New York Times*, and *Life* magazine, which called him "a shy, amiable young man" who had "already reached the stature of a major literary figure."[61]

Even more pleasing was the recognition Lowell received from other writers. Friendships were begun with many of the literary giants he had long idolized from afar: W. H. Auden, T. S. Eliot, William Empson, Robert Frost, Marianne Moore, Ezra Pound, George Santayana, and William Carlos Williams. Upon first looking into *Lord Weary's Castle*, his mentor Allen Tate wrote to him enthusiastically: "The immense advance that you have made in the past three years is one of the most astonishing things in modern poetry." T. S. Eliot, in his role as editor for Faber, assumed a personal interest in Lowell's career. He wrote to Lowell's American publisher in 1946 that he thought it wise not to introduce the young poet to the British public with a reprint of *Lord Weary's Castle* but rather to wait awhile and publish a substantial selection, adding "I am really very interested in watching Lowell's progress." (Their personal relations were somewhat ambiguous; Lowell wrote after first meeting Eliot, "When I finally said goodbye to him—I felt I could say nothing to him and be understood and sympathized with. . . . There are many layers to be gotten under, when you do there's something warm and human.") In early 1948 Lowell paid a call on Ezra Pound at St. Elizabeth's, and according to a witness "dazzled him out of all countenance." Lowell thereafter visited frequently. Pound wrote a letter of introduction for him to Huntington Cairns ("Cairns, this guy iz a seeryus character"); later wrote Lowell pleasant letters (one ends "*like* yu"); and praised him to visitors as the best of a generally poor crop of younger poets. In 1949 Robert Frost told readers of the *New York Herald Tribune Book Review* that Lowell was one of the "most promising young poets," along with Wilbur, Viereck, Shapiro, Bishop, and Ciardi. As proof of Lowell's literary arrival he was selected for inclusion in Louis Untermeyer's next edition of his modern American poetry anthology. Lowell, who had first seen modern poetry in Untermeyer's anthology at St. Mark's, wrote to Untermeyer telling him that he was flattered to be included.[62]

Yet despite this surface triumph, Lowell's inner life was deeply troubled in the years following *Lord Weary's Castle*. His moment of artistic transcendence, in which passion found its appropriate form, had ended. Personally, he entered into a period of painful change. In the late 1940s he lost his faith, his politics, his wife, and his mind. And his poetry drifted.

Lord Weary's Castle had been largely written in the aristocratic, traditionalist ambiance provided by Tate and the Agrarians. Now living in Washington and New York, Lowell found himself in a very different world. He was surrounded and greatly stimulated by liberal literary intellectuals, people like Randall Jarrell, Philip Rahv, Delmore Schwartz, and John Berryman, whose ideas were based on Freud, Marx, and modern science rather than Christopher Dawson. In this milieu, Lowell found his Christian mythmaking out of place and even under attack. Jarrell, in fact, had chided him about it in his review of *Lord Weary's Castle*: "It is hard to enjoy the ambergris for thinking of all those suffering whales." Further, Lowell's relationship to Allen Tate, his guide in orthodoxy, lost its intimacy in the years following his success. And his marriage to fellow Catholic Jean Stafford, a woman with some of the force and personality of his mother, was bitterly dissolved in 1948. (The following year he married the social and literary critic Elizabeth Hardwick, who was politically on the left and not religious.) Finally, Lowell was very aware that the global apocalypse he had prophesied with confidence in *Land of Unlikeness* and with growing hesitance in *Lord Weary's Castle* had failed to occur.[63]

Perhaps Lowell's radical-feudalist politics and militant religious faith had been willed and insecure acquisitions all along, desperate attempts to ward off a personal chaos. In 1949, however, he broke down; violent and out of control, he underwent the first of his periodic institutionalizations, which would recur throughout the rest of his life. He emerged from his experience of the late 1940s stripped of his politics and his theology, indeed stripped of all his bases for making sense of his world, and for making poetry out of it. Deprived of the beliefs that once inspired him, he lost his inspiration.

The most interesting and consequential development in Lowell's intellectual life during this period was a renewal of his interest, after a decade of neglect, in the work of William Carlos Williams. With the alteration of his religious and political views he found that Tate (and by extension Eliot) had ceased to function as a usable artistic model or "master." Casting about for a solution to a growing artistic dilemma, he began to look again at Williams, the poet he had found so exciting at Harvard but whom Tate had dismissed as merely a "byline" to modern poetry. In 1947 Lowell published an enthusiastic review of book one of

Paterson in the *Sewanee Review*. The review ends with a revealing comparison of Williams to the poets who had previously served as his culture totems—Tate, Ransom, Eliot, and Pound. Seemingly disturbed at the increasing division of his own loyalties, Lowell attempts to play down the differences between Williams and the more conservative writers. Eager for a reconciliation, he argues that Williams, despite himself, is a conservative too:

> Williams is liberal, anti-orthodox, and a descendant of Emerson and Whitman. But if a man is intense and honest enough, the half-truth of any extreme position will in time absorb much of its opposite. Williams has much in common with Catholic, aristocratic and Agrarian writers. For all his sympathy with his people, he makes one feel that the sword of Damocles hangs over Paterson, the modern city and world. As with Yeats, "things fall apart." The educated lack connection, and the ignorant are filled with speechless passion.

But on the issue of nativism versus cosmopolitanism, Lowell surprisingly defends Williams's side without reservation: "In *Paterson* his position has paid off, when compared with Pound's. It is a sort of anti-Cantos rooted in America, in one city, and in what Williams has known long and seen often. . . . Its details [are] enriched and verified by experience." And in summation, Lowell suggests that of all the modern masters Williams is the supreme poet of experience: "It would be fruitless to compare *Paterson* with the best writing of Eliot, Stevens, Tate, or Auden, for the ways of writing very well are various; but for experience and observation, it has along with a few poems of Frost, a richness that makes almost all other contemporary poetry look a little second hand."[64]

In a second essay on Williams published the following year in *The Nation*, Lowell enthusiastically compared the first two books of *Paterson* to *Leaves of Grass* as great poems of American experience. This essay shows him grappling with the whole "redskin" tradition in American poetry, which under the guidance of Tate he had previously rejected as tending toward ethnocentrism and artless effusion. Now, however, he found himself fascinated by the redskin poets Whitman and Williams, and by the ambiguity of their relationship to America, which seemed to correspond to his own:

> "Paterson" is an attempt to write the American Poem. It depends on the American myth, a myth that is seldom absent from our literature—part of our power, and part of our hubris and deformity. At its grossest the myth is propaganda, puffing and grimacing: Size, Strength, Vitality, the Common Man, the New World, Vital Speech, the Machine; the hideous neo-Roman personae: Democracy, Freedom, Liberty, the Corn, the Land. How hollow, windy, and inert this would have seemed to an imaginative man of another culture! But the myth is a serious matter. It is assumed by Emerson, Whitman, and Hart Crane; by Henry Adams and Henry James. For good or for evil, America *is* something immense, crass, and Roman. We must unavoidably place ourselves in our geography, history, civilization, institutions, and future. . . .
>
> "Paterson" is Whitman's America, grown pathetic and tragic, brutalized by inequality, disorganized by industrial chaos, and faced with annihilation. No poet has written of it with such a combination of brilliance, sympathy, and experience, with such alertness and energy. Because he has tried to understand rather than excoriate, and because in his maturity he has been occupied with the "raw" and the universal, his "Paterson" is not the tragedy of an outcast but the tragedy of our civilization.[65]

In these two essays Lowell has clearly made a *rapprochement* with Williams. The superficial reason for his change of attitude was probably Randall Jarrell, who had been championing Williams in print and in his private correspondence with Lowell.* But the more profound reason lay in Lowell's own artistic quandary. Williams seemed able to portray the "tragedy of our civilization" within the liberal agnostic tradition that Lowell now found himself entering almost against his will. Further, Williams offered a model for stylistic innovation just at a time when Lowell's own neo-English Renaissance style was becoming outworn. In the late 1940s, however, Lowell was far from ready to throw over his past and begin anew under the tutelage of Williams. Williams wrote to Lowell after reading Lowell's first *Paterson* review, and the two poets established a literary friendship similar to the ones Lowell had established with Eliot and Pound. At first the two were attracted to each other precisely because their manifest differences seemed to make any possibility of influence or competition out of the question. Williams, who forgave Lowell his "rhymed couplets" because of their "naive" un-English quality, wrote to him early in their relationship: "Cal, we're not alike but that's a good thing. I think we annoy each other the less for that and I can speak freely to you whereas if we were more similar I couldn't do it." Over the years Lowell's acquaintanceship with Williams would blossom into an almost father-son relationship, replacing the one he had previously enjoyed with Tate. But for now Lowell admired Williams without suspecting that he could emulate him.[66]

Instead Lowell took to heart the advice of his close friends Randall Jarrell and Delmore Schwartz that he introduce plot, drama, and character into his poetry. Jarrell,

---

* In his review of *Paterson I* Jarrell summarized the book at length and said that if the next books were as good "the whole poem will be the best very long poem that any American has written." In his own review of *Paterson I,* Lowell states that he only repeats "poorly but in different words" what Jarrell had already written. Privately Jarrell wrote to Lowell that "the people that think *Paterson* either mediocre or bad would bewilder me if I weren't used to such fools."

who liked poems that possessed "accessibility to experience" and scorned "poems that might have been written *by* a typewriter *on* a typewriter," wrote that Lowell was " at his best a dramatic poet." Similarly, Schwartz complained in his essays about an "absence of narrative or dramatic writing" in modern verse and personally counseled Lowell to open his poetry to "direct experience" by getting "people talking in a poem." Recognizing the need to bring humanity into his poetry, to avoid falling back on the desiccated abstractness of *Land of Unlikeness*, Lowell worked on dramatic and narrative poems open to all experience—all experience, that is, except his own. The result was *The Mills of the Kavanaughs*, published in 1951.[67]

This slim volume contains seven poems, Lowell's entire output for five years. Five of them are stunning failures. The problem with *The Mills of the Kavanaughs* is that Lowell mistook his gift and obsession to be fiction when in fact it was autobiography. Resisting a growing autobiographical impulse, he sought to evade the riving conflicts of his life in the utter impersonality of dramatic monologue and verse narrative. Yet he could prevail upon himself to remain reasonably anonymous in only two of the poems, "Falling Asleep over the Aeneid" and "Mother Marie Therese." Significantly, these are the only effective poems in the book. In them Lowell tried to achieve the vitality of Chaucer's and Frost's monologues, which he had been reading with great admiration. The dramatic monologue form seemed to offer him a way to narrow the distance between life and art without sacrificing his prized detachment. Yet although "Falling Asleep" and "Mother Marie Therese" are among the more brilliant dramatic poems of this century, they are not entirely successful on Lowell's own terms. He later said of "Mother Marie Therese": "I don't believe anybody would think my nun was quite a real person. . . . She has a lot of color to her and drama, and has some things that Frost's characters don't, but she doesn't have their wonderful quality of life." Lowell had

striven to emulate Chaucer and Frost but he had only succeeded in emulating Browning—achieving manifestly
theatrical *tours de force* in which there is a "glaze between
what [the poet] writes and what really happened." The
kind of "poetry of experience" aimed at by Lowell differs
from that later described by Robert Langbaum in his study
of the monologue convention. Rather than Browning-like
performances, Lowell had hoped for something more inte-
grally related to life itself.[68]

In the two best poems of *The Mills of the Kavanaughs*,
Lowell did achieve a limited, though ultimately unsatisfy-
ing, success in the dramatic mode. In the five weaker
poems, however, he allowed details from his personal life
to invade his impersonal structures, resulting in a debilitat-
ing distortion of both the manifest impersonal content and
the latent personal content. One may detect a disguised
subjectivity in all of the lesser poems—the incest in "The
Mills of the Kavanaughs" and "Her Dead Brother"; the
failure of love and marriage in "The Mills," "David and
Bathsheba in the Garden," and "Thanksgiving's Over";
the loss of faith in "Thanksgiving's Over"; the self-hatred
in "The Fat Man in the Mirror"; the threat of disabling
mental illness present to some degree in all the poems.
Sabotaged as fiction and stifled as autobiography, these
poems refuse to come to life.

The most spectacular failure is the title poem "The Mills
of the Kavanaughs" (*MK*, 1-21). This poem was originally
written during Lowell's first stay with Allen Tate in 1937
and called "The Kavanaughs of the Mills." The fact that
Lowell felt impelled to return to this product of his sopho-
more days is a sign of his artistic desperation. His letters
written while revising it reveal the terrible lack of inspiration that can make composition into pure drudgery, "a hell
of a job." Essentially Lowell took his original work (which
became, virtually unchanged, stanzas 2, 12, 13, 15, 34, 35,
and 37 of the published version) and added to it stanzas
describing his parents' unhappy marriage and his own

even unhappier marriage to Jean Stafford. He overlaid the whole with obtrusive parallels to Ovidian myth, sinking the poem. Lowell's imagination was not well suited to myths in which he did not personally believe, and "The Mills of the Kavanaughs" fails to bring its pagan myth to life.[69]

Equally defective is the story itself, which comes to nothing as a fiction though possessing some interest as half-concealed family gossip. The Kavanaughs share the Winslow family motto "Cut down we flourish," the Winslow farm in Damariscotta, Maine, and the Winslow ancestral curse of Indian killing. Harry Kavanaugh's military failure and consequent deterioration are drawn from the life of Lowell's father. The dragonlike snowplow, the bedroom fight, and perhaps Harry's mental collapse are drawn from Lowell's own life. (The same materials appear in Stafford's short story "A Country Love Story.") Once these autobiographical incidents are finished, the poem loses its real reason for being and soon grinds to a halt. In "The Mills of the Kavanaughs" Lowell erred in trying to weave his own experiences into a traditional, impersonal artifice. As Randall Jarrell wrote in his withering critique of the poem (which must surely have shaken Lowell's confidence in his ability to continue in its vein):

> The people too often seem to be acting *in the manner of* Robert Lowell, rather than plausibly as real people act (or implausibly as real people act). I doubt that many readers will think them real; the husband of the heroine never seems so, and the heroine is first of all a sort of symbiotic state of the poet. (You feel, "Yes, Robert Lowell would act like this if he were a girl"; but whoever saw a girl like Robert Lowell?)

Only by tearing off his disguises, by writing openly of his own exposed experience, would Lowell discover a true subject matter and style, renewing his art by revolutionizing it.[70]

Drift

Frank Parker's frontispiece to *The Mills of the Kavanaughs* prophetically portrays a swan, a *Symboliste* metaphor for the poet, singing its song of death. *The Mills of the Kavanaughs* was indeed a swan song. It showed that Lowell had lost hold of his subject and had become trapped in a mannered and devitalized style. In her sensitive review of the book, Louise Bogan suggested that Lowell's development had reached some "dark mid-point" that "must in some way be transcended." Lowell would indeed transcend this point, and create himself and his poetry anew; but only after many bitter years of artistic silence.[71]

§ III ?

Photographs of Experience

Starting Over: Learning from Williams

> We study to utter our painful secret.
> —*Emerson*, "The Poet"

> —Were you up here last night?
> Yes.
> What were you doing?
> Writing.
> What did you write?
> The story of my life—
> —*The Autobiography*
> *of William Carlos Williams*

For Lowell the 1950s were a time of parental death, marital strain, and recurrent mental illness. Beginning in 1949 he had become subject to episodes of severe manic-depression, which in 1954 began to occur "once yearly," causing him to check in at regular intervals to McLean's hospital outside Boston. Rooted in the emotional conflicts of his early childhood, Lowell's illness included periods of manic delusions and erratic behavior, but its most characteristic symptom was a hollow despondency in which "one wakes, is happy for about two minutes, probably less, and then fades into dread of the day." Depression being "no gift from the muse," he found himself unable to write.[1]

Indeed, Lowell's growing sense of artistic failure may well have contributed to his intense depression. The creative crisis which had been implicit in *The Mills of the Kavanaughs* was now upon him. In reviewing that volume, his friend Jarrell had satirically pictured him "gritting his teeth and working away at All the Things He Does Best." Lowell felt the justice of this remark and, fearing repetition and mannerism, reduced himself to silence: "I didn't want to go just cranking the same machine." He later described the years following *The Mills of the Kavanaughs* as "six or seven years ineptitude—a slack of eternity. I remember a cousin proving to someone that I was finished—at only thirty-nine! Five Messy poems in five years!" The "five messy poems" were actually seven: early versions of the poems that eventually appeared as parts one and three of *Life Studies*. In their original versions, these poems seemed to Lowell symbol-ridden and obscure. After their appearance in little magazines in 1953 and 1954, he published no poetry at all. Curiously enough, his problem during this period was essentially technical. Lacking a language and prosody with which to express his inspiration, he lacked inspiration itself. He wrote letters to Allen Tate filled with complaints against "this old jungle of used equipment" and "the inertia of our old rhetorics and habits." But Tate could no longer help him. Lowell obliquely described his dilemma in an interview years later: "It's a terrible struggle, because what you really feel hasn't got the form, it's not what you can put down in a poem. And the poem you're equipped to write concerns nothing that you care very much about." In truth, he was in painful transit from the use of tight metrical forms, which could no longer contain and express his experience, to free verse, which could.[2]

Even in the late 1940s, Lowell had been developing an esthetic of plain speech quite contrary to his own practice at that time. In an essay written in 1948, he said: "How few modern poems—however obscure, fierce, sonorous, pretentious, million-dollar worded—have the distinction of good conversation. . . . Literary people as a rule have less of their own to say and consequently use words with less subtlety and precision than a Maine farmer." During this same period, he praised Elizabeth Bishop and William Carlos Williams for the plainness of their language and condemned Dylan Thomas (whose style rather resembled Lowell's own) for his excessive "rhetoric." Lowell was clearly at odds with his own style of poetry for at least a decade before *Life Studies*. It is no accident that when, in the summer of 1957, he finally turned to free verse, he entitled his first effort "Inspiration." In this unpublished version of "Skunk Hour," the poet pictures himself "writing verses like a Turk," inspired by the ugly, brute reality around and within him—and implicitly inspired by the discovery of a poetic technique that could accurately convey that reality.[3]

Viewing this period of his career in retrospect, Lowell commented, "I think I was a professional who was forced, who forced myself, into a revolutionary style in writing *Life Studies*, the biggest change in myself perhaps I ever made or will." His revolution was twofold: shifting to an intensely personal subject matter, and finding a style perfectly suited to such subject matter—free enough to express the poet's "personal vibrance," yet subtly crafted, capable of giving the "vibrance" meaning and form. Of course, the sources of Lowell's achievement lay deep within his own creative imagination, but they were helped to flow by the example (and in some cases encouragement) of numerous other poets. Among these were Delmore Schwartz, Allen Ginsberg, Ezra Pound (the *Pisan Cantos*), D. H. Lawrence (his animal poems), Ford Madox Ford (*Buckshee*), and most importantly, Lowell's friend Elizabeth Bishop, his former student W. D. Snodgrass, and the poet he would come to call first among his "masters," William Carlos Williams.[4]

Lowell's growing personal and artistic affinities with Williams during the 1950s made his *Life Studies* "revolution" possible. By 1950, what had begun in 1947 as a purely literary relationship had become a real friendship, marked by visits, compliments, and personal favors. Williams assumed his wonted role of master poet, alternately advising and reassuring Lowell, who in turn more and more assumed *his* wonted role of apprentice. Lowell needed help, and Williams alone among the modernist masters was willing and able to give it. Unlike Tate, Ransom, Eliot, Stevens, Frost, and Moore, Williams was emotionally warm and openhearted; and unlike Pound (who *was* warm and openhearted), he was relatively unegotistical.* Even more important, Williams in the period following World War II continued to develop his art and his theories about art, and was eager to share his discoveries with all who might profit from them.

For several seasons Lowell periodically visited Williams in Rutherford, bearing bottles of bourbon and set to "wallow in prosody." His poetry running dry, Lowell sensed that Williams's ideas of prosody spoke to his problem. After all, Williams's primary goal, as he wrote in "The Poem as a Field of Action" (1948), was a technique to "let our feelings through." On his side, Williams welcomed the younger poet's visits and told him that he hoped their talk would help to "dislodge us from our prejudices." But in 1950 Lowell decided to escape his dilemma by taking an extended tour of Europe with his new wife Elizabeth Hardwick. This was not so much a search for a fresh way of writing (as Williams had said of Auden's move to America), as a quest to renew the *old* way. Williams continued to advise and encourage Lowell in his private correspondence and in print.[5]

When *The Mills of the Kavanaughs* appeared in 1951, Williams wrote an enthusiastic notice for the *New York Times Book Review*, but included hints of dissatisfaction with its form and feeling, qualities which both Williams and Lowell perceived as intimately connected. "When [Lowell] does under stress of emotion break through the monotony of the line, it never goes far, it is as though he had at last wakened to breathe freely again, you can feel the lines

---

* Obsessed with his own concerns, Pound in his letters showed li.tle interest in Lowell's poetry, even after Lowell sent him a packet of the "Life Studies" poems in manuscript. Pound's only personal inquiries related to what he termed Lowell's "mixed race." Insisting that Lowell's resemblance to William Carlos Williams resulted from their both having had a Jewish ancestor, Pound demanded to see Lowell's "fambly treee."

breathing, the poem rouses as though from a trance." Williams also questioned the narrowness of Lowell's "range of feeling." Despite such doubts, he conceded that "the rhymes are necessary to Lowell. He must, to his mind, appear to surmount them," and he generously summed up the volume as "excellent work. What can one wish more?" Yet Williams's stated reservations clearly indicated that he did wish something more: Lowell's liberation from self-imposed, and perhaps now damaging, prosodic restraints.[6]

In thanking him for the review, Lowell revealed that he shared something of Williams's hinted-at dissatisfaction. He had been reading Williams's recently published *Collected Later Poems* (1950), a volume brimming with vividly observed people, objects, and events. He was struck by the way the intricate, rich sentences, in a poem like "The Semblables," were given clarity and simplicity by being arranged in stanzas of short lines. "Reading over your volume," he wrote to Williams, "I've been wondering if my characters and plots aren't a bit trifling and cumbersome," somehow too remote from "what one lives." Clearly, even as *The Mills* was being published, Lowell had begun to consider Williams's poetry as a possible model, an alternative to such previous, and now exhausted, models as Tate and Eliot. Yet at this point, he was unable really to contemplate taking the leap to Williams's open forms: "But I'd feel as unhappy out of rime and meter as you would in them." A year later, still in Europe, he wrote that he wished "rather in vain" that he could absorb something of Williams's way of writing. Lowell was to spend the next five years preparing to absorb Williams, preparing to invent a poetry without regular meter or rhyme which would nevertheless satisfy his powerful yearning for form.[7]

Lowell returned from Europe (as Williams had hoped he would) in 1953, spent a year teaching creative writing at the University of Iowa, a semester at the University of Cincinnati, and the remainder of the decade living on

Marlborough Street in Boston and teaching at Boston University. During that time, Lowell and Williams continued to correspond and to pay each other visits. Their regard for each other grew. "Cal Lowell," Williams wrote to Pound, "is a man I respect and for whom I feel a strong bond of sympathy." He wrote to Lowell himself: "For spite of differences in our poetic styles I feel that we are close brothers under the skin." For his part, Lowell wrote to Williams upon hearing that he was ill, "I feel more love for you than for any man of your age."[8]

Lowell's personal affection was paralleled by his growing artistic admiration. When *The Desert Music* appeared in 1954, he wrote Williams that "To Daphne and Virginia" and "Work in Progress" (a draft of "Asphodel, That Greeny Flower") were inexpressibly moving to him: "They are poetry and go beyond poetry." The book's advertisements quoted Lowell calling Williams "one of the best poets in the world." Lowell especially admired the brilliance and seeming ease of the poet's self-liberation from the modernist idea of the poem as impersonal object. In this last, great phase of his career, Williams's poems had become openly, movingly personal. They went "beyond poetry" to the emotional reality of life itself, closing the spaces between self, word, and world. When *Journey to Love* appeared in 1955, containing the completed "Asphodel," Lowell wrote to Williams, "I've read *Journey to Love* many times. You are pouring out, and I know I shall be hearing your voice speaking the words to some inner ear in me, for as long—for as long as I journey myself."[9]

Lowell's process of internalizing Williams's way of writing was boosted by two weekend visits from Williams, which coincided with speaking engagements at Wellesley in 1956 and Brandeis in June of 1957. At Wellesley, Williams read his recent poetry, ending with the Coda to "Asphodel." The audience, as he later remembered it, "practically carried me off on their shoulders. I was speechless." Seated in the audience, Robert Lowell was overwhelmed by Williams's reception and, even more, by the power of "Asphodel" itself. He wrote to Williams afterward to say that it was the best reading he had ever heard. In his essay "William Carlos Williams," Lowell vividly recalled the event: "It couldn't have been more crowded in the wide-galleried hall and I had to sit in the aisle. The poet appeared, one whole side partly paralyzed, his voice just audible, and here and there a word misread. No one stirred. In the silence he read his great poem 'Of Asphodel, That Greeny Flower,' a triumph of simple confession."[10]

At Brandeis, Williams characteristically lectured on the rejection of traditional poetic forms, "the break from old arrangements of the words." His ideas must have seemed directly aimed at Lowell, sitting in the lecture hall.

> In this country it started, mainly, with Whitman. . . . He compared the past with the columns of a classic temple, that is to say the poems of the past, and the poems of the present to the waves of the sea: both have a certain metrical (or measured) regularity but the modern is far more flexible than the old. . . .
>
> [The contemporary poet] refuses to return to the past and yet doesn't quite know (he is alive and himself unexplained) where to go for a new design with which to reaffirm the old life. He will then proceed by instinct rather than to acknowledge defeat, and write as he at least feels that he wants to do. Finally a conscious design must evolve, all new, to be broken down later into whatever the succeeding development out of chaos requires.

Williams concluded his speech by claiming that since Whitman, an important development had occurred: the appearance of the "American Idiom" as a unique modern language. The "American Idiom," Williams said, replaced the "fixed standard foot" with a "variable foot," thereby restoring to measure the dignity it had lost in modern times. As in his earlier essay "On Measure," he was suggesting that free verse need not be formless, but that its form must result from the poem's organic, internal pressure rather than from traditional patterns externally applied.[11]

Lowell, obsessed as he was by the dialectic of freedom and form, wrote afterwards to Williams that his speech "went to the heart," by which he may have meant both the heart of the problem and his own emotional center. He finally began to see a way out of his dilemma, a way to write unscanned lines without relinquishing meaningful form—for, as Williams had said, "the form IS the meaning (if it is a poem)." In the weeks immediately following Williams's speech, Lowell began to write *Life Studies*, bolstered by Williams's family chronicles, *In the Money* and the Preface to *The Dog and the Fever*. Prosodically, Lowell did not specifically adopt Williams's own triadic stanza. Rather, he took from him the idea of freedom: the idea that form is only *"an* arrangement of the words for the effect, not *the* arrangement, fixed and unalterable," the idea that if form is meaning then "the new form is the new meaning."[12]

On September 30, 1957, Lowell wrote to tell Williams that his artistic block had been overcome:

> Your best work couldn't be more perfect and it has that life-blood of the arts, the real world. Well, we all get it in our different ways, according to our calling. I've been writing poems like a house afire, i.e. for me that means five in six weeks, fifty versions of each. I've been experimenting with mixing loose and free meters with strict. . . . I feel more and more technically indebted to you.

In December, after his first flood of inspiration had abated, he sent Williams a packet of fifteen poems along with a note: "At forty I've written my first unmeasured verse. . . . I've only tried it in a few of these poems, those that are most personal. It's great to have no hurdle of rhyme and scansion between yourself and what you want to say most forcibly." Following this breakthrough, his letters to Williams all brim with feelings of admiration, gratitude, and comradeship. (Soon after sending the poems, he wrote, "I have no master, only masters, you are about first among them." He was surely aware that a century before, Whitman had addressed Emerson as his "Master" in a note accompanying a packet of his poems.) Lowell pleased himself by thinking that he had "crossed the river" into Williams's world. After years of wishing in vain to absorb Williams's way of writing into his own, he had finally succeeded. Following a visit to his new mentor after *Life Studies* was finished but before its publication, Lowell wrote to him, "I'll go down to my grave in time thanking God that I have met Williams. . . . Ah, we are brothers."[13]

Unlike Allen Tate, who was horrified by the manuscript of *Life Studies* and insisted that it not be published, Williams was frankly overwhelmed by Lowell's "terrible wonderful poems." When his wife Floss read to him aloud the packet of fifteen new poems (including "Skunk Hour"), he impulsively wrote to congratulate Lowell on his achievement: "You have opened a new field. You needed that break, rhyme could not contain you any longer, you have too much to say for that. . . . [This] brings one of my dreams for you into full fruit." Later when Floss read the completed manuscript of *Life Studies* to him, Williams wrote to Lowell, "You have piled accomplishment upon accomplishment until there is nothing to be said to you in rebuttal of your devastating statements or the way you have uttered them. . . . The book must have caused you some difficulty to write. There is no lying permitted to a man who writes that way." Williams, who was by 1958 rather infirm, broke the letter off here, resuming the following day with the explanation that he "couldn't go on" for the book had taken too much out of him.[14]

At the risk of oversimplifying, we may say that Lowell absorbed three different but closely related lessons from Williams's poetry. The first was Williams's "variable foot," which he defined as "*relatively* stable" but not "rigid"—a relative measure to describe a relative universe. Williams (along with Charles Olson and Robert Creeley who helped him formulate his idea) was here returning to Emerson's theory of a poetry that is neither conventionally metered nor unmetered, but one in which the argument makes its own meter. For Williams, this idea became in practice the "triadic stanza," in which each line is a foot containing a variable number of syllables followed by an unrhymed pause:

> For our wedding, too
> the light was wakened
> and shone. The light!
> the light stood before us
> waiting!
> I thought the world
> stood still.
> At the altar
> so intent was I
> before my vows,
> so moved by your presence
> a girl so pale
> and ready to faint
> that I pitied you
> and wanted to protect you.
> As I think of it now,
> after a lifetime,
> it is as if
> a sweet-scented flower
> were poised
> and for me did open.
>
> ("Asphodel")

For Lowell, the idea resulted in a very different prosody, a line seemingly close to prose yet more rhythmical, and free to include rhymes and even passages of regular meter:

Oh my *Petite*,
clearest of all God's creatures, still all air and nerve:
you were in your twenties, and I
once hand on glass
and heart in mouth,
outdrank the Rahvs in the heat
of Greenwich Village, fainting at your feet—
too boiled and shy
and poker-faced to make a pass,
while the shrill verve
of your invective scorched the traditional South.

Now twelve years later, you turn your back.
Sleepless, you hold
your pillow to your hollows like a child;
your old-fashioned tirade—
loving, rapid, merciless—
breaks like the Atlantic Ocean on my head.

("Man and Wife")

Lowell's line, like Williams's, eliminates initial capitaliza-
tion and regular rhyme and meter. It is, however, more
proselike than Williams's, and at the same time more connected to traditional English prosody (the irregular
rhymes, the underlying iambic rhythm). Lowell adapted
his mentor's formal insights to suit his own particular
needs. Williams in his essay "On Measure" had exhorted
his followers to "invent new modes to take the place of
those which are worn out," and Lowell's mode necessarily
differed from Williams's own. But essentially their purposes were identical: to achieve a balance between freedom and order by basing the poetic line on a flexible
"rhythmic unit" dictated by the poem's inner dynamic.[15]

Secondly, Lowell adopted the "American Idiom" to replace the obscure, charged rhetoric of his earlier poems.
The "American Idiom," which Williams thought must
"shape the pattern" of the poem, entailed a rhythmic pace
equivalent to the pace of speech and a diction akin to "the

local American way of speaking." Williams's poetic language, as he told a hostile British questioner in an exchange recorded in his *Autobiography*, came "from the mouths of Polish mothers." Now Lowell sought a similar plainness of speech. Ignoring the seven types of ambiguity, Lowell in *Life Studies* deliberately aimed for "a tone that sounded a little like conversation." His new style was an Emersonian mixture of sophisticated diction ("my *Petite*, clearest of all God's creatures") and colloquial speech ("too boiled to make a pass"). In "My Last Afternoon with Uncle Devereux Winslow" Lowell typically varies "bibulous," "ingenu" and "Agrippina" the younger with such colloquialisms as "stogie" and "crummy," and with the clichés for which he has been criticized:

> That's how I threw cold water
> on my Mother and Father's
> watery martini pipe dreams.

The voice speaking in *Life Studies* is that of Lowell himself, off his stilts. By his metrical experimentation and his emphasis on the language of common speech, he left what Edwin Fussell has called the "conservative" tradition of American poetic technique and moved toward Williams's own more "radical" tradition. [16]

These technical lessons that Lowell learned from Williams directly relate to what is most important of all, the lesson he learned concerning content. For Williams had stated plainly that the only real purpose of his stylistic innovations was to "liberate the possibilities of depicting reality in a modern world that has seen more if not felt more than in the past." Lowell used his new technical freedom to depict the reality of his own life history. He had, of course, been tempted by autobiography from the beginning of his writing career, but had lacked a poetics that would make undisguised autobiography possible. But now that he had developed a rhythm and language seeming to derive organically, even spontaneously, from his self, he could effectively confront his own authentic experience, and thereby return his poetry to its source.[17]

In diminishing the space between himself as human being and himself as speaker of his poem, Lowell turned toward the poetic tradition of personal witness called for by Emerson in his essay "The Poet" and exemplified by such works as *Leaves of Grass*, *The Pisan Cantos*, and Williams's poems beginning with *Paterson*. In the poems of *The Desert Music* and *Journey to Love* in the mid-1950s, Williams relinquished his modernist pose of anonymity and objectivity and instead, in James Breslin's phrase, turned "increasingly inward, often into personal memory." In "Asphodel," Williams regales his wife with memories of their life together and assertions of abiding love, all as their "eyes fill / with tears." When Lowell called this poem "both poetry and beyond poetry" he was reiterating Whitman's point about *Leaves of Grass*: that it is more than a literary performance, it puts *"a Person* . . . freely, fully and truly on record." *Life Studies* in a similar way bridges the gap between poetry and life. Lowell said that the book was "about direct experience, and not symbols"; it tells his "personal story and memories." He called *Life Studies* "confessional" just as he called "Asphodel" a "confession." As is clearly shown by the contrasting passages of "Asphodel" and "Man and Wife" quoted above, Lowell's savagely ironic self-revelation differs tonally from Williams's confession, which radiates a sense of achieved wisdom and joy. Yet Lowell's poetry of the 1950s shares with Williams's the knowledge that "nothing can grow unless it taps into the soil." Williams once wrote to Lowell that he wanted to compose poems that would " 'say' what I am." Beginning with *Life Studies*, Lowell determined to do likewise (though in fact his poems more often say "what am I?").[18]

Whereas Lowell's association with Allen Tate had once led him to adopt a style and viewpoint virtually synonymous with Tate's, his association with Williams led him to discover a style and viewpoint that were uniquely his own. Lowell the paleface donned the garb of the redskin, ceasing to think of art as discipline and beginning to think of it as a means of liberation. By precept and example, Williams persuaded Lowell finally to rebel against the authority of the past, English literary tradition, Boston, and his teachers at Kenyon. He persuaded Lowell to trust in the authority of the self. In his review of *Lord Weary's Castle* Jarrell had observed that Lowell's poems occupied a "kingdom of necessity" filled with "everything that is closed, turned inward, incestuous, that blinds or binds," but that "struggling within this like leaven" was "everything that is free or open, that grows or is willing to change." Jarrell called this latter impulse "accessibility to experience" and a "realm of freedom." Under the guidance of William Carlos Williams, Lowell in *Life Studies* departed from "the kingdom of necessity" and entered into "the realm of freedom." In 1952 Lowell had written Williams that he lacked Williams's "eye, experience and sense of language." In *Life Studies* he rediscovered his own eye and his own experience, and invented an appropriate language by which to convey them.[19]

A second major influence on Lowell's development of a new style was W. D. Snodgrass. Snodgrass personally had little interest in Williams, but his poetry independently and concurrently reinforced the lessons Lowell derived from Williams. Lowell met Snodgrass in 1953 during his year teaching in the Creative Writing Program at the University of Iowa. A graduate student in one of Lowell's classes, Snodgrass himself was struggling under the confining orthodoxies of the academy, writing complex, erudite poems on themes remote from his own experience. Indeed, at this time the book he admired most and modeled his poetry upon was Lowell's own *Lord Weary's Castle*.

But following a divorce, mental crisis, and a subsequent period of psychotherapy, he came to feel his poetry insincere and unfelt. The self, and the self's interactions with the world, began to seem the proper focus for poetry. Further influenced by the emotional intensity of Renaissance songs, Mahler's "Songs on the death of infants," and the straightforward poems of a fellow student named Robert Shelley, Snodgrass started to write poetry he later labeled "domestic" (rather than "confessional"), in a new unclotted style.[20]

The entire movement of "Confessional poetry" may be said to have commenced on the evening of November 18, 1953, when during a piano concert Snodgrass scribbled on the back of his program lines which eventually became the beginning of "Heart's Needle":

> Child of my winter, born
> When the new soldiers died
> On the ice hills, when I was torn

The essentials of Confessional poetry are all present in these three lines: an undisguised exposure of painful personal event (in this case Snodgrass's divorce and separation from his child), a dialectic of private matter with public matter (the Korean War), and an intimate, unornamented style. The kind of writing Snodgrass initiated that evening would eventually come to include much of the best poetry in the 1950s and '60s: Snodgrass's own *Heart's Needle* (1959) and *After Experience* (1968), Lowell's *Life Studies* (1959) and much of his later work, Sexton's *To Bedlam and Part Way Back* (1960) and later volumes, Jarrell's *The Lost World* (1965), Plath's *Ariel* (1966), Berryman's *Dream Songs* (1969), and Kunitz's *The Testing Tree* (1971). (Ginsberg's *Kaddish* [1960], which certainly belongs to this group, might be said to have an independent line of origin.)[21]

After leaving Iowa, Lowell continued his friendship with Snodgrass through correspondence and occasional meetings. At first Lowell seemed to disapprove of the new direction to Snodgrass's work, thinking it overly personal and sentimental. But by the time he began to write *Life Studies* (just after a selection of Snodgrass's poems appeared in the Hall-Pack-Simpson anthology *New Poets of England and America*), he had become an enthusiastic admirer of his former student. Writing to the poet Isabella Gardner, he called him the best of the younger poets. Viewing the matter in retrospect, Lowell told his *Paris Review* interviewer that Snodgrass "did these things before I did. . . . He may have influenced me though people have suggested the opposite."[22]

Lowell had returned to Boston from the midwest after his mother's death in 1954, apparently with the intention of writing about his family. *Time* quotes an anonymous friend as commenting, "The idea was to recapture some roots." Following an incapacitating manic-depressive episode, he began to work on a prose autobiography, but found prose "an awful job." He eventually broke off writing and published the completed fragment, entitled "91 Revere Street," in the *Partisan Review* in fall, 1956. Although the proposed autobiography was aborted, the generative idea of making literary use of autobiographical material was not abandoned. Further, the experience of writing prose intensified his desire to write a poetry assimilating the language and cadences of prose. Prose seemed in many ways "better off than poetry" because "less cut off from life." Lowell had long admired the vitality of the prose passages in *Paterson* and had been newly impressed by the proselike qualities of Williams's and Snodgrass's most recent poetry. Now he began to think that "the best style for poetry was . . . something like the prose of Chekhov and Flaubert."[23]

In March of 1957, Lowell went on a speaking tour of the west coast. Reading his poems in San Francisco, in "the era and setting of Allen Ginsberg," he was again struck by the insufficiencies of his poetic style: "I felt my old poems hid what they were really about, and at times offered a stiff, humorless and even impenetrable surface. . . . [They] seemed like prehistoric monsters dragged down into the bog and death by their ponderous armor. I was reciting what I no longer felt." Though "no convert to the 'beats,' " Lowell did like "bits of Ginsberg" and thought *Howl*, like Snodgrass's poetry, a breakthrough to "direct utterance." Ginsberg said that he had ceased to make "a distinction between what you tell your friends and what you tell your Muse."*[24]

Lowell returned from the west in April, attended Williams's Brandeis lecture on the new measure in June, and left that same month with his family for his annual summer stay in Castine, Maine. In Maine, his mind churned with the new ideas he had encountered and with the new possibilities they seemed to open up. He carefully read and reread Williams's family narratives and also Elizabeth Bishop's personal yet coolly descriptive poems. Bishop was a long-time friend of Lowell's, along with Jarrell the closest friend he had. Moreover, Lowell admired her poetry more than that of any of his other contemporaries. Rereading her poems, especially "The Armadillo," he found yet another model for himself. The important aspects of Bishop's poetry for Lowell were its open forms, conversational diction, precise descriptions, and receptivity to human experience. Bishop's poetry, like that of the Beats, was "exploratory" and "original"; unlike theirs, hers was "controlled."[25]

As early as his 1947 review of Bishop's *North & South*, Lowell had associated her "bare objective language" with that of Williams. But Bishop, possibly in contradistinction

---

* In the last year of Lowell's life, the two poets gave a joint reading in New York City. According to Charles Molesworth, when Lowell was introduced he mentioned a notice in the *New York Times* that spoke of Ginsberg and himself as representing "opposite ends of the spectrum." Lowell commented that they were not really that different, and added that, if anything, they were simply opposite ends of William Carlos Williams.

to Williams, was "one of the best craftsmen alive." As Lowell's better craftsman, she seems to have made fully legitimate for him the key elements of Williams's esthetics—the American Idiom, the minute description yielding frequently to personal reflection, the scaled-down, profoundly individual voice and vision. "You can see," Lowell later told Stanley Kunitz, "that Bishop is a sort of bridge between Tate's formalism and Williams' informal art." Using that bridge, Lowell crossed into a new poetic world. "At times," he wrote to Williams, "I felt frightened of the journey." Snodgrass and Ginsberg had lent impetus, and Bishop a sense of legitimacy. But it was William Carlos Williams, through his encouragement, ideas, and work, who had inspired Lowell to reinvent his art and hence himself.[26]

Life Studies

> The experience of each new age requires a new confession.
> —*Emerson*, "The Poet"

> Memory is a kind
> of accomplishment
> a sort of renewal
> even
> an initiation . . .
> —*Williams*, "The Descent"

> Home is where one starts from. As we grow older
> The world becomes stranger, the pattern more complicated
> Of dead and living. . . .
> There is a time for the evening under starlight,
> A time for the evening under lamplight
> (The evening with the photograph album).
> —*Eliot*, "East Coker"

> Whatever [the writer] beholds or experiences comes to him
> as a model and sits for its picture.
> —*Emerson*, "Goethe; or the Writer"

Lowell began "pouring out poems" in August 1957, working on several at once. By the start of December, he had virtually completed seven of the fifteen poems of the

"Life Studies" sequence: "My Last Afternoon with Uncle Devereux Winslow," "Commander Lowell," "Terminal Days at Beverly Farms," "Sailing Home from Rapallo," "Man and Wife," " 'To Speak of Woe That Is in Marriage,' " and the poem he had finished first, "Skunk Hour." The intensity of this creative surge sent him back for a brief rest at McLean's, a stay described in "Waking in the Blue." That poem and the remaining "Life Studies" were written in 1958. In little over a year from the time Lowell began writing, *Life Studies* was essentially complete. About half the poems appeared in magazines in 1958 and 1959, and the volume itself appeared in April of 1959, about two years after his west coast speaking tour.[27]

Life Studies, along with Snodgrass's *Heart's Needle* which was published in the same month, became the poetry event of the year. It immediately provoked a critical controversy. Joseph Bennett, missing Lowell's ironies, attacked the book as "lazy and anecdotal . . . more suited as an appendix to some snobbish society magazine," and Desales Standerwick, in a review indicatively titled "Pieces too Personal," found the subject matter of the poems "embarrassing." The laudatory reviewers were in the majority, but they too seemed to find it hard to verbalize a literary response to the book. A. Alvarez, for example, wrote that "poetry of this order needs neither to be justified nor explained; one should simply be thankful that there is still someone to write it." Alfred Kazin and M. L. Rosenthal were able to be more precise. Kazin praised Lowell for having achieved "freedom from the suffocating traditions of fine style" and for having brought twentieth-century poetry back "to its sister, life." And in his influential and widely reprinted review in which he coined the phrase "confessional poetry," Rosenthal explained that Lowell "removes the mask" in *Life Studies*, emerging as neither egotist nor bored family anecdotalist but as "the damned speaking-sensibility of the world." The 1959 Pulitzer Prize went to Snodgrass, but Lowell received the Guiness

Poetry Award (along with Auden and Edith Sitwell), the Longview Foundation Award, and the National Book Award.[28]

The first three parts of *Life Studies*, all written earlier, serve as preparation for the crucial "Life Studies" themselves. Although Lowell seems to have hoped that the poems of part one would provide historical perspective for the breakdowns described later on, they do not fulfill this intention with equal success. The title characters of "The Banker's Daughter" and "A Mad Negro Soldier Confined at Munich" are the first among many exiles, madmen, and prisoners populating the pages of *Life Studies*, all in some measure standing for Lowell himself; but this thematic linkage cannot save the poems. Originally written at the tail end of his dramatic monologue period in the early 1950s, both poems lack the power Lowell admired in Frost of getting within a character's skin and language. Of the poems in part one, "Beyond the Alps" alone is a fitting introduction to the book. It suggests not only the disintegration of a world, but also the disintegration of the poet's former beliefs.

On its literal level, "Beyond the Alps" describes a train ride from Rome to Paris taken during Lowell's European sojourn in the early 1950s. On its metaphoric level, the poem describes his loss of faith, a loss that underlies the horror of the later poems. Alluding to St. Augustine's distinction between City of God and Earthly City, Lowell writes that "much against my will / I left the City of God where it belongs." A spirit devoted to Divine truth in *Lord Weary's Castle*, he has now joined the other society, the City of Man, which has its own, if lesser, values. Faithless, Lowell belongs to the "monstrous human crush" in the fragmented region he once contemptuously termed, echoing Augustine, the land of unlikeness. He has given up his home in the eternal for an existentialist stay within time,

among his fellow human beings. Augustine's God of res-
cue has not rescued *him*. Indeed the process of St. Augustine's *Confessions* has been reversed. Instead of seeking
God's hidden face, Lowell accepts, reluctantly but defi-
nitely, its absence. Instead of remembering and confessing
unto God His mercies, Lowell remembers and confesses to
human strangers (the reading audience) his own forsaken-
ness.[29]

"Beyond the Alps" embodies an esthetic renunciation as
well as a theological one. For Lowell, the Alps stand for the
traditions of high art: "that altitude / once held by Hellas."
Artistic ascension, like religious ascension, has come to
seem impossible for him. Just as Roman Catholic dogma
goes unbelieved (line 23), so classical poetry now seems
"wasted"; there are no longer "tickets for that altitude." In
place of the goddess Minerva, our genius is Mussolini,
"pure prose." Lowell's sense of himself as artistically "Beyond the Alps" is clarified by a remark he made about
Robert Penn Warren's verse-novel *Brother to Dragons*. Reviewing the book at the same time as he was composing
"Beyond the Alps," and apparently thinking in the images
of the poem, he wrote: "Warren . . . has crossed the Alps
and, like Napoleon's shoeless army, entered the fat populated riverbottom of the novel." In *Life Studies*, Lowell
likewise intended to stress experience over form, and enter
"the fat, populated riverbottom" of life. His train, once
mountain-climbing, "had come to earth" (line 29). Henry
James, complaining to Howells of his own artistic problems, once refused to make an identical journey: "I shall
probably not . . . be beyond the Alps. . . . That way Boston
lies, which is the deadliest form of madness."[30]

"91 Revere Street," the second part of *Life Studies*, is
Lowell's complex and beautifully written prose reminiscence of his blasted childhood, and of a family and culture
in decline. Despite some shared narrative details, it bears a
largely ironic relation to the long tradition of Bostonian
(and quasi-Bostonian) reminiscences which includes *The*

Education of Henry Adams and Henry James's autobiographies. In contrast to the concealments that typify the genre, Lowell focuses precisely on the family disgraces, tensions, neuroses, and failures. No "labor of love and loyalty" (James's description of *A Small Boy and Others*), no effort to memorialize distinguished friends or loved relations, "91 Revere Street" attacks the genteel traditions, even to the point of overtly parodying (and exposing the rhetorical evasions implicit in) Henry James's style.* Lowell's memoir opens with an irony which sounds gentler than it in fact is: in the family "Biographical Sketches," one ancestor "has no Christian name and is entitled merely Major M. Myers" (*LS*, 11). M. (for Mordecai) Myers, being Jewish, has "no Christian name" in a double sense. The family refuses to acknowledge what it does not like, but Lowell's own biographical sketch will operate according to a different method. It reveals in rich and ironic prose the demeaning property disputes of his mother, whose cousin Cassie "only became a close relative in 1922. In that year she died" (*LS*, 13); the financial and moral decline of his father, his earnings more or less decreasing year by year (*LS*, 16); his parents' bedroom clashes, to which their son listens as though to a movie (*LS*, 19); and his own boyish signs of instability and alienation.**[31]

The internal failure of the Lowells coincides with social change. The "seated and rooted social order" of the Boston of Henry James's youth has given way to the collapsing civilization Adams foresaw in the *Education* and James himself in *The American Scene*. In the boy Lowell's night-

---

* "Amy Lowell . . . had been so plucky, so *formidable*, so *beautifully and unblushingly immense*, as Henry James might have said" (*LS*, 38). Appropriately, Lowell tells us that the cousin who compiles his family's "Biographical Sketches" is a "Julian-James," implying a possible connection to the Jameses.

** Lowell's ironic perspective on his family is underlined by the fact that the poems of *Life Studies* are written in free verse, a form his family viewed as a symptom of modern anarchy, "like playing tennis without a net" (*LS*, 38).

mare, the Social Register symbolically yields to the cash register (*LS*, 24). The "people of the right sort," having lost cultural dominance, are reduced to shopping for a bargain at Filene's basement, and to learning from an encyclopedia "the gentlemanly talent" of carving (*LS*, 32, 34). They have been left with only their repugnance intact. For the Lowells, "historic Boston Common" is now on the wrong side of the tracks: "Everywhere there were grit, litter, gangs of Irish, Negroes, Latins" (*LS*, 31). But the Lowells themselves are threadbare, out of sync, worthless, like the pieces of furniture they have inherited (*LS*, 43-44). In his autobiographies, Henry James deliberately squeezed "the sponge of memory" and relived his past with strangely mixed pleasure; the past was a "ragbag" or a "spring," a source of surprise, delight, refreshment. But Lowell's memories are "fixed in the mind" and "rocklike," neither random nor refreshing (*LS*, 12-13). "Urgent with life and meaning," these memories are not merely facts of a childhood now long past, they are present realities, that part of the past that weighs on the present, having lost none of its emotional significance. In "91 Revere Street," Lowell ironically surveys the wreckage of a self, family, and civilization (a wreckage he will photograph close up in the "Life Studies" sequence). He concludes by imagining his great-great-grandfather Mordecai Myers, the Jewish outsider with no Hawthornean "allegory in his eyes, no *Mayflower*," passing judgment: "My children, my blood, accept graciously the loot of your inheritance. We are all dealers in used furniture" (*LS*, 45).[32]

The group of four poems following "91 Revere Street" prepares us for the "Life Studies" sequence in a different way. They establish Lowell's sense of spiritual kinship to brilliant and tormented writers—Ford Madox Ford, George Santayana, Delmore Schwartz, and Hart Crane—all of whom in some way contributed to his growth as a poet, and all of whom endured an exile from society prefiguring his own. These poems, comprising a kind of parabolic autobiography, then yield to the explicit auto-biography of the "Life Studies" themselves, which directly expose Lowell's own particular set of circumstances, his own flawed being. The first three parts of *Life Studies* have provided the necessary contexts in which to place the primary text.

As we have seen, the "Life Studies" poems are written in a radically new style and treat a radically new subject matter. Seeking what he later described as a "break-through back into life," Lowell abandoned the traditional rhetoric and meter that seemed to proclaim "I am a poem." At the beginning of the decade Randall Jarrell had advised him that his poetry needed "spontaneity," Delmore Schwartz had advocated "openness to direct experience," and Williams had counseled that "assertion of origins is the more fertile basis for thought—and technique." In the "Life Studies" sequence he took all of this advice: "I wanted to see how much of my personal story and memories I could get into poetry. To a large extent it was a technical problem, as most problems in poetry are. But it was something of a cause: to extend the poem to include, without compromise, what I felt and knew." Nevertheless, Lowell understood full well that "the flux of life is not poetry." Although the "Life Studies" deliberately re-pudiate "the artifice that removes poetry from life," they are nonetheless subtly and powerfully artful. In order to begin distinguishing the *kind* of artistry at work here—in order to develop a suitable critical vocabulary to describe Lowell's strange, new, seemingly nonpoetic poetic—let us look at two of his poems in their manuscript development, the first a failure and the second a success.[33]

Seeking his new style and subject matter in early summer 1957, Lowell struggled with and then left off writing a quasi-autobiographical poem beginning:

Photographs of Experience

My daddy was chief engineer
On the Pensy, when he engendered me;
My mother bore me by Boston Common—
I wish I could die or live off the sea.

The poem is not without wit: the play on "engineer" and "engendered"; the travestied grandeur of "my mother bore me"; the possible pun on "bore" which reinforces the poem's theme of ennui. But ultimately the poem is all wrong. The wit serves as disguise, falsifying Lowell's experience. His father was actually an engineer for the navy, not a railroad engineer. Further, the speaker of the poem is an invented persona, a jaded esthete such as one finds in early Eliot:

I have the sacraments to help me die:
Women's conversation, hi fi.
.   .   .   .
If your hearing's good at forty, you can hear your
    heart flutter
Like the pigeons taking a roll in the hay of my gutter.

The society-verse couplets, the wit, and the elegant urban despair, all in the mood of *Prufrock and Other Observations* and the song of the third Thames-daughter in *The Waste Land*, show Lowell trying to express his Confessional impulse in a language sanctified by Pound and Eliot. The effort convinced him that he had in fact no appropriate language at all. Realizing that "most of what I knew about writing was a hindrance," he turned in new directions and started to write successfully.[34]

Finally accepting Williams's advice (given in 1952) to "make the new meter out of whole cloth," Lowell found his immediate inspiration in prose. "My Last Afternoon with Uncle Devereux Winslow," the first poem of the "Life Studies" series, was initially written as "four or five prose pages" intended for Lowell's memoir. By December 1957, he had "cut things out and re-arranged it and made differ-

Life Studies

ent transitions and put it into verse.''* An analysis of his revisions of section three of the poem, the portrait of Great Aunt Sarah, reveals his progress toward a fully developed Confessionalist poetry. (See Appendix B for texts of three versions of this section.) Even in the first draft, Lowell had achieved the technical freedom and human interest he sought. As in Williams's poems, the sentences, if written out in paragraphs, have the density of good prose:

Up in the air,
by the sunset window in the billiards-room,
my Great Aunt Sarah
was learning the *Overture to the Flying Dutchman*,
and thundered on the keyboard of her dummy piano.
With gauze skirts like a boudoir table,
accordion-like, yet soundless,
it had been bought to spare the nerves
of my Grandmother Winslow,
tone-deaf, quick as a cricket—
now grousing through a paper-bound *Zola*, and saying:
"Why does Sally thump forever
on a toy no one can hear?"

Forty years earlier,
twenty, auburn-headed, a virtuoso
wept over by Liszt,
Aunt Sarah, the Winslows' only "genius,"
had lifted her archaic Athenian nose,
and jilted an Astor.

* Other of the "Life Studies" poems were composed differently: Lowell would begin in a regular rhythm and rhyme scheme and then irregularize the poem in revision. "Commander Lowell," for example, was originally patterned after the tetrameter couplets of Marvell's "Nymph Complaining for the Death of Her Faun," and in the final free-verse version many of the couplets remain as rhymes. Other poems composed in this manner are "Man and Wife," "To Speak of Woe" and "Skunk Hour." The poems Lowell composed last, including "During Fever," "Waking in the Blue" and "Home after Three Months Away," were written in free verse and required no metrical revision at all. Although he used three distinct methods of composition, the poems are all of a piece.

109

Photographs of Experience

Each morning she had practiced
on the grand piano at Symphony Hall,
deathlike in the off-season summer—
its naked Greek statues draped with purple
like the saints during Holy Week . . .
On concert day, Miss Winslow could not appear.

Now her investments were made by her Brother.
Her career
was a danger-signal for the nieces.
High above us,
Aunt Sarah lifted a hand
from the dead keys of the dummy piano,
and declaimed grandly:
"Barbarism lies behind me;
mannerism is ahead."[35]

Although close to prose in diction, syntax, and subject
matter, this passage possesses poetic virtues as well: its
concision; its telling images and symbols (the sunset window, the dummy piano); its understated use of rising
rhythms and unaccented line-endings; its bare hints of
rhyme (air / Sarah, soundless / nerves, forever / hear, earlier / Astor, Liszt / practiced, Hall / purple, summer / appear, Brother / career, nieces / us, grandly / me, and hand /
ahead). The technical art of the passage is covert, rather
than overt as it was in "My daddy was chief engineer."
Further, the wit is subtler and therefore both more pointed
and less intrusive. The poem gives the impression of being
spoken not by an anonymous persona but by the great-
nephew of the actual Sarah Winslow. Finally, the "I" remains relatively neutral and transparent, a camera eye.
The density of the poem resides in the material that the "I"
handles; the world is admitted to the poem.

A second version of the poem, written in 1958, included
several significant changes. In general, this version is
closer to the poem as printed in *Life Studies* (though it retains the third verse-paragraph which was ultimately de-

leted). The "sunset window" has become at once more perceptual and more symbolic, a "lakeview window . . : / lurid in the doldrums of the sunset hour"; the aunt's playing is now referred to as "grasshopper notes of genius," adding a nervous, insect image to coincide with the description of the grandmother as "quick as a cricket"; and the comic rhyme of the aunt "risen like the Phoenix / from her bed of troublesome snacks and Tauchnitz classics" has been introduced, deflating its subject by its ironic allusions to the Phoenix myth and perhaps Hamlet's celebrated "sea of troubles," yet also nostalgically evoking a specific lost culture, *fin de siècle* Boston. One significant change, however, was a damaging turn in the wrong direction: Lowell renamed Sarah "Aunt Laura," disguising her identity. When he sent the virtually completed manuscript of *Life Studies* to Williams in November 1958, he had written "Sarah" back in by hand.[36]

As published, "My Last Afternoon with Uncle Devereux Winslow" demonstrates most of the qualities quintessential to Lowell's Confessional poetry (and qualities frequently observable in the Confessional poetry of Snodgrass, Ginsberg, Berryman, Plath, Jarrell, Sexton, and Kunitz as well). An analysis of the principal qualities of the poem will take us some distance toward a working definition of the new poetic genre Lowell helped create.

A description of Lowell's childhood stay at his grandfather's house during which he first learned of death, "My Last Afternoon" is entirely and openly personal. It abandons the personae, masks, and anonymity of Modernism in order to reestablish the self as a realm of primary literary interest. More, the poem is not merely personal in the manner of most lyric poetry; it is frankly autobiographical, with real-life characters and elements of plot. It seems to maintain a scrupulous factuality throughout, specifying names, dates, and places. Lowell's maternal relatives, Sarah and Devereux Winslow, are given their true names as is the grandfather's farm, *"Char-de-sa* / in the Social Register." Even the date is carefully supplied (appropriately, 1922, the year of *The Waste Land*). Time is recorded with Franklinesque precision:

> I was five and a half
> My formal pearl gray shorts
> had been worn for three minutes.
>
> (*LS*, 61)

Indeed, Lowell is careful to give his age in almost every one of the "Life Studies," so that the reader is firmly placed in the world of historical time and objective event. The poem cleaves not to the timeless and universal sphere of the imagination but to the literal, particular, time-bound world of fact.

The reader, as Lowell later explained, "was to believe he was getting the *real* Robert Lowell." The poem may or may not be literally true in its details—like many autobiographers Lowell admits to having "invented facts" in order to give the whole a greater coherence—but the seeming factual precision gives the poem the *impression* of being true. At the very least, one may say that the necessary fiction of *Life Studies* is that it is nonfictional. Lowell has said that "if a poem is autobiographical—and this is true of any kind of autobiographical writing and of historical writing—you want the reader to say, this is true." Thus critics like George Herndl who claim that "interest in 'confessional' poetry as True Confessions is different from interest in it as poetry" oversimplify a complex problem and betray a distaste for the autobiographical mode. As autobiographical writing, *Life Studies* exists in order to allow us entrance into its author's actual life and mode of consciousness. We as readers need to feel that we have gained access to Lowell's real self if the work is to serve its double function of satisfying our legitimate curiosity and giving us greater insight into our own selves. Further, it is possible to argue that literary confession, like religious confession, has its very source in veracity. As Lowell has said, "the needle that prods into what really happened may be the same needle that writes a good line." For instance, the verbal brilliance of his description of "Aunt Sarah, risen like the Phoenix / from her bed of troublesome snacks and Tauchnitz classics" cannot be separated from his intense emotional-intellectual response to his actual memory of Aunt Sarah. Just as Catholic belief provided the inspiration for *Lord Weary's Castle*, so psychological truth provides the inspiration for *Life Studies*.[37]

"My Last Afternoon" not only presents autobiographical truth, it presents that truth unvarnished. It resists the euphemisms, evasions, deceptions, and self-deceptions often found in autobiographical writing. In "My Last Afternoon," Lowell clearly indicates for the reader the family conflicts and failures normally kept politely hidden. Indicatively, the poem begins by plunging us into the child Lowell's rebellion against parental authority: "I won't go with you. I want to stay with Grandpa!" Setting the stage for the poet's later mental collapse, the poem suggests the instability of all the family elders described: "overbearing" Grandfather, pathetic Great Aunt Sarah, and emotionally stunted Uncle Devereux. The method of Wordsworth's *Prelude* and the 1891-1892 *Leaves of Grass* has been reversed: objects of embarrassment and shame are not excluded but focused upon. In a time when most social and religious verities have been called into question, Lowell has been impelled to place ultimate value on absolute fidelity to the actual. He has eliminated (dubious) generalities in favor of the known particulars of his life, ugly though those particulars prove to be. In a sense possibly unintended by Emerson, *Life Studies* fulfills his definition of poetry as "the condition of true naming."

The emphasis in "My Last Afternoon," and even more in such poems as "Waking in the Blue" and "Skunk Hour," is on the extreme experience or psychological state. We are told about Aunt Sarah maniacally thundering on her soundless piano, Uncle Devereux "dying of the incurable

113

Hodgkin's disease," and young Lowell himself cowering in terror at family disputes. The sequence concludes with an unsparing depiction of his mental collapse as an adult. Lowell's premise is the William Jamesian one, more recently reenunciated by the psychoanalyst R. D. Laing and the literary critic A. Alvarez, that madness and the experience of extremity have meaning for the sane. Often there is reason in madness. As Melville explained, "Tormented into desperation, Lear the frantic king tears off the mask, and speaks the sane madness of vital truth." For Lowell, as for many other poets past and present, madness may be another name for "Inspiration" (the original title of "Skunk Hour") and divinest sense.[38]

"My Last Afternoon," like all of "Life Studies," has its orientation in both existential philosophy and Freudian psychology. In existentialist terms, Lowell is alienated from his environment and his own existence, and must therefore undergo a descent into the abyss of his self if he is to find renewed wholeness and authenticity. Like Ellison's *Invisible Man*, he is in search of his lost identity. Such a search leads inevitably to the past, to memory, for time is inseparable from the sense of selfhood. In *Time in Literature*, Hans Meyerhoff argues that "the quest for a clarification of the self leads to a *recherche du temps perdu*. And the more seriously human beings become engaged in this quest, the more they become preoccupied with the consciousness of *time* and its meaning for human life." Having lost his religious faith, Lowell lacks access to the eternal; and so for him only time, as Sartre says, confers meaning. In "My Last Afternoon," Lowell is in quest of his own self lost within time: "What in the world was I wishing?" he wonders about his five-and-a-half-year-old alter ego. One of the poem's first images is of an inexorably ticking cuckoo clock. In seeking to reconnect his past and present selves via memory, Lowell's goal is a sense of continuity, an identity that has withstood time's incomprehensible flow. The goal is to find what he now seems to lack, a unified, enduring, and valuable "I am."[39]

This concern with memory and time is reinforced by Freudian psychology, which teaches that self-examination can yield insight, which in turn can yield self-transformation. Self-examination must begin in the past, in childhood, which contains the seeds of the adult personality. As in existentialism, the goal of Freudian analysis is both self-realization and self-alteration. Freud, Lowell has said, "provides the conditions that one must think in" and is "very much part of my life." Like Berryman compulsively making his "awful pilgrimage" into his past, like Jarrell looking over the fence of his "Lost World," like Ginsberg "dreaming back thru life" in quest of "the key," Lowell must relive his childhood and reexperience its pain fully. He thereby recovers what Roethke called "the lost self," not the past self only but present self as well.[40]

Lowell's dual theme of the connections and disconnections between past and present gains force from his use of a narratorial double-consciousness; the authorial awareness includes both the consciousness of the remembered child and that of the remembering adult poet. Often the double-consciousness appears within a single phrase: "*Tockytock, tockytock* clumped our Alpine, Edwardian cuckoo clock," the childlike mimicry contrasting with the adult knowledge capable of identifying the clock as Alpine and Edwardian (*LS*, 59). A more complex yoking of dictions, and the mentalities they represent, appears in this description of Grandfather's farm:

> Diamond-pointed, athirst and Norman,
> its alley of poplars
> paraded from Grandmother's rose garden
> to a scarey stand of virgin pine,
> scrub, and paths forever pioneering.
>
> (*LS*, 59)

Child and adult are both uneasily present here, the child who perceived the pines as "scarey," the adult who conceives the poplars as "Norman." Further, the adult poet's barely-heard suggestion of Spenser's "Wandering Wood,"

115

with its "pathes and allaies wide" among "sayling pine" and "poplar never dry," serves to validate, on a higher plane of erudition, the child's feeling that untamed nature, and implicitly untamed human nature, is "scarey." This feeling, of course, proves to be the central theme of Lowell's volume.

Structurally, "My Last Afternoon" vibrates between child and adult points of view. The story of Great Aunt Sarah, jilting an Astor, failing to appear at Symphony Hall, could only have been understood and related by the adult Lowell; the passage that directly follows, describing fantasies of a sail-colored horse and of a flight over the house, is a product of the child Lowell's mind (*LS*, 62). Part of the drama of the poem resides in the adult poet's attempt to enter into the imagination of the child, to envision him internally as well as externally.

Lowell's inner-outer view of his past self gives him a Jamesian complexity of perspective. In *The Ambassadors*, James's narrator is both inside and outside of Lambert Strether's consciousness, the inside view supplying sympathy for Strether, the outside view allowing for a more objective judgment. In the same way, Lowell achieves sympathetic identification with his childhood self, sharing his perceptions, fantasies, fears, even his language; yet he at the same time maintains an ironic detachment from that self. He notes, for example, that in a basin's reflection, the misfit child resembled "a stuffed toucan" (*LS*, 61). The adult, objective consciousness is also capable of attaching appropriate meaning to the events described. He detects the child's transition from innocence to terrified knowledge of conflict and death:

> I wasn't a child at all—
> unseen and all-seeing, I was Agrippina
> in the Golden House of Nero
>
> (*LS*, 63)

Lowell's balance between sentimentality and irony, or emotion and understanding, appears in his treatment of all

116

of his characters. Great Aunt Sarah and Uncle Devereux are objects of both affection and derision, as are, in succeeding poems, Lowell's parents. In "Sailing Home from Rapallo," for example, tears run down Lowell's cheeks when he learns of the manner of his mother's death, but they do not keep him from noting that even as a corpse she insisted on her privileges: "Mother travelled first-class in the hold." Irony, frequently quite savage irony, attends his treatment of all his family members, and of his own feelings of love for them. Even his weeping is subjected to disdain: "Tears *smut* my fingers" (*LS*, 69). Yet the irony ultimately reinforces the impression of Lowell's love: the object of scorn is not Great Aunt Sarah playing her dummy piano, or Father booming "Anchors aweigh" in the tub, or Mother "wrapped like *panetone* in Italian tinfoil," but the cruelty of fate, circumstance, and inevitable human frailty which reduce human beings to such indignities (*LS*, 61, 71, 78). Within the complex phenomenology of the "Life Studies" sequence, a creative tension is achieved between past and present, between the remembered and the rememberer, and between the rememberer's own irony and pity.

Further, there is, as M. L. Rosenthal first noted, a tension between Lowell's individual and social awareness. Unlike Sylvia Plath who uses political atrocity as a metaphor for her personal anguish, or Allen Ginsberg who views his madness as a perfectly valid response to the madness of the age, Lowell merely observes that personal and cultural disturbance are in some sense related. As he himself breaks down, he gives us an interior view of a social system that is also breaking down. *Life Studies* contains both psychic testimony and national socio-economic history. It looks inward and outward at once, its inwardness deriving from Freud, its historicism from Marx ("the two thinkers . . . who are never out of one's mind"). Lowell's multiplicitous point of view in *Life Studies* can be seen in the same terms Ian Watt has applied to James's later style: "A supremely civilized effort to relate every event and every moment of life to the full complexity of its circumambient conditions."[41]

"My Last Afternoon" proceeds in a movement characteristic of several of the "Life Studies" (for instance "Skunk Hour"), beginning with a catalogue of almost random details and eventually homing in on its real subject, in this case the death of Uncle Devereux. Upon completion, the poem reveals that the décor which had seemed intended merely to create a naturalistic surface was in fact highly symbolic as well. The clock "slung with strangled, wooden game" and the puppy "paralyzed from gobbling toads" are grotesque images of inanition and death reflective of the family members themselves (LS, 60). Moreover, the poem's recurrent allusions to burnt and decaying substances turning back to Earth prepare the reader for the death of Uncle Devereux, who is not even mentioned until the poem's last section. These images also suggest the physical and moral decay of the Lowell family, a primary topic of Life Studies. The trees are "diamond-pointed," the ponds like "sapphires," the porch screens "as black as coal," the tiles "sweaty with secret dank, crummy with ant-stale," the dead puppy is named "Cinder," the clothing store, in a fine combination of surface and symbol, is called "Rogers Peet's" (LS, 59-61). The farm itself includes the word "char" in its name. At several points throughout the poem, Lowell describes himself as "mixing black earth and lime," an image of decomposition specifically bearing on the fate of Uncle Devereux.

Thus, the Image is as crucial to the success of "My Last Afternoon" as it is to an imagist poem. But Lowell's imagistic methodology has broken from the traditions of Modernism, and from his own practice in Lord Weary's Castle. The natural object alone is no longer an adequate symbol, and the bare juxtaposition of images no longer sufficiently elucidates. Following Williams's lead in "Asphodel," Lowell is willing to fill in the gap between image and image, to explain the image's meaning:

118

My hands were warm, then cool, on the piles
of earth and lime,
a black pile and a white pile. . . .
Come winter,
Uncle Devereux would blend to the one color.

                                                    (*LS*, 64)

Lowell here combines the sensuous surface of poetry with
the accessibility of prose. By adding the final two explana-
tory lines, he has broken with the Modernist esthetic. He
has replaced the verbal "tension" of *Lord Weary's Castle*
with a "prose calm" in which objects and their meanings,
as both exist in the poet's consciousness, are recorded. In
place of the chaotic energy of bare forces in conflict, this
poetry displays a sense of relation, an achieved understanding. [42]
    The visual element is supreme in the first section of the
"Life Studies." Indeed, the poems were written, as the
title suggests, according to the metaphor of portraiture or
photography. In manuscript Lowell emphasized this
metaphor by capitalizing only the initial letter of poem titles, as if they were captions in a family album. Stylistically
the poems exemplify a "displaced mimetic" mode of iconography. They attempt to imitate in verbal form the visual effect of a photograph. They therefore seem to lack
depth. We learn from them what Lowell's eye has seen but
we do not learn directly what his heart has felt. Unlike *Lord
Weary's Castle*, where the outer world was at times blocked
from view by the presence of the poet's own gesticulating
consciousness, *Life Studies* gives us a world of characters in
full view, with the consciousness of the poet reduced to
the thickness of a camera lens. Yet this effect of two-
dimensionality is somewhat misleading. The surfaces of
the poems may seem flat, but just below the surface one
senses the poet's immense emotional pressure, which once
or twice forces through in the form of tears and anguished
exclamations ("Grandpa! Have me, hold me, cherish me!"

[LS, 69]). Lowell's photograph-like portraits of his relatives are meant to resemble the portraits of M. Meyers and other ancestors in the attic of his childhood house. This resemblance, however, is a gesture of pure irony. These photographic life studies are neither flattering nor seemly; they are brutally frank revelations of extremity. As Lowell once wrote of Robert Penn Warren's characters in *Brother to Dragons*, he assumes in *Life Studies* the posture of "Lizzie Borden braining the family portraits with an axe." Or to change the metaphor, he becomes the Diane Arbus of poetry, finding his grotesque subjects not on the streets of New York but in his own family circle—and ultimately in himself.[43]

The picture-like poems in section one of the "Life Studies" comprise an elegiac family record. The chronicle describes Lowell's uncle, grandparents, and parents, in the order of their deaths, and then Lowell's own suicidal mental crisis and partial recovery. A world of faded gentility and failed hopes is delineated. Uncle Devereux lived on memories of former glory; Grandfather Winslow shunned human society and "raked leaves from our dead forbears"; Lowell's father, revealingly drinking "old fashioneds," was fixated in his naval past; and his mother yearned for "those settled years of World War One" (LS, 66, 73, 80). Even the elm trees are dusty and "fatigued" (LS, 68). All of Lowell's ancestors are tired, removed from life, nostalgic for the nineteenth century. They all resemble his mother, mooning in a window "as if she had stayed on a train / one stop past her destination" (LS, 76).

This familial history of social tension, defeat, lovelessness, guilt, and repression is Lowell's inheritance and burden. He collapses under its weight. In his mental breakdown we witness the fall of the house of Lowell, past glory turning to present ruin. The poet, returning to a favorite image, feels like a whale pursued by the whale-killer, that prime symbol of all that is wrong with his personal and national past: "My heart grows tense / as though a harpoon were sparring for the kill" (*LS*, 81). He and the other patients in the mental ward are "Mayflower screwballs," "thoroughbred mental cases." This is the end of the line. Or perhaps not quite. Pathetically, his infant daughter has already been taught to carry on the family tradition of guilt and failure: " 'Sorry,' she mumbles like her dim-bulb father, 'sorry' " (*LS*, 79). Lowell's past and the American past have both culminated in mania and despair. Like his "pedigreed" flowers that have become indistinguishable from weeds, Lowell now keeps "no rank nor station" (*LS*, 84). Divested of the burdens and glories of the past, he faces the terrors of existence alone, diminished, his future unclear: "Cured, I am frizzled, stale and small" (*LS*, 84).

The second section of the "Life Studies" sequence, consisting of four poems, is quite different from the family chronicle of the first section. That difference has generally been overlooked or mistaken by Lowell's critics. It has been thought, for example, that the first group deals with the past and the second with the present. Actually, Lowell is only "forty" in the first poem of section two, whereas he was "forty-one" in the last poem of section one. The final three poems of the first section, which portray Lowell's mental decline, institutionalization, and partial recovery, are clearly intended to take place *after* the harrowing psychotic episode described in section two. Biographical and textual evidence coincide: the first three poems of section two take place in Boston in winter and spring of 1957; and the fourth, "Skunk Hour," takes place in Castine, Maine in summer of 1957. "During Fever" occurs later that year when Lowell, in his obscurely sarcastic phrase, is "home from the healthy country"; "Waking in the Blue" occurs at McLean's hospital in Waverly, Massachusetts in January of 1958; and "Home After Three Months Away" occurs in early spring of the same year. There may well be,

121

as Lowell has said, some "tinkering with the fact," but a chronology has been carefully established which provides at least the illusion of reality. To fail to note the chronology is to mistake the narrative structure Lowell has so carefully implemented and to fail to experience and understand the sequence as he intended.[44]

Sections one and two of "Life Studies" are not divided according to time but to tone and subject matter. I believe that section one constitutes the "Life Studies" per se, the family album, and section two centers, much more subjectively, on the breaking-apart of Lowell's mind. Finally he lays aside his metaphor of the objective photograph and openly asserts his anguish. The sequence, which began as external and calm, even (in Lowell's term) "gentle," concludes as a tortured and brutal journey to the interior.[45]

In "Memories of West Street and Lepke," Lowell presents himself suffocating in the respectable conformity of upper-class Boston's "hardly passionate Marlborough Street" (LS, 85). This quoted phrase has been credited to Henry James by some commentators, but the actual source is William James, who once gave his classes the sentence, "Marlborough is hardly a passionate street" as an example of understatement. Regardless of its source, the phrase suggests just those Brahmin standards of propriety that the revelations of Life Studies set out to subvert. On the surface Lowell seems as "hardly passionate" as Boston, as "tranquillized" or "lobotomized" as the mausoleum-hearted Republic itself. Yet beneath the surface calm lurks his other rebel self, "fire-breathing" and "manic." This is the self who in his "seedtime" (ironically Wordsworthian word) went to jail to protest war; who is about (in "Skunk Hour") to explode again.[46]

Lowell's description of his bizarre former jailmates, all of whom are partial images of himself, recalls Pound's similar descriptions in the *Pisan Cantos*. Ever since voting to give the first Bollingen award to Pound, Lowell had been a staunch admirer of the *Pisan Cantos*, thinking it (as he once wrote Williams) Pound's "most human and nuttiest work." It was the heartfelt personalism of the *Pisan Cantos* that he especially admired: in "those magnificent reveries of recollection," he told interviewers, Pound "let the heart break through his glass ribs." When he came to write a volume of his own that featured immediacy of experience, a mixture of present time and memory, and a poet-self writing (in Pound's phrase) "as a lone ant from a broken ant-hill," Lowell naturally turned to Pound, to pay homage. *Life Studies* rings with Poundian notes, especially in its vivid portraits of writers and of inmates in mental and penal institutions. For example, the "Fordie" of Cantos 74, 80, and 82 prefigures the "Fordie" of Lowell's "Ford Madox Ford"; and Pound's all-too-human fellow prisoners, Mr. Edwards, Mr. G. Scott and the rest, prefigure the Negro boy, Abramowitz, and the other "jailbirds" of "Memories of West Street and Lepke." Lowell's prison poem inevitably echoes Pound's, though stylistically the two are dissimilar. For both poets, prison is a center of human quirkiness and also, somehow, of moral honor; outside is the world of politics, of armies "whose only right is their power" (Canto 76), of John Foster Dulles's "agonizing reappraisals" (*LS*, 86). "Beyond the stockade," Pound wrote in Canto 80, "there is chaos and nothingness." It is this chaos that Lowell inhabits on Marlborough Street, a chaos thinly disguised as order.[47]

In "Man and Wife," Lowell and his wife Elizabeth Hardwick are literally drugged, yet Miltown cannot touch Lowell's inner distemper. He perceives a world homicidally antagonistic: the sunlight appears as "war paint"; even the magnolia trees of Marlborough Street "ignite" with "murderous" flower; and his wife's tirade is as "merciless" as a wave breaking on his head (*LS*, 87). This suppressed violence erupts in "To Speak of Woe That Is in Marriage," a Catullan monologue spoken by his wife (*LS*, 88). As in *The Dolphin*, Lowell makes Hardwick a sympathetic character, though the title derived from the Wife of

123

Bath and a note of self-righteousness within the poem itself allow for the possibility of irony. "To Speak of Woe"
portrays a maniacal Lowell "free-lancing out along the
razor's edge." This madness is primarily personal, of
course, but it also carries with it the failure of the entire social tradition summed up by "hardly passionate
Marlborough Street," and the failure of a political system
that has achieved only tranquilization at home and
"agonizing reappraisals" abroad. Surrounded by collapses
of all sorts—moral, spiritual, social, cultural—Lowell's
mind itself gives way.

The cultural context of Lowell's psychological malady is
made clear in the first four stanzas of "Skunk Hour,"
which describe a physical and moral landscape in which
madness occurs. In his essay on this poem, Lowell claimed
that the first four stanzas were written after the last four
were almost complete, but the manuscript evidence does
not fully support this claim. Although the early draft of the
poem, entitled "Inspiration," contains more lines which
eventually appeared in the second half of "Skunk Hour"
than in the first, Lowell's plan to combine psychological
confession with cultural observation was already clear. Indeed, "Inspiration" begins with the line, "The season's
ill," indicating a clear intention to link inner conditions
with outer. In revising, Lowell's only real change of direction was metrical: he abandoned the nearly regular 24442
ABCBCA stanza form of "Inspiration" for a freer form,
narrowing the distance between the poem and the experience that triggered it. (See Appendix B for the text of "Inspiration.")[48]

The first four stanzas of "Skunk Hour" describe the
Maine seacoast village of Castine (and nearby Nautilus Island and Blue Hill), where Lowell spent the summer of
1957.

Nautilus Island's hermit
heiress still lives through winter in her Spartan cottage;
her sheep still graze above the sea.

Life Studies

Her son's a bishop. Her farmer
is first selectman in our village;
she's in her dotage.

Thirsting for
the hierarchic privacy
of Queen Victoria's century,
she buys up all
the eyesores facing her shore,
and lets them fall.

The season's ill—
we've lost our summer millionaire,
who seemed to leap from an L. L. Bean
catalogue. His nine-knot yawl
was auctioned off to lobstermen.
A red fox stain covers Blue Hill.

And now our fairy
decorator brightens his shop for fall;
his fishnet's filled with orange cork,
orange, his cobbler's bench and awl;
there is no money in his work,
he'd rather marry.

(*LS*, 89)

Lowell remarked of these stanzas, "Sterility howls through
the scenery, but I try to give a tone of tolerance, humor,
and randomness to the sad prospect." The amiability of his
tone is a ruse. He is describing more than scenery, he is
describing the rótting of a whole social structure. The
"hermit heiress" longs for "Queen Victoria's century" and
is senile. Her social successor, the "summer millionaire,"
is also past his prime—his yawl has been auctioned off.
Even nature has grown old and sinister, covered with
"stain" (though literally Lowell must only mean that the
leaves on Blue Hill have begun to change color). The once
vibrant New England culture and economy have been de-
graded: their traditional implements—nets and corks of

125

fishermen, cobbler's bench and awl—are now only items displayed by an interior decorator to attract wealthy tourists.[49]

In stanza five the "sterility" howling through the landscape is given its point. "You dawdle in the first part and suddenly get caught in the poem." The observation in stanza three that "the season's ill" might have referred innocently to seasonal change, but by stanza six its full implication is manifest: this season of human habitation on earth is ill—decadent and debased. And Lowell, his spirit "ill" (st. 6), personifies that disease. Just as he embodies his ailing civilization, so the town inhabitants turn out to have prefigured Lowell himself, who is as isolated and demented as the heiress, as fallen as the ruined millionaire, and as loveless and artistically failed as the decorator. (In the early draft of the poem, he applied the line "there's no money in this work" to himself.) Lowell's soul, in William James's term, is sick:

> One dark night,
> my Tudor Ford climbed the hill's skull;
> I watched for love-cars. Lights turned down,
> they lay together, hull to hull,
> where the graveyard shelves on the town. . . .
> My mind's not right.
>
> A car radio bleats,
> "Love, O careless Love. . . ." I hear
> my ill-spirit sob in each blood cell,
> as if my hand were at its throat. . . .
>
> (LS, 90)[50]

Lowell has entered a monstrous world akin to the world of "For the Union Dead" in which automobiles and steam-shovels appear as creatures out of the Mesozoic era. The monsters of both poems embody the inner truth of the observed scene and, equally frightening, make manifest his own disordered feelings. In "Skunk Hour" he sees the graveyard hill itself as a "skull," an expressionist figure of death. He projects his feelings of lovelessness and balked lust into a scene of automotive sexuality, in which not only the car's occupants but the "love-cars" themselves couple "hull to hull," while bleating like sheep of "careless Love." Disconnected from the observed scene and even from his own inner self, Lowell perceives *himself* to be a "skull" of death, an empty "hull" in which his spirit chokes.

The self-portrait Lowell has created calls to mind other sexually and emotionally withdrawn characters in our post-Puritan literature, preeminently those of Hawthorne and Henry James. Lowell portrays himself as an un-spiritualized Paul Pry, a Miles Coverdale reduced to spying on Zenobia through a window, or a John Marcher spying on himself spying on himself. The experience he so feelingly recounts is precisely that of the inability to experience or feel. The Puritan introspector has become at last mere voyeur. As in Hawthorne, Lowell's depiction of psychological separateness manifests a cosmic condition. Because he is now exiled from God as well as human society, he is constrained, in the manner of Ethan Brand, to judge and punish himself:

> I myself am hell;
> nobody's here—

Lowell has written of his stanzas, "This is the dark night. I hoped my readers would remember John of the Cross's poem. My night is not gracious, but secular, puritan, and agnostical. An Existential night. Somewhere in my mind was a passage from Sartre or Camus about reaching some point of final darkness where the one free act is suicide." Like Christ on Golgotha, the "place of a skull," Lowell confronts death on the "hill's skull" near the graveyard; not a death leading to resurrection, but an existential death, yielding nothingness.[51]

These stanzas of "Skunk Hour" combine religious and agnostic imagery because, as William James has said, doubt and hope are sisters. Indeed, if it is true, as James

127

claimed, that religious experience involves uneasiness and its solution, then "Skunk Hour" may be seen as a variety of religious poem—a position held by Lowell himself when he said that though *Life Studies* lacks the Christian trappings of *Lord Weary's Castle*, it seemed to him "in many ways more religious" than the earlier work. "Skunk Hour" resembles many testaments of the complete destitution that frequently precedes union with God. Hopkins' "terrible sonnets" and (at a lesser intensity) part three of Eliot's "East Coker" chronicle a dark night of the soul in which the poet wrestles with his isolation, unbelief, and suicidal impulses. A prototype of this genre, of course, is the sixteenth-century mystical poem "The Dark Night" by St. John of the Cross. Lowell picks up several phrases from this poem—"one dark night," "they lay together," "nobody's here"—as well as St. John's use of nocturnal darkness and sexual longing as vehicles to communicate a sense of spiritual emptiness. William James, who frequently quotes St. John of the Cross when discussing mystical experience in *The Varieties of Religious Experience*, refers to this feeling of negation or desolation as "the salvation through self-despair, the dying to be truly born." Yet for Lowell negation does not lead to Godhead. His poem, unlike those of Hopkins, Eliot, and St. John of the Cross, describes not a passage *through* but a passage *into* the void. He can no longer find his salvation in a Christian tradition that has come to seem to him "chalk-dry."[52]

Lowell communicates his sense of Christian apostasy in the line "I myself am hell," which simultaneously echoes Marlowe's Mephistophilis and Milton's Satan. Mephistophilis explains in *Dr. Faustus* that for the damned, "Where we are is Hell," and Milton's Satan similarly observes, "Which way I fly is Hell; myself am Hell." Lowell, now an image of Lucifer, suffers the tortures of the damned. In his terrible isolation—from God, from divinely ordained standards of conduct, from his fellow human beings, and even from his own sane self—he experiences the full terrors of an unsheltered existence. He has entered into the heart of the land of unlikeness.

Yet if in Christian terms Lowell is damned, in existential terms he displays the qualities of a hero. As he indicated, "Skunk Hour" owes something to both Jean-Paul Sartre and Albert Camus. Sartre insists that all acts are free, not merely the act of suicide; but despite this important difference from Lowell's postulation of a "point of final darkness where the one free act is suicide," Sartre does describe the suicidal occurrence in terms very similar to Lowell's own. In *Being and Nothingness*, an anguished Sartre considers throwing himself down a precipice, but that impulse only leads him on to intensified self-scrutiny and self-creation. For Sartre this is a moment of existential authenticity. It ends not in the suicidal act itself—he retreats from the edge of the precipice and resumes his way—but in a renewed obligation to "remake the *Self* which designates the free being." During his moment of "anguish" when he felt "cut off from the world and from my essence by this nothingness which I *am*," he was able to apprehend himself "at once as totally free and as not being able to derive the meaning of the world except as coming from myself." Sartre celebrates anguish, the self's isolated sufficiency and radical freedom, and suicide itself as an "absurd" choice and "affirmation of being"; in this celebration we see the philosophical honoring of the experience undergone so harrowingly, and with so little sense of honor, in Lowell's poem.[53]

"Skunk Hour" is equally indebted to Camus. In *The Myth of Sisyphus* Camus calls the question of self-murder "the one truly serious philosophical problem," one which may produce a valuable "awakening" of consciousness. For Camus the earth is a "desert" and the human relation to it at best "absurd." The absurd inevitably results from human reason's confrontation with a world unreasonably silent—a world where, as Lowell says, "nobody's here." Yet Camus argues that suicide ultimately be rejected because suicide itself kills the absurd; it reconciles mind and world, which ought to remain always unreconciled. The height of human consciousness is to be forever contemplative of the absurd, and hence of the possibility of suicide, without ever yielding to suicide's temptation. Camus tells us that "the important thing . . . is not to be cured, but to live with one's ailments."[54]

The conclusion of "Skunk Hour" conforms to the dicta of Sartre and Camus. Like Sisyphus, Lowell consents to Earthly existence, a futile labor whose only reward is consciousness itself. Echoing the existentialists' characterization of suicidal contemplation as "absurdity" and "affirmation," Lowell has said of his ending: "Out of this comes the march and affirmation, an ambiguous one, of my skunks in the last two stanzas. The skunks are both quixotic and barbarously absurd, hence the tone of amusement and defiance."

nobody's here—

only skunks, that search
in the moonlight for a bite to eat.
They march on their soles up Main Street:
white stripes, moonstruck eyes' red fire
under the chalk-dry and spar spire
of the Trinitarian Church.

I stand on top
of our back steps and breathe the rich air—
a mother skunk with her column of kittens swills the
    garbage pail.
She jabs her wedge-head in a cup
of sour cream, drops her ostrich tail,
and will not scare.

(*LS*, 90)

The skunks' strong will to survive, their steadfast ransacking of the garbage pails, implies the poet's parallel will to live. Although Lowell, skunk-like, is reduced to feasting on carrion, it is not the carrion of self-annihilation, but of endurance.[55]

Lowell has said that he modeled the march of the skunks on Elizabeth Bishop's brilliant poem "The Armadillo." Bishop's armadillo is observed fleeing a fire, "head down, tail down," like Lowell's skunks a symbol of survival. Yet the armadillo is harmless and pathetic in its defiance of a hostile universe, "a weak mailed fist / clenched ignorant against the sky!" Lowell's skunks are domineering and "moonstruck," a bestial, morally repugnant occupation army. These skunks anticipate Ted Hughes's "Crow." In the modern waste land, devoid of even the hope of rain, all is abnormality, self-assertion, ugliness, violence, madness, monstrosity. "Nobody's here— / only skunks." The skunks "march," "bite," "jab," stink, refuse to be scared off. They are the militant, brutish new order, commanding the ruins of the former civilization (symbolized by the chalk-dry church). They swill the garbage pail, the refuse of the past. The skunks are an image of the new world Lowell has entered, and an image of Lowell himself, having entered. He breathes the "rich air," accommodating himself to this present, this future.[56]

In "Skunk Hour" Lowell stares deeply into an interior abyss, but keeps himself from plunging into it by means of his art. The poem counters the solipsism of suicide by establishing temporal relations to past (St. John of the Cross, Milton) and future ("will not scare"), and a spatial relation to the Maine locale it describes so carefully. Most importantly, the poem connects Lowell in discourse to his readers (his confessors). In Emerson's phrase, Lowell utters aloud his painful secret. He *confesses*, a word which derives from *com* plus *fateri*: to *speak completely*, and also, to *speak with*, to *speak together*. He thereby reverses his journey into the nothingness within. As Stephen Spender argued in an essay on "Confessions and Autobiography" published in 1955,

Even the most shamelessly revealed inner life yet pleads its cause before the moral system of an outer, objective life. One of the things which the most abysmal confessions prove is the incapacity of even the most outcast creature to be alone. Indeed, the essence of the confession is that the one who feels outcast pleads with humanity to relate his isolation to its wholeness.

As a literary confession "Skunk Hour" relieves the poet's subjective burden and restores the connection between self and world. The poem proves, as Lowell hoped it would, not a "deathrope" but a "lifeline."[57]

Rooted in Lowell's painful personal life, *Life Studies* affirms the value of human experience. Alfred Kazin wrote that in *Lord Weary's Castle* Lowell seemed "more intense about life than intimate with it." In flight from his personal experience, he made the cosmos reverberate with his cries. In *Life Studies* his cries of defiance and praise ring out to something a little nearer. And as a result the dove of experience has brought him new wisdom, a new olive branch to eat. Lowell's rebellion in the "Life Studies" sequence is familial and social; he rebels against "Mother and Father" in the initial poems (both as disobedient child and satirical adult poet) and against social norms in the later poems. Yet by having expressed and acknowledged his rebellion, he moves to a new state of consciousness, beyond rebellion. "Frizzled, stale and small," he ultimately chooses contemplation over agony, endurance over apocalyptic gestures. He leaves us with a wry double image of himself, as the inept figure incapable of scaring a skunk, and, symbolically, as the quixotic skunk itself, refusing to be scared. By facing the tensions of his inner being in its interplay with outer world, Lowell has come to terms with himself. He is now beyond needing an external authority to justify and protect him. He has become his own father. He survives.[58]

In *Life Studies* Lowell breaks through to the tradition of Emerson and Whitman, in which the poet speaks for his community and yet remains a single identifiable individual. He has become Emerson's ideal "Poet," unfolding "a whole new experience" which the reader recognizes as an allegory of his own. Yet if Lowell's new insistence on his own "personal story" is Emersonian or Whitmanian, his sensibility continues to be shaped by what Melville called (referring to Hawthorne) the power of blackness. Lowell resembles the later, disillusioned Emerson, who in essays significantly titled "Experience" and "Fate" learned to discern "ferocity in the interiors of nature"; or the Whitman of 1860 who saw in himself "ashes and filth"; or the Williams of *Paterson* and "Asphodel," stunned by signs of social "divorce," "breakdown," and "waste." Lowell is a prophet who has paid the price of experience. He appears to us not as a god, but a beast. His wisdom derives not from any visionary gleam, but from the desolate market and withered field of the world.[59]

❧ IV ❧
Impressions of Experience

For the Union Dead as a Sequence

To write down that which happens at that time— To perfect the ability to record at the moment when the consciousness is enlarged by the sympathies and the unity of understanding which the imagination gives.
—*Williams, Spring and All*

After *Life Studies* appeared, Lowell's former student Anne Sexton sent him a poem entitled "To a Friend Whose Work Has Come to Triumph," in which she portrayed him (rather in her own image) as an Icarus whose ultimate misfortune was dwarfed by the grandeur of his flight. Yet he did not particularly relish the prospect of plunging into the sea, nor did he perceive himself as even momentarily triumphant. *Life Studies* had indeed been very successful; it proved to be the most *noticed* book he ever published. But after its publication Lowell was left, as he commented in accepting the National Book Award, "hanging on a questionmark." He was faced with the problem of the future: what to do now. [1]

In 1960 Lowell and his wife decided to move the family from Boston to New York. It was to be a new start. In Boston Lowell had begun to feel "stranded" in a city that was "now a museum." The poem "For the Union Dead," which he completed before the move and read in a ceremony on Boston Common in June of 1960, represented his farewell to New England and to his ancestral and personal roots. He was done with looking backward into his past. New York, a city "with no past . . . no landmarks," stood for the rootless future. Lowell was later to say that New York "has a great sheer feeling of utter freedom. And then when one thinks back a little bit, it seems all confused and naked." Confused and naked himself, he began to explore the new artistic world he had opened up for himself in *Life Studies*.[2]

Lowell at first felt hampered by the feeling that he had "done enough personal poetry," and spent most of 1960 and 1961 writing free translations for a volume he hoped would be "a small anthology of European poetry." Despite his Drydenesque intention in *Imitations* to "do what my authors might have done if they were writing their poems now and in America," the volume became at last nearly as personal a document as *Life Studies*; he himself acknowledged this in his introduction by calling the book "partly self-sufficient and separate from its sources . . . a sequence, one voice running through many personalities." The voice, inevitably, was his own. Disguised as a collection of translations, the volume in actuality exposes Lowell's crisis of consciousness resulting from his contemplation of suicide. The sequence proceeds from death-wracked terror in its initial poems, into black despair and self-loathing in its central Baudelaire poems, and then, in a movement typical of most of Lowell's books, back out again toward the light. Abandoning its pretense to chronological order, the volume ends with a poem very loosely based on Rilke's "Die Tauben." In this poem Lowell acknowledges a powerful death-wish yet also affirms survival as the ultimate absurd and painful value in a world without absolutes:

> Still only by suffering the rat-race in the arena
> can the heart learn to beat.
>
> (*I*, 149)[3]

Imitations, the "anthology" that became a confession, taught Lowell that his poetic gift was now firmly wedded to the personal. It also taught him that he was able to produce an art acceptable to both of his "masters," Allen Tate and William Carlos Williams. Tate thought Lowell's poems "brilliant" and Williams called them "the real thing."* In

* *Imitations*, however, was unsuccessful with most reviewers, who chided Lowell for his "mistranslations" and declined to treat the volume

contemplating his future, Lowell realized that "continuous autobiography" in the manner of *Life Studies* "was impossible"—that vein of silver had for now given out. Instead he determined to combine the undisguised personal quality of *Life Studies* with the inward probing of *Imitations*, producing poems that contained the whole of his present self.[4]

In *For the Union Dead* Lowell quietly but significantly altered the "revolutionary" style of *Life Studies* by giving his poems a density lacking in the earlier book. In most of the "Life Studies" sequence Lowell looked steadily, as through a thin pane of transparent glass, at scenes from his past. In the poems of *For the Union Dead*, however, he moves easily back and forth between past and present. He interposes between himself and his ostensible subject the thick, translucent glass of his whole being, an opaque medium that shapes, adds, and alters as it transmits. In place of ironic, realistic photographs of past events, Lowell now gives us the rich, intermingled impressions of past and present events upon his own consciousness. Growing out of his full awareness at the moment of writing, the poems of *For the Union Dead* manifest the indeterminacy and incompleteness, the mixture of inarticulateness and eloquence, common to consciousness. In *For the Union Dead*, therefore, Lowell initiated his third distinct manner of handling his experience in poetry, supplanting the manipulative rhetoric of *Lord Weary's Castle* and the plainly exposed surfaces of *Life Studies* with a poetry of and about consciousness itself. This third major phase of Lowell's poetry—continuing, with modifications, for the rest of his career—reflects Henry James's insight in "The Art of Fiction" that "if experience consists of impressions, it may be said that impressions *are* experience."

in any way as new creation. Even the general public was annoyed. When Lowell read from the volume at the YMHA in New York in 1961, a woman in the audience complained that she had paid to hear new poems and insisted upon her money being refunded.

Immediately following his completion of *Imitations* in spring of 1961, Lowell wrote to Allen Tate and Tate's new wife Isabella Gardner that he was "in one of those dreadful empty vacation periods between bursts of writing." Several months later he wrote to Gardner again, to congratulate her on her first book of poetry, *The Looking Glass*, and to complain of his own desolation (in language that prefigures the conclusion of "Eye and Tooth"): "Writing's hell, isn't it? I tire of my turmoil, and feel everyone else has, and long for a Horatian calm." His state of artistic exhaustion resembled his condition following *Lord Weary's Castle*, but instead of turning to stale self-repetition as he had in *The Mills of the Kavanaughs*, Lowell this time was willing to try something new: "I find that you plan one thing and something unforeseen breaks through it and carries you God knows where. So there's always surprise, adventure and imperfection, much better, I guess, than a tame certainty." Suffering from episodes of intense depression and feeling devoid of the inspiration that had produced *Lord Weary's Castle* and *Life Studies*, he nevertheless began to work on the bulk of the poems that were published in 1964 in *For the Union Dead*.[5]

Having learned above all else to "write directly about what mattered" to him, Lowell decided to focus on his own dejection and lack of artistic inspiration and to make this very sense of "witheredness" his poetic subject. In place of artistic silence on the one hand, or Ungaretti's lovely "flower gathered" on the other, he produced poems he termed "gathered crumbs." The mood of his book resembles that caught in the title of W. D. Snodgrass's second book: *After Experience*. *For the Union Dead* exposes Lowell's emotional sterility following the conflicts of *Lord Weary's Castle* and the harrowing confessions of *Life Studies*. In his early work he inflated himself into a figure equivalent to Cain and inflated his family situation into high tragedy and even (in a poem like "Rebellion") cosmic allegory. In *Life Studies* he finally came to terms with his par-

137

ents and himself as comic and pathetic, half-repellent and half-attractive figures; that is to say, as merely human. The experience left him "soured and dry." Except in its vivid title-poem, *For the Union Dead* reveals inner exhaustion, reveals "the drouth I had touched with my own hands."[6]

The "drouth" in *For the Union Dead*, however, is as much cultural as it is individual. Much more than *Life Studies*, Lowell's new volume reflects the politics of its time. Mary Jarrell remembers that Lowell's letters to her husband Randall during this period "were full of the grim realities of the bomb and mass death." In *For the Union Dead* Lowell reveals to us the struggle of an individual to bear the double burden of his existence, social as well as personal. His point is that public and private worlds are interconnected, each affecting and being affected by the other. Lowell as private man may be alienated from the hostile social world, but he is not therefore isolated from it. In *For the Union Dead* he expresses the terrors of human life in modern urban society, a society technologically advanced but spiritually empty. He describes the experience of the contemporary Waste Land, a place of unprecedented wealth and pollution, where individuals are powerless, faithless, isolated, and, in their inchoate rage, even antagonistic to one another; and where all stands threatened at every moment by nuclear annihilation.[7]

It would be tempting to say that *For the Union Dead* superimposes the manner of *Lord Weary's Castle* upon the manner of *Life Studies*. Perhaps there is some truth in that. But *For the Union Dead* differs from *Lord Weary's Castle* in that its speaking voice is fallibly human rather than oracular. "Confused and naked," "hanging on a question-mark," wanting to "splash in the waters of life" but discovering only "drouth," Lowell stared deeply into a personal and communal void and gathered poems out of it. *For the Union Dead* commences his period of artistic maturity, in which his poems are "involved in the contemporary world" yet responsive to the quirks and contradictions of his own individual psyche. As the book was being published, he told A. Alvarez that American poets had entered into a new cultural situation:

> We are free to say what we want to, and somehow what we want to say is the confusion and sadness and incoherence of the human condition. . . . I don't know why the arts say this so strongly. It may be a more miserable time, more than others, with the world liable to blow up. We're in some transition domestically: I mean in one's family and everything else. There are new moral possibilities, new moral incoherence. It's a very confused moment. And for some reason it's almost a dogma with us: we'll show that confusion.

In *For the Union Dead* Lowell exposed the private and public confusions he had undergone firsthand. Out of the wealth and poverty of his own experience he created his poetry of consciousness.[8]

Although Lowell intended the poems of *For the Union Dead* to be "separate entities," the book as a whole takes the form of a rough sequence, much like *Lord Weary's Castle* and *Imitations*. On its primary level of meaning the sequence is intensely personal, even (in its pivotal central section) solipsistic. It enacts a Sartrean existential drama: Lowell's prolonged encounter in shame and disgust with his own flawed being and then an affirmative movement out of the self's isolation toward reconnection with the world. In a letter to Williams, Lowell once pictured himself loafing "as freely as Walt Whitman," but *For the Union Dead* reveals that in fact his sense of freedom was rigidly circumscribed. If Whitman felt himself to be a child going forth every day, Lowell felt himself to be fully adult, weighted with a cultural and personal past that insistently pressured and controlled his present. If Whitman felt himself to be a kosmos, Lowell felt himself to be in pieces. If Whitman was man on the open road, Lowell was sentenced to solitary confinement in the cell of himself. Yet as

Andrei Voznesensky wrote to him, "All around—a maximum-security prison . . . / and still you must sing like a child." In *For the Union Dead* Lowell sings the unlovely songs of a trapped soul in praise of freedom. And in his concluding title-poem he ultimately attains his freedom, just at the point where Whitman lost his: in the face of evil. Whereas "the meanness and agony without end" reduced Whitman to the alienated silence of "I Sit and Look Out," they inspire Lowell in "For the Union Dead" to rediscover the power of the human spirit to resist its own degradation.[9]

For the Union Dead begins quietly with poems memorializing two past failures in love. In "Water," a poem of monochrome bleakness modeled on Hardy's "Neutral Tones," Lowell ruefully recalls a moment when he and an unnamed woman proved unable to connect. (The *Notebook/History* revision of this poem reveals that the woman was Elizabeth Bishop and the time 1948.) In "The Old Flame" he remembers the last days of his marriage to Jean Stafford, retelling events he had earlier mythologized out of recognition in "The Death of the Sheriff" and "The Mills of the Kavanaughs." This poem exhibits a willed optimism—"everything's changed for the best"—that attests to Lowell's suppression of his violent emotions. As the sequence continues, however, he slowly abandons his control. Each succeeding poem is written at a different level of intensity, but the movement is generally a descent into his naked psyche, and therefore into bitterness, remorse, incoherence, self-hatred, and yearnings for death. These poems express Lowell's deepest despair during a period he described to Tate as "a stretch of dark, post-manic and pathological self-abasement."[10]

As the book progresses, Lowell's remembered sexual loneliness develops into a present separation from all things. Eyes and eyesight are a crucial image in *For the Union Dead*, signifying both human communication and poetic vision. Early on, Lowell describes himself gazing "like a bird-watcher" at the surrounding landscape (*FUD*, 10). But by the middle of the sequence, in poems significantly titled "Eye and Tooth," "Myopia: a Night," and "The Severed Head," he has become almost totally immersed in his own isolated and painful consciousness: "the old cut cornea throbbed, / I saw things darkly" (*FUD*, 18). At a point near autism, he perceives the outside world as little more than a bad dream. Yet the relationship of subjective consciousness to the objective world is precisely what constitutes the functioning self. By shutting tight his doors of perception, by withdrawing his consciousness from the world it inhabits, Lowell approaches the nothingness that Sartre says is coiled in the heart of being like a worm.

Lowell's existential journey to the heart of darkness reaches its furthest point in "Myopia: a Night," at the precise numerical center of the book (*FUD*, 31-33). Dislocated and inturning, this poem resembles the last suicidal poems of Plath, Jarrell, and Berryman. It describes a sleepless night which inexorably becomes a dark night of the soul. His glasses removed, Lowell's vision, his primary link to the world, fails him: "all's / ramshackle, streaky, weird." This myopic divorce from the external world is more than physical, it is metaphysical as well. Lowell feels alienated from his life and surroundings, which seem threateningly dense, dark, and strange. He sees only "a dull and alien room." Even his own room, a mediator between self and indifferent universe, now seems itself indifferent and foreign. The "cell of learning," the artist's special place and a metonymy for intellectual activity itself, proves just as unintelligible as the universe it was meant somehow to order.

Struck by the futility of his life and apparent failure of his art, Lowell turns away from both life and art: "My eyes avoid / that room. No need to see." Here he contemplates death. He recalls that once (perhaps in the period of *Lord Weary's Castle*) he had wished for a purifying, transcendent artistic vision to "burn away the blur" of mortal existence, while his "senses clenched / their teeth, thought stitched to thought, / as through a needle's eye." This apocalyptic quest itself was implicitly suicidal, involving the cessation of perception ("senses clenched"), and a giving over to a disordered mental world in which senses have teeth to clench, and thoughts are stitched together as if by thread yet go through a needle as if they *are* thread. This hoped-for mystic oblivion has failed, however, and Lowell is left to discern in Satan's metamorphosis a metaphor for himself: all that "blinding brightness" changed into a dark creature "grovelling on its gut."

"Myopia: a Night" may be viewed as Lowell's naturalistic answer to Roethke's "In a Dark Time," which Roethke had mailed him in manuscript several years before. Roethke's poem claims that "in a dark time, the eye begins to see," but in Lowell's dark time, the eye sees nothing, learns nothing. For Lowell, extreme depression (as he later told an interviewer) is not "a visitation of the angels but dust in the blood." Approaching the conclusion of "Myopia: a Night," he fully equates ego and vision, "I" and "eye," and declares himself ready for suicide: "The things of the eye are done." And yet he does not kill himself. The poem fades into the morning's light. Death listens for Lowell's voice, but for no apparent reason he refuses to call. He just waits.[11]

In the second half of the *For the Union Dead* sequence, Lowell gradually recovers from his suicidal crisis by connecting with egos outside his own—first by sympathetically identifying himself with great writers of the past (in poems about Hawthorne and Jonathan Edwards) and finally by rediscovering his love for his wife, Elizabeth Hardwick. The three poems at the end of the sequence which affirm this love, "New York 1962: Fragment," "The Flaw," and "Night Sweat," balance the two poems of past lovelessness at the beginning. These sets of counterpoems frame Lowell's progression from alienation to human relation. By the end of the sequence he has recovered from his solipsistic self-confrontation and, somehow purged and strengthened, has tentatively reentered the world.

"Night Sweat," the penultimate poem of the book, concludes Lowell's mental torments. In the first half of this poem he describes himself in a fever, sleeping apart from his wife. For one last time he struggles with his "will to die," again imaged as isolation in darkness. For Lowell, as for Yeats in "Nineteen Hundred and Nineteen," "the night can sweat with terror." This part of the poem contrasts ironically with Yvor Winters's lovely poem 'The Marriage," which Lowell singled out for praise in a 1961 essay on Winters. "The Marriage" concludes with an image of Winters and his wife in eternal spiritual union:

> And, in commemoration of our lust,
> May our heirs seal us in a single urn,
> A single spirit never to return.

Lowell, on the contrary, images himself as utterly alone in the heavy black urn of himself:

> my life's fever is soaking in night sweat—
> .   .   .   .
> one universe, one body . . . in this urn
> the animal night sweats of the spirit burn.
>
> (*FUD*, 68)

But in the second half of "Night Sweat" both light and lightness return, as Lowell feels "the light / lighten" his leaded eyelids. The "soot of night" gives way to his Hopkinsian delight in the "dapple of the day." He experiences a spiritual recovery that is actually caused less by the returning daylight than by the return of his wife: "my wife . . . your lightness alters everything." The poem has thus moved from night to day, sightlessness to vision, heaviness to lightness, isolation to hoped-for connection. He pleads with his wife, "Absolve me, help me Dear Heart, as you bear / this world's dead weight and cycle on your back." A cry for help is as hopeful as this sequence gets. Lowell is essentially a poet of trapped awareness; and yet his struggle for vision, for a humanizing relation to the surrounding world, provides the very subject matter of the poetry. Escaping the dark cocoon of self, he at the last recovers the ability to "see" himself and his surroundings "washed with light." Vision, and all that it implies, has been regained.[12]

In his review of *For the Union Dead*, Christopher Ricks helpfully observed that the volume married "the three contexts" of Lowell's imagination: "personal experience," "the way we live now, a social and political web," and "the outer context, historical, literary and religious." As we have seen, the poems of *For the Union Dead* are indeed deeply personal. Several have historical, literary, and religious sides as well, most notably the pair of poems on Hawthorne and Edwards. But Lowell's striking innovation in *For the Union Dead* is his creation of poems focusing directly on social and political themes. He no longer treats politics as part of a religious myth (as in his first books) or as an undercurrent (as in the "Life Studies" sequence), but as an important area of experience in its own right. In *For the Union Dead* he reveals to us a consciousness shaped not just by individual experience and cultural inheritance but by its continuing exposure to our collective social and political ills.[13]

Lowell, unlike Harry Truman, "lost sleep about the atom bomb." Pollution "disgusts" him. These concerns, growing ever stronger in his poetry of the 1960s, appear in two groups of political poems positioned almost symmetrically toward the beginning and end of *For the Union Dead*. The first group consists of "The Mouth of the Hudson" and

1. A bas-relief by Augustus Saint-Gaudens depicting Colonel Robert Gould Shaw and the Massachusetts Fifty-fourth infantry regiment. The monument, dedicated in 1897, is located in a corner of Boston Common on Beacon Street. *Photo by C. P. Curtis, June 1955, courtesy of the Boston Athenaeum.*

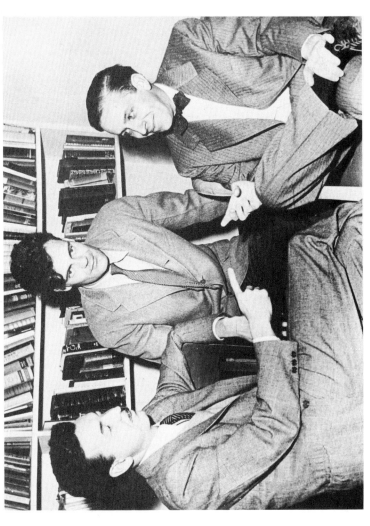

2. From left: Randall Jarrell, Robert Lowell, Peter Taylor. Taken in Jarrell's office at the University of North Carolina Women's College (Greensboro) in 1948. *Courtesy of Mrs. Randall Jarrell and the University of North Carolina, Greensboro.*

3. Staff of the Kenyon School of English, summer 1950. From left, top row: Arthur Mizener, Robert Lowell, Kenneth Burke, Delmore Schwartz; bottom row: Philip B. Rice, William Empson, John Crowe Ransom, L. C. Knight, Charles Coffin. *From* KENYON COLLEGE—ITS THIRD HALF CENTURY, 1975, *by Thomas B. Greenslade, courtesy of Kenyon College.*

4. William Carlos Williams in the late 1940s. *Photo by Charles Sheeler, courtesy of New Directions Publishing Corp.*

5. W. D. Snodgrass at the University of Iowa in the early 1950s. *Courtesy of W. D. Snodgrass.*

6. Robert Lowell and Mary McCarthy at a picnic in Parc de St. Cloud, France, August 1963. *Photo by Loomis Dean,* LIFE MAGAZINE, © TIME, *Inc.*

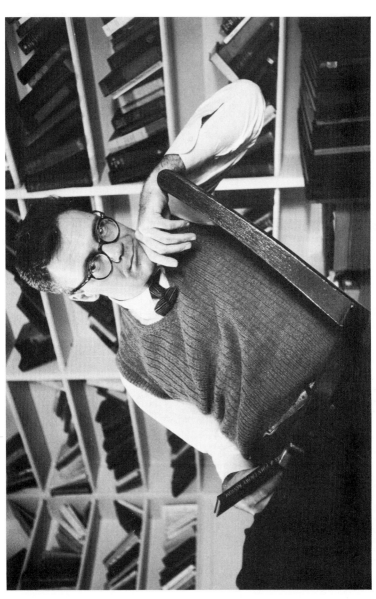

7. Robert Lowell in his study in New York, early 1962. *Photo by Alfred Eisenstaedt,* LIFE MAGAZINE, © TIME, *Inc.*

8. Senator Eugene McCarthy and Robert Lowell on the campaign trail, spring 1968. *Photo by Leonard McCombe, LIFE MAGAZINE, © TIME, Inc.*

9. Robert Lowell reading his poetry at Sanders Theater, Harvard, May 1977.
Photo by Stan Grossfeld, BOSTON GLOBE *Photo.*

For the Union Dead as a Sequence

"Fall 1961," and the second of "July in Washington," "Buenos Aires," and "Dropping South: Brazil." The ability to write a political poem represents a certain degree of mental stability for Lowell. These poems show him coping with his environment, rather than withdrawing into himself as he does in the deathlike center of the sequence. He feels strong enough to assume the role of conscience (as well as consciousness) of his age.[14]

In "The Mouth of the Hudson," for example, he observes the polluted Hudson River and the wasted surrounding countryside and is repelled by what he sees. This poem is a powerful expression of outrage at the "suburban factories" causing "chemical air" and "salt and pepper snow." The physical pollution of the environment points toward society's interior moral and spiritual decay: the transient Negro of the poem, toasting wheat-seeds over coke-fumes, has been discarded by society just as surely as the old cable drums and condemned freight trains. The poem gains added depth and authenticity, however, because it is not *simply* a poem of political protest. It is one of the poems of *For the Union Dead* Lowell intended to be "close to symbolism." Originally entitled "From the Presbyterian Hospital Windows (October 1962)," the poem objectifies his mental disturbance. On this level, the blighted external scene functions as a symbol of his own mind, alienated by society's baseness and betrayed by his own failings as well. The "unforgivable landscape" is an inscape. In that half-observed and half-introspected scene, Lowell describes a man like himself, who "has trouble with his balance." "The Mouth of the Hudson," then, is not merely an angry attack on American industry for polluting and wasting, though it is that. It is more profoundly a vision of Hell that images the poet's inner being—and in some measure the inner being of us all. For the Hell we have created around us gives sign of the Hell we carry within.[15]

Lowell follows "The Mouth of the Hudson" with "Fall

145

1961," his major poem of the Cold War and one of the strongest political poems he ever wrote. Composed in the period it describes, this poem captures the sense of nuclear anxiety that overwhelmed America during the Berlin crisis of the autumn of 1961. In an interview given just before it broke (in July 1961), Lowell had praised W. H. Auden for expressing in his poetry of the 1930s the "neurotic tension" of that prewar period: "He caught the air and it was air in which events were hovering over your shoulder at every point, the second war was boiling into existence." He had added, however, that this poetic possibility was not available to himself: "I don't think this is a period of parties and politics the way the thirties were. . . . I don't meet people who are violently anti-Russian very often. That doesn't seem to be the air." Yet even as this interview was being published, in August, these last remarks were proven wrong: the air was suddenly blown, in Nehru's phrase, by "the foul winds of war." On August 13th, East German troops sealed off the border between East and West Berlin. This act commenced a prolonged confrontation between American and Soviet troops in Berlin and a psychological war of nerves that included the mutual resumption of nuclear testing after a three-year moratorium. Just four months after Lowell's July interview, the political scientist Louis J. Halle could seriously argue that "we are living today in a prewar period—like those that led up to 1914 and 1939."[16]

Like Auden twenty-three Septembers before, Lowell now found himself thrust into historical crisis "uncertain and afraid." Writing for a *Partisan Review* symposium on the Cold War, he passionately condemned what he called "crusading nationalism" and an "amoral power struggle."

> No nation should possess, use, or retaliate with its bombs. I believe we should rather die than drop our own bombs. . . . The sovereign nations, despite their feverish last minute existence, are really obsolete. They imperil the lives they are credited to protect.

For the Union Dead as a Sequence

"Fall 1961" expresses the peril of that moment in history. Yet like all of Lowell's public poems, it is at the same time a quite personal poem; its topic is the suffering, private human being exposed to the horrors of contemporary history. For political events impinge on the individual's reality whether he wills it or not, and nuclear extinction is as real an individual death as any other kind. In most of his poetry Lowell stands as a metaphor for any person at the extreme limits of existence, whose very being has been brought into question. In the fall of 1961, however, all people had their being brought into question, courtesy of the state. Lowell functions in "Fall 1961" not merely as metaphor but as representative human voice. [17]

The poem began to take form in late September, as Lowell sat in his studio and looked out across Central Park toward the Carlyle Hotel, where President Kennedy was temporarily ensconced in a suite nicknamed by the press "the little White House." Kennedy, in a speech on September 25 about the international crisis, warned the United Nations General Assembly: "Today, every inhabitant of this planet must contemplate the day when it may no longer be habitable. Every man, woman and child lives under a nuclear sword of Damocles, hanging by the slenderest of threads, capable of being cut at any moment." Struck by the contrast between Kennedy's Jonathan Edwards-flavored warnings and the cyclical recurrences of nature observable in Central Park, Lowell began to compose his poem. [18]

> Back and forth, back and forth
> goes the tock, tock, tock
> of the orange, bland, ambassadorial
> face of the moon
> on the grandfather clock.
>
> All autumn, the chafe and jar
> of nuclear war;
> we have talked our extinction to death.

147

Impressions of Experience

I swim like a minnow
behind my studio window.

Our end drifts nearer,
the moon lifts,
radiant with terror.
The state
is a diver under a glass bell.

A father's no shield
for his child.
We are like a lot of wild
spiders crying together,
but without tears.

Nature holds up a mirror.
One swallow makes a summer.
It's easy to tick
off the minutes,
but the clockhands stick.

Back and forth!
Back and forth, back and forth—
my one point of rest
is the orange and black
oriole's swinging nest!

(*FUD*, 11-12)

"Fall 1961" revives Lowell's theme of apocalypse—not, however, as a feature of religious myth (as in *Lord Weary's Castle*) but as an imminent historical possibility. That fall, phrases like "atomic holocaust," "atomic annihilation," "the very continuation of human life on this Earth," "the generation that turned this planet into a flaming funeral pyre," and "Armageddon" were commonly and even casually used. Prodded by *Time*, *Life*, and billboard advertising, millions of Americans dutifully constructed family fallout shelters. Daily headlines vexed readers with Yeatsian nightmares of blood-dimmed tide and rough slouching beast. Lowell's poem captures the dread, monotony, and sense of powerlessness experienced by those living through the crisis. Like a Norman Mailer "non-fiction novel," it closes the gap separating journalism from art:

> Across the nation last week, there was endless conversation about the threat of nuclear war. There was apprehension and an edge of sadness as women looked at their children and wondered about their chances of survival. *(Time)*

> All autumn, the chafe and jar
> of nuclear war;
> we have talked our extinction to death.
> .   .   .   .
> A father's no shield
> for his child.

Further, Lowell carefully integrates the public diction of the day into his poem. His phrase "nuclear war" was obviously a common one, but other more specialized words do even more to evoke the particular moment. "A father's no shield / for his child," in addition to its apparent meaning, probably refers punningly to the North American Air Defense Command's "Sky Shield," a defense against nuclear attack from over the North Pole. A heavily publicized exercise of "Sky Shield" against simulated Soviet attack occurred on October 14, and Lowell added the phrase to his poem soon after. His sentence "Our end drifts nearer, / the moon lifts, / radiant with terror" includes several prevalent terms: "drift" (connoting the atmospheric movement of atomic fallout, as in the phrase "nuclear drift"); "radiant" (suggesting radioactivity); and "terror" (a word on the lips of every editorialist that fall, appearing, for instance, dozens of times in *New York Times* editorials in such phrases as "Khrushchev's strategy of terror"). Lowell has assimilated the terms and preoccupations, the general "air" of the time, into the verbal texture of his poem.[19]

Lowell places these public allusions in a highly personal context. He suggests his psychic anxiety through Hal-

149

loween-like imagery of orange and black, and through the symbol of a ticking grandfather clock. The ticking has several implications. First, it reminds us of the ticking of a time-bomb, a perfect image of silent tension preceding explosion. Second, the clock's sound makes clear that the present crisis can only be understood as a historical and time-bound (rather than mythic) event. And finally, the ticking suggests that Lowell is experiencing what William James called "the feeling of bare time": when time is empty of experience, and consciousness is primarily directed upon itself. At such moments of heightened awareness time seems almost to stop still. "The clockhands stick." Utterly divorced from the objective world, Lowell is frozen in his own subjective fear. He communicates his sense of things gone massively wrong through a series of reversals and ironies: extinction has been "talked to death," he himself is but a "minnow," the state is "a diver" taking chances, the human race is a lot of "spiders." (This last metaphor, incidentally, reminds us of Jonathan Edwards's portrait of the future punishment of the wicked, though Lowell has said he appropriated it from the musings of his young daughter.) Terror has turned the world upside down: "Nature holds up a mirror. / One swallow makes a summer."[20]

Lowell ultimately finds relief from his fear in the swinging of an oriole's nest in the park outside his window. The nest's rhythms counterpoint the rhythms of the grandfather clock at the beginning of the poem. The clock with its mechanical ticking belongs to the historical moment, and therefore summons up thoughts of the potentially deadly nuclear crisis. Its face reminds Lowell of the "bland, ambassadorial" faces at the United Nations, or of the "face of the moon," that lifeless satellite lifting "radiant with terror" in the radioactive sky. The oriole's nest, on the other hand, with its natural rhythm belongs to the eternal cycle of life, and summons up comforting thoughts of renewal. Whereas the "back and forth" of the clock reminds

For the Union Dead as a Sequence

Lowell of the "chafe and jar" of nuclear war, the "back and forth" of the nest is a "point of rest," in the manner of a cradle endlessly rocking. Lowell has complained that in modern industrialized society "mechanical time is replacing organic time." In "Fall 1961" he recovers, if only for a moment, the spiritual comfort of organic time, of the rhythmic cycles of nature. The poem records his progress from a state of severe alienation, in which he perceives the outer world as cold, threatening, and disordered, to a more humanized state, in which his senses and emotions open to the world. Lowell remedies his Tate-like ego-confinement with a Williams-like union with the realm of natural objects. At a moment of intense human crisis he negotiates, for one of the few times in his poetic career, a leap into the nonhuman universe. Where once the dove of Jesus brought him wisdom, the orioles of nature now provide a "point of rest."[21]

This rest, however, is only momentary, for despite Lowell's reverence for nature's infinite gentleness he remains a creature of our civilization, the living voice of its discontents. He elaborates upon those discontents once more in his second group of political poems, toward the end of the book. These poems, "July in Washington," "Buenos Aires," and "Dropping South: Brazil," were written following a tour he made of South America in 1962 sponsored by the Congress of Cultural Freedom. When he subsequently discovered that the Congress was a conduit for Central Intelligence Agency funds, he was plagued by "unhappy thoughts" of his own "gullibility, shallowness and opportunism." Nevertheless, his frowning portraits of Brazilian and Argentine totalitarianism could scarcely have been what the CIA had in mind when it picked up his tab. Further, by grouping these three poems together, Lowell strongly implies that the United States government is akin to the provincial dictatorships of South America. In place of the City upon a Hill envisioned by the Puritans, the

United States proves only "some equatorial / backland that will inherit the globe" (*FUD*, 58). Although these three political poems are sensitive and intelligent, they lack the quality of intense personal involvement present in "The Mouth of the Hudson" and "Fall 1961." These three poems offer politics as a subject for thought and irony, but not, as in Lowell's best public poems, as a nightmare he has lived through.[22]

I believe that Gabriel Pearson was right when he began his fine essay on Lowell with the assertion that *For the Union Dead* is "the nub of the matter." For it is here, in this drouthy, problematical book, that Lowell tests for the first time his fully matured poetic voice. Developing beyond the partly derivative verbal panache of *Lord Weary's Castle* and the brilliant but limited ironic objectivity of *Life Studies*, he here speaks in a voice that will last him a lifetime, a voice capable of transmitting the full range and intensity of his unique sensibility and experience, a voice indebted to Tate and to Williams but ultimately liberated from both. It is appropriate that Lowell, having arrived at this point, should try to pay homage in this book to his two poetic fathers.[23]

Through the years Lowell maintained an attachment to Tate, though the two were never again as close as they had been in the early 1940s in Tennessee. Tate regarded *Life Studies* as something like a fall from grace, but approved the denser textures of Lowell's subsequent work. In the November 1961 "Robert Lowell" issue of the *Harvard Advocate*, Tate published a paragraph praising his "old and dear young friend" for producing "a body of work which to my mind is not equalled by anybody else of his generation." While he noted Lowell's originality, he depicted his former protégé as essentially "a formalist and traditionalist." Lowell, moved by the tribute, now sought to acknowledge in some way his continuing artistic debt to Tate. He first thought to begin *For the Union Dead* with a translation of "Pervigilium Veneris," dedicated to his former mentor. But realizing that a new translation of the poem Tate himself had laboriously translated would constitute a dubious compliment at best, he dropped this idea and concentrated instead on writing an original poem in the manner of Tate's late style. Tate's last published poems, appearing in literary quarterlies in 1953, were "The Swimmers" and "The Buried Lake," both originally conceived as parts of a long, never-finished autobiographical sequence in terza rima. When Lowell first read these deeply personal poems in manuscript, he wrote to his former mentor that they were his "best poems." Rereading them a decade later in Tate's collected *Poems*, he felt inspired to "write a pure Tate pastiche" himself. He began to compose "The Severed Head" (*FUD*, 52-53). Although Lowell had some reservations concerning the "Allenisms," or contorted phrases, of "The Buried Lake," he oddly chose that poem rather than the more lucid "The Swimmers" as his primary model, perhaps because it struck him as the more characteristic work. That his imitation does not really succeed suggests that he had by this time moved too far from Tate ever to return. "The Severed Head" superficially resembles "The Buried Lake" in both form and content: both terzinas describe a surrealist dream in which the dreamer descends into the dark "buried lake" of the unconscious in quest of mystic illumination and a reintegration of self. But whereas Tate's Dantesque dreamer awakens convinced that he has redemptively experienced "enduring love," Lowell's dreamer has been granted only a dreary vision of his own decapitation. Whereas "The Buried Lake," as Tate's last published poem, serves as a fittingly impassioned conclusion to his poetic career, and perhaps even (as Radcliffe Squires has suggested) to the whole Modernist movement in poetry, Lowell's poem seems merely contrived, its symbolism and verbal agitation dully formulaic. "The Severed Head" is indeed, as Lowell has said, a "pastiche," proving only that he could not—at some level did not want to—recapture his own Modernist origins.[24]

The consciously Williams-like effects of *For the Union Dead* are more effective than the imitation of Tate, but they too show that Lowell was by now no poet's apprentice but rather a master himself, having forged his own masterly style. In the years following *Life Studies* his personal ties to Williams grew ever stronger. He dedicated his translation of Villon's "Great Testament" in *Imitations* to Williams, enthusiastically praised Williams's newly published *Many Loves and Other Plays*, and recited parts of *Paterson* aloud at public readings. The two continued to correspond regularly and affectionately. In the 1961 "Lowell" issue of the *Harvard Advocate*, Williams paid tribute to Lowell not as Tate's "formalist and traditionalist" but as a creative individualist on the order of Williams himself: "Here is a poet who knows what he is doing, devoted to the best in his language, with courage to go ahead with his own tasks, and a cultured addiction to his native way of speaking. You can't fool such a man because he will make up his own mind." Almost immediately after writing these words, Williams's health began to fail. Meetings now were impossible, and soon Williams, confused and weak, lost even the ability to answer Lowell's letters. Realizing that his friend was dying, Lowell wrote his lovely prose tribute called "William Carlos Williams," which he said "was more my personal feelings than a piece of formal criticism." In the essay Lowell recalled his last visit to Williams in Rutherford: "The town seemed to know him and love him and take him in its stride, as we will do with his great pouring of books, his part in the air we breathe and will breathe."[25]

For the Union Dead breathes the Williamsian air. "The Mouth of the Hudson" elaborates upon Williams's description of the squalid Hudson in *Paterson IV*, and "Fall 1961" concludes in a Williams-like state of openness to the world. It is probably no coincidence that Lowell wrote part of the latter poem on the back of one of the typescript sheets of his essay on Williams. Perhaps his most deliberate effort to internalize the lessons of the master occurs in the poem "Eye and Tooth." In his essay on Williams, Lowell wrote:

> When I think about writing on Dr. Williams, I feel a chaos of thoughts and images. . . . When I woke up this morning, something unusual for this summer was going on!—pinpricks of rain were falling in a reliable, comforting simmer. Our town was blanketed in the rain of rot and the rain of renewal. . . . An image held my mind during these moments and kept returning—an old fashioned New England cottage freshly painted white. I saw a shaggy, triangular shade on the house, trees, a hedge, or their shadows, the blotch of decay. . . . Inside the house was a birdbook with an old stiff and steely engraving of a sharp-shinned hawk. The hawk's legs had a reddish brown buffalo fuzz on them; behind was the blue sky, bare and abstracted from the world. . . .
> An image of a white house with a blotch in it—this is perhaps the start of a Williams poem.

"Eye and Tooth"—with its "simmer of rot and renewal," its house and hedge blotched with decay, its "sharp-shinned hawk" (*FUD*, 18-19)—is clearly that "Williams poem." Yet no one would mistake Lowell's agony-laden lines for Williams's. The two poets differ temperamentally. Even in anger and despair Williams adjures himself, "Be reconciled, Poet, with your world." Lowell will *not* be reconciled with *his* world, still less with himself. Nevertheless, this difference in their sensibilities ultimately counts for little. Like a latter-day Whitman, Williams served Lowell as "a model and a liberator"—a model of artistic self-expression and a liberator of the self. He privately and publicly encouraged Lowell "to go ahead with his own tasks," though fully aware that Lowell's tasks did not always accord with his own.[26]

Williams knew that in the deepest sense their tasks did indeed accord. When the elder poet died on March 4, 1963, Lowell was hard at work completing the poems of *For the Union Dead*, poems which resemble Williams's own in being designed to reveal and justify the consciousness that gave them rise. In *Paterson III* Williams writes,

> Nothing is so unclear between man and
> his writing as to which is the man and
> which the thing.

In "Night Sweat" Lowell affirms, "One life, one writing!"

"For the Union Dead"

> Some invest in the past.
> —*John Berryman*, "Dream Song 15"

When *The House of the Seven Gables* appeared in 1851, James Russell Lowell wrote to Hawthorne that it was the most valuable contribution yet made to New England history, adding that "the true office of the historian is to reconcile the present with the past." In the late 1950s Robert Lowell had Hawthorne's art much on his mind, and in exactly the terms his great-granduncle had applied to it a century before. He wrote to William Carlos Williams in 1958 that *The House of the Seven Gables* "has enough economic history to set the Commonweath of Massachusetts back on its toes." Within the next few years he completed several Hawthornean projects: two historical plays based on "The Maypole at Merrymount" and "My Kinsman, Major Molineux" (in *The Old Glory*); an introduction to a new edition of Hawthorne's tale of Pegasus; and the poem "Hawthorne" for the Hawthorne centenary (*FUD*, 38-39). Perhaps his most Hawthorne-like work of all during this period was the poem "For the Union Dead," which contains enough political history to set Massachusetts and the nation back on its toes. Like Hawthorne, Lowell reconciles the present with the past, and private experience with the movements of history. He becomes, in Richard Poirier's apt phrase, "our truest historian." [27]

Soon after completing "For the Union Dead" Lowell said, "I've always wanted to write a Civil War poem. And finally at forty-three I did." "For the Union Dead" is a Civil War poem and more. It unites the personal, historical, political, and literary materials episodically present throughout the *For the Union Dead* sequence into a single grand entity, an emanation of total consciousness. In "For the Union Dead" Lowell treats American history and culture as if they were part of his personal life story, as of course they are. As Ernst Cassirer has said, "In history man constantly returns to himself; he attempts to recollect and actualize the whole of his past experience." The poet as historian aims neither to retrieve data nor to provide a rationale for a political program, but rather to give us essential knowledge of ourselves. Perhaps more than any other single Lowell work, this poem captures the fullness of that knowledge. When he was asked in the early 1970s to choose his "best" poem, Lowell protested, "If I knew my best poem I think I would be so elated that I would keep the secret," and then he chose "For the Union Dead."[28]

Perhaps it was the brilliance of Tate's "Ode to the Confederate Dead" that caused Lowell to want to write an abolitionist counterpart, "a northern Civil War poem." Or perhaps he took his inspiration from a remark Williams made during a discussion of politics and history in 1958: "When I look at the faces of the drivers of our oversized and really inconvenient cars . . . I see how much they resemble each other. There is no liberality of mind." Lowell's immediate impetus, however, was an invitation to read a new poem in the Public Garden at the 1960 Boston Arts Festival. He began to work on the poem following the publication of *Life Studies* in spring of 1959; "cut, added and tinkered" all the following winter; and completed the poem only a few days before the Arts Festival "poetry night" on June 5, 1960. The *Christian Science Monitor* reported the following day that "Mr. Lowell, rebellious scion of the famed proper-Bostonian family" had read his new poem "to an enthusiastic audience" that included Eleanor Roosevelt. He had introduced the poem by satirically describing modern Boston as "a rapidly emerging center of highways and parking places," and as if to underline the point, his recitation was interrupted by the sounds of "airplane engines and airbrakes on Boylston Street." Nonetheless, the occasion was sweet. Overwhelmed by applause, Lowell told his audience of 4,000 that as a boy he had been ejected from the Public Garden for misbehavior but that "tonight partly makes up for it."[29]

Like "The Quaker Graveyard in Nantucket" before it, "For the Union Dead" began as several separate poems which Lowell "pulled together." One of these initial poetic sketches was a deeply personal evocation of childhood memories entitled "The Old Aquarium." In this sketch, he contrasted the life-teeming aquarium of his childhood to the disused aquarium of the present, and contrasted his own childhood self, tingling "with careless confidence," to his present self, "midway in the next day's night / mid-way in life toward death." This sketch depicted, as Lowell later said, "a child growing to courage and terror."[30]

His other initial sketch was primarily public and historical, an ode entitled "One Gallant Rush: The Death of Colonel Robert Shaw." It had for its subject, "the evisceration of our modern cities, civil rights, nuclear warfare and more particularly Colonel Robert Shaw and his Negro regiment, the Massachusetts 54th." This second sketch evidently owed its genesis to the work of Elizabeth Hardwick, who at this time was in the midst of two projects relating to Colonel Shaw and to modern Boston. One of these was an edition of William James's letters, including one to his brother Henry in which he described his oration at the dedication of Saint-Gaudens's memorial to Colonel Shaw in 1897. The other was an article called "Boston: The Lost

"For the Union Dead"

Ideal" appearing in *Harper's* in late 1959. Hardwick's vision of Boston in this article foreshadows Lowell's: a "pathetic old city now feeding on its own smugness, snobbery, and wilted traditions . . . wrinkled, spindly-legged, depleted of nearly all her spiritual and cutaneous oils, provincial, self-esteeming." Lowell's sketch on Shaw shared this jaundiced view of a city whose "fraudulent posture of traditionalism" was belied by its thoughtless desecration of the past, but he deepened his attack by bringing in Colonel Shaw as a symbol of the ideal that had been lost.[31]

As Lowell worked his materials, his two sketches became one. From the start their subjects were parallel. "One Gallant Rush" contrasted the pampered and adolescent Shaw—disguising himself as a girl at a society ball or packing his uniform only at his mother's insistence—with the suddenly matured soldier he became, "powder-lit, sword in hand, crouching like a cat" as he led his men toward certain death. Thus, just as much as "The Old Aquarium," "One Gallant Rush" in its own way described "a child growing to courage and terror." Lowell brought his two sketches together in order to examine his theme of the fall from innocence from both the inside (as in "The Aquarium") and the outside (as in "One Gallant Rush"). He has said that he added the "early personal memories because I wanted to avoid the fixed, brazen tone of the set-piece and official ode," but perhaps his real intention was more complex: not only to personalize Boston but to depersonalize his own life, to explore self and culture each in the context of the other.[32]

For the Union Dead
"Relinquunt Omnia Servare Rem Publicam."

The old South Boston Aquarium stands
in a Sahara of snow now. Its broken windows are
    boarded.
The bronze weathervane cod has lost half its scales.
The airy tanks are dry.

Impressions of Experience

Once my nose crawled like a snail on the glass;
my hand tingled
to burst the bubbles
drifting from the noses of the cowed, compliant fish.

My hand draws back. I often sigh still
for the dark downward and vegetating kingdom
of the fish and reptile. One morning last March,
I pressed against the new barbed and galvanized

fence on the Boston Common. Behind their cage,
yellow dinosaur steamshovels were grunting
as they cropped up tons of mush and grass
to gouge their underworld garage.

Parking spaces luxuriate like civic
sandpiles in the heart of Boston.
A girdle of orange, Puritan-pumpkin colored girders
braces the tingling Statehouse,

shaking over the excavations, as it faces Colonel Shaw
and his bell-cheeked Negro infantry
on St. Gaudens' shaking Civil War relief,
propped by a plank splint against the garage's
    earthquake.

Two months after marching through Boston,
half the regiment was dead;
at the dedication,
William James could almost hear the bronze Negroes
    breathe.

Their monument sticks like a fishbone
in the city's throat.
Its Colonel is as lean
as a compass-needle.

He has an angry wrenlike vigilance,
a greyhound's gentle tautness;
he seems to wince at pleasure,
and suffocate for privacy.

"For the Union Dead"

He is out of bounds now. He rejoices in man's lovely,
peculiar power to choose life and die—
when he leads his black soldiers to death,
he cannot bend his back.

On a thousand small town New England greens,
the old white churches hold their air
of sparse, sincere rebellion; frayed flags
quilt the graveyards of the Grand Army of the Republic.

The stone statues of the abstract Union Soldier
grow slimmer and younger each year—
wasp-waisted, they doze over muskets
and muse through their sideburns . . .

Shaw's father wanted no monument
except the ditch,
where his son's body was thrown
and lost with his "niggers."

The ditch is nearer.
There are no statues for the last war here;
on Boylston Street, a commercial photograph
shows Hiroshima boiling

over a Mosler Safe, the "Rock of Ages"
that survived the blast. Space is nearer.
When I crouch to my television set,
the drained faces of Negro school-children rise like
     balloons.

Colonel Shaw
is riding on his bubble,
he waits
for the blessèd break.

The Aquarium is gone. Everywhere,
giant finned cars nose forward like fish;
a savage servility
slides by on grease.

(FUD, 70-72)

This poem does many things at once: it contemplates Colonel Shaw and through him the ambiguities of the American past; it elaborates upon and plays against a strong literary tradition of works concerning Shaw; it depicts the contemporary cityscape as a wasteland inhabited by dehumanized, brutal beasts of survival; it tells of Lowell's personal growth from childhood moral innocence to adult moral anguish; and it projects his continuing psychic battle of life against death. In this poem, then, the outmost in due time becomes the inmost. Before we enter into its interior personal layers we must first understand the poem at its outmost—as a poem containing history. Even when self-consciously renouncing past traditions, as in *Life Studies*, Lowell has always been a traditional and historical poet. "For the Union Dead" represents his most concentrated meditation on a particular historical event, and probably his most deliberate attempt to address a well-defined literary topos.

In contemplating the doomed, heroic charge of Colonel Robert Gould Shaw and his men upon a Southern fortress, Lowell consciously placed himself within a remarkably rich, century-long artistic tradition that includes poems by Ralph Waldo Emerson, James Russell Lowell, Paul Laurence Dunbar, William Vaughn Moody, John Berryman, and many others; orations by Frederick Douglass, Booker T. Washington, William James, and Oliver Wendell Holmes Jr.; a program by Charles Ives; and the bas-relief in Boston Common by Augustus Saint-Gaudens. "I knew," Lowell said, "that Colonel Shaw was a heroic, an overworked subject." In composing "For the Union Dead" he entered deliberately into literary history—into dialogue with his respected predecessors and with his comrade in art, John Berryman. His poem demonstrates the survival of literary tradition by breathing life into one of its branches.

By its very existence the poem reinforces those values of civilization which are its essential concern. In retrospect it seems almost a matter of destiny that Lowell should have contributed to this tradition of artworks about Shaw, and, as seems possible, completed its development. Colonel Shaw, whose sister married Lowell's favorite ancestor Charles Russell Lowell Jr., is an altogether suitable subject for a poem in his most characteristic mode, the family elegy. But far more important, Robert Lowell, with his sense of history and his moral sensitivity, was perfectly suited by temperament to engage the themes suggested by Shaw's story.[33]

In spring of 1863 Robert Gould Shaw, a twenty-five-year-old Boston Brahmin and family friend of the Lowells, was given command of the Negro Fifty-fourth Massachusetts Volunteers. The Fifty-fourth Massachusetts was the first Union Army regiment to be composed below officer rank entirely of free northern blacks. On July 18, 1863, after being in combat for just a few weeks, Colonel Shaw and his regiment were ordered to lead the advance on Fort Wagner, the outermost defense of the Charleston harbor. The assault proved suicidal. Almost half of the members of the Fifty-fourth were killed, including Shaw who was shot with a dozen of his men after having scaled the parapet wall of the fort. By all accounts Shaw and his soldiers had fought gallantly, proceeding with their charge even after realizing that they were caught in an ambush. Because his soldiers were black, the Confederate commander of Fort Wagner refused Shaw the honorable burial to which his rank entitled him, and instead had him buried with his men in a common grave. Later, when efforts were initiated in the North to rebury him more ceremonially, Shaw's father quietly forbade this to be done, holding that "a soldier's most appropriate burial place is on the field where he has fallen."[34]

Colonel Shaw's "picturesque and gallant death" made an immense impact on a northern public confused about the war and eager for heroes. Shaw came to represent for the North, and especially for New England, its own capacity for idealism and courage. His life and death were taken as justification for the Union cause and, more importantly, as justification for the essential Yankee character. Because of the symbolic quality his story assumed and indeed invited, it became a subject for poems, all of which serve as a matrix for "For the Union Dead." Characteristic of the works composed in the months immediately following the assault on Fort Wagner is Phoebe Cary's "The Hero of Fort Wagner," in which a fallen black soldier selflessly exhorts a white officer, "I'm done gone, Massa; step on me; / And you can scale the wall!" In a similar bathetic spirit, Anna Cabot Lowell Quincy Waterston, a friend of both the Lowell and Shaw families, wrote an ode to Shaw entitled "Together," four lines of which were later incribed on the Saint-Gaudens memorial:

> O fair-haired Northern hero,
> With thy guard of dusky hue,
> Up from the field of battle
> Rise to the last review.

Less pretentious were many anonymous and widely circulated pieces of doggerel, one of which purported to describe Fort Wagner's commanding officer ordering his troops to bury Shaw "with his niggers," a phrase Lowell alludes to in stanza thirteen of "For the Union Dead."[35]

Two of the earliest poems took the form of generalized tributes. Ralph Waldo Emerson had young Shaw in mind when he composed these famous lines for his Civil War dirge "Voluntaries":

> In an age of fops and toys,
> Wanting wisdom, void of right,
> Who shall nerve heroic boys
> To hazard all in Freedom's fight?
>
> .   .   .   .

"For the Union Dead"

So nigh is grandeur to our dust,
So near is God to man,
When Duty whispers low, *Thou must*,
The youth replies, *I can*.

In an early version of "For the Union Dead," Robert Lowell
wrote that Shaw "replied" to his general "I will," a possible echo of Emerson's "I can." Although the published
version contains no verbal echoing of Emerson, its portrayal of Shaw accords with Emerson's depiction of him as
an exemplar of duty in an age of "sloth and ease." The second generalized tribute was James Russell Lowell's "Ode
Recited at the Harvard Commemoration," which he contributed to a volume of *Harvard Memorial Biographies* containing a life of Shaw written by his mother. Although the
"Ode" names no soldier specifically, its fervid rhetoric was
doubtless inspired by the death of Shaw as well as the
deaths of two of Lowell's nephews. This poem, however,
is just the kind of "set-piece and official ode" that Robert
Lowell sought to avoid in "For the Union Dead," just the
kind of poem that caused him to call his great-granduncle a
poet "pedestalled for oblivion."[36]
Perhaps the most impressive of all the Shaw poems written during this period was another poem by James Russell
Lowell called "Memoriae Positum R.G.S." This poem,
begun in the weeks following Shaw's death and published
in the following year, shows its author for once descended
from his pedestal. A result of intense "brooding in [the]
heart," it possesses a quiet dignity and pained self-ques-
tioning very different from the inflated tone of the "Commemoration Ode." In "Memoriae Positum" the poet attempts, with very little self-assurance, to justify both
Shaw's death and his own survival, and to renew his
shaken faith in his country at a time when the country's
future was still in doubt. Complex, ambiguous, and ultimately quite personal, "Memoriae Positum" is perhaps
James Russell Lowell's most "modern" poem. Foreshad-

owing "For the Union Dead," the poem contrasts Colonel Shaw's ideal of moral purity with society's reality of moral bankruptcy. It pictures Shaw as a "saintly shape of fame" whose memory now will goad survivors into goodness. But it also expresses a deep fear that the masses will prove "heedless" of Shaw, and heedless of poetry celebrating him. The poem thus takes the form of a dialectic between James Russell Lowell's constitutional need to affirm and his underlying philosophical fears and doubts. Predictably, the lines chosen to be inscribed on the Saint-Gaudens memorial are the most yea-saying of the poem, ending "death for noble ends makes dying sweet." Yet two stanzas later, Shaw and his band are pessimistically termed "Hope's *forlorn-hopes* that plant the *desperate* good." (Robert Lowell similarly referred to Shaw's "forlorn hope" in one draft of "For the Union Dead," but ultimately abandoned the image.) By allowing his compassion for Shaw to radiate outward to include all of life's innocents, James Russell Lowell is able to end his poem with renewed faith in America and the future. He thus makes an affirmation that Robert Lowell cannot. His earnest hopes for a union reborn are answered a century later by his descendant's lamentations for a union dead.[37]

Three decades later, the dedication of Augustus Saint-Gaudens's bronze bas-relief memorial to Shaw and his regiment in Boston Common inspired a second spate of poems and recitations on the topic. The memorial itself, completed in 1897, was obviously intended in part as a compliment by the Boston cultural elite to itself. The monument is scrupulously inscribed with the names of every one of the killed white officers but none of the killed black soldiers. Its epigraph, "Omnia Relinquit Servare Rempublicam," is the motto of the Society of the Cincinnati, the exclusive military club to which Shaw belonged by right of descent. Yet both the overall conception of Saint-Gaudens's design, giving prominence as it does to the individuality of each of the black soldiers, and the pas-

sionately egalitarian speeches given at the unveiling cere-
monies, attest to Boston's real moral fervor. The Shaw family itself refused initial plans for an equestrian statue of
Shaw alone, insisting that the memorial give equal importance to the black soldiers. William James, in the major address of the unveiling, called the black soldiers "cham-
pions of a better day for man" and said that they and Shaw
"represent with such typical purity the profounder meaning of the Union cause." Thomas Bailey Aldrich recited a
grandiloquent dedicatory poem entitled "Shaw Memorial
Ode," and speeches suitable to the occasion were given by
Booker T. Washington and several government officials.
The next several years saw the publication of poems about
Shaw by Richard Watson Gilder, Benjamin Brawley, Percy
MacKaye, Paul Laurence Dunbar, and William Vaughn
Moody. Of these, the most enduring are Dunbar's eloquent sonnet "Robert Gould Shaw," which laments the
lack of racial progress since Shaw's time, and Moody's
idealistic, angry "Ode in Time of Hesitation." Like Emerson and James Russell Lowell before him, Moody presents
Shaw as a moral example whose heroism contrasts tell-
ingly with endemic civic corruption (specifically, American
imperialism). To this basic contrast, however, he adds a
new historical dimension. He associates Shaw's heroic
ideal with the past, and unheroic reality with the present,
thus suggesting a pattern of moral degeneration similar to
that suggested by "For the Union Dead."[38]

Apart from "For the Union Dead" itself, the only later
addition to the tradition of Shaw poems is "Boston Common" by John Berryman, Lowell's friend and an acknowledged influence on his work. Writing during World War II,
Berryman portrays Colonel Shaw in even a darker aspect
than Moody does. His Shaw can no longer even speak to
us: "Fiery night consumes a summoned ghost." For Berryman, the mass slaughter of modern war has rendered
Shaw and his regiment obsolete, even as symbols. Whereas James Russell Lowell once looked hopefully to a nobler

future, William Vaughn Moody and John Berryman and finally Robert Lowell himself all lament, with increasing bitterness, the passing of a nobler past. This alteration signals a dimming of hopes, a process of disillusionment, the darkening glass of the twentieth century.

"For the Union Dead" clearly responds to the themes and motifs present in the previous poems on Colonel Shaw. It even more openly echoes two eloquent speeches on the subject: William James's oration dedicating the Shaw memorial and a short address by Justice Oliver Wendell Holmes called "Harvard College in the War." In a sense, Lowell's poem may be viewed as an ironic commentary on both these speeches, which were several notches more optimistic in their idealism than any of the major poems about Shaw dared to be. James, for example, had consecrated "Shaw's beautiful image to stand here for all time, an inciter to similarly unselfish public deeds." Holmes had thought Shaw's example "necessary" to future generations. Instead, Lowell sees Shaw as being "out of bounds now" (st. 10), both literally and spiritually. His beautiful image incites only civic hostility. He "sticks" in the city's throat (st. 8).[39]

Both of Lowell's descriptions of statuary in "For the Union Dead" echo phrases from William James's speech. He remarks of the Saint-Gaudens bas-relief that "William James could almost hear the bronze Negroes breathe" (st. 7), an allusion to James's description of them as "so true to nature that one can almost hear them breathing." And he goes on to describe the "stone statues of the abstract Union Soldier" which are found "on a thousand small town New England greens" (st. 11-12), a paraphrase of James's statement that "the abstract soldiers'-monuments have been reared on every village green." In both of these borrowings Lowell deliberately turns James's words of hope and praise into lament. He comments that the Union Soldier statues "grow slimmer and younger each year" in contrast to the increasingly fat and venal general populace (st.

12). And now, far from almost hearing Saint-Gaudens's blacks breathing, the general populace roundly ignores them; values them less than parking places; seeks half-consciously to rid itself of their symbolic reproach. James had written that nothing "can save us from degeneration if the inner mystery is lost," defining this inner mystery as "trained and disciplined good temper" and "fierce and merciless resentment toward every man or set of men who break the public peace." Lowell, however, everywhere sees savagery rather than good temper and servility rather than righteous resentment. The degeneration James feared has become Lowell's theme.[40]

"For the Union Dead" stands in a similarly ironic relation to Justice Holmes's speech. In its initial drafts, the poem included explicit quotations from this speech, but by the time the poem assumed its final form Holmes had become merely another of the figures standing dimly behind it, his own possibly facile optimism corrected by Lowell's re-vision. Holmes had professed to believe that succeeding generations would continue to heed Shaw as "a symbol of man's destiny and power for duty," and of the willingness "to toss life and hope like a flower" before the feet of one's country. Lowell, of course, tells us that Shaw goes generally *un*heeded by succeeding generations. Further, Lowell intends his statement that Shaw "rejoices" in man's "peculiar power to choose life and die" (st. 10) as a faint parodic echo of several characteristic Holmes remarks. Holmes once said of the casualties of the Civil War that "our dead brothers still live for us, and bid us think of life, not death," and on another occasion proclaimed that "life is action, the use of one's powers. . . . To use them to their height is our joy and duty." Yet Lowell believes that this justification of the heroically strenuous life masks an unconscious urge toward its opposite: "How we mean the opposite of what we first say or habitually say." "For the Union Dead" makes manifest the note of suicidalism implicit but unacknowledged in Holmes's remarks. Lowell's

Shaw finds his joy and duty in his power not merely to think of life or "choose life" but also to "die," and even to lead others "to death." Thus, Lowell converts Holmes's attractive but simplistic affirmations into a vision more richly ambiguous. His poem praises the military valor of Shaw, but also suggests dark, mixed motives beneath that valor.[41]

"For the Union Dead," then, is first of all a poem about American history. It pays a complex but sincere tribute to a humanitarian Civil War hero, and it responds to and subtly alters a distinguished tradition of works of art about that hero, through a process Emerson would term "creative reading." Lowell's purpose in harkening to the past is to expose and dramatize the moral squalor of the historical present. Colonel Shaw's heroic idealism and the preservation of his honored memory in various works of art contrast devastatingly with the only memento Boston cares to keep of World War II: a commercial photograph of the Hiroshima mushroom cloud with a caption advertising the Mosler Safe as "the 'Rock of Ages' that survived the blast" (st. 15). (Paul C. Doherty has reported that the Mosler Safe Company entitled this advertising display "The Hiroshima Story Comes to Life with a Bang.") In contrast to nineteenth-century Boston, which cheered Shaw and his men off to war in 1863 and celebrated their valor in memorials, orations, and poems after their death, the "New Boston" can only pride itself blasphemously upon a receptacle for lucre sturdy enough to "survive" atomic explosion— unlike 80,000 human beings. Colonel Shaw's "civic courage" (in James's phrase) has given way to a complacent merchandising of nuclear annihilation.[42]

Yet in Lowell's complex vision, the past explains as well as rebukes the present. The circumstances of Shaw's brutal death and burial, in what Lowell called "the first modern war," suggests that Fort Wagner and Hiroshima are both part of the same historical curve of increasing technological barbarity. Equally disturbing, the hidden homicidal or suicidal strain that Lowell detects in Shaw himself (and in some of his nineteenth-century celebrators) corresponds to the Ahab-like spirit he finds deep in the American character, a spirit of "violence and idealism" capable in our day of producing nuclear holocaust.[43]

Nevertheless, there is another, more hopeful historical comparison in "For the Union Dead": that between Shaw's black regiment and the black students of the desegregation battles of the 1950s. These students, nonviolent counterparts of the Massachusetts Fifty-fourth, are the only unambiguous heroes in the poem. Lowell has said of the political aspect of "For the Union Dead": "In 1959 I had a message here; since then the blacks have found their 'break,' but the landscape remains." This landscape is one of continuing injustice and increasing political terror. The flawed but very real idealism of Shaw and his celebrators has given way to a "commercial optimism" (in a phrase from one of the poem's drafts) which serves as a cover for mass murder, for servility, for savagery. Yet however dark the prospects, the black schoolchildren, lonely but determined disciples of Gandhi, provide reason for hope.[44]

In "For the Union Dead," Lowell has substituted a prophetic historicism for the prophetic mythology of his earliest public poems. The poem is literally born of time, focusing on various historical moments: Colonel Shaw and his regiment marching through Boston in 1863 and then dead at Fort Wagner two months later; William James dedicating their monument in 1897; Hiroshima "boiling" in 1945; the Boston Common being torn open "one morning last March"; the teeming city thoroughfares of time present. Even within the poem itself, the process of time, Philip Rahv's "powerhouse of change," can be observed: in the first stanza the aquarium still "stands" but by the last it "is gone." By his act of historical memory, Lowell seeks to counter the prevailing mood of his age, which is fiercely antagonistic to traces of the past—aquarium, Shaw memorial, and all else. By obliterating its own past, mod-

171

ern society has become a stranger to itself, without identity or inherited moral values (such as those promulgated by James and other writers about Shaw). As a result we ignorantly repeat the worst sins of our ancestors: Shaw's brutal death and burial become, immensely magnified, the bombing of Hiroshima. But by applying his historical consciousness to a land actively hostile to history, Lowell hopes to redeem time by restoring its significance. He identifies Colonel Shaw and the Massachusetts Fifty-fourth, William James, and (above all) the black school-children as models of a humane and liberal tradition; one which, however flawed and beleaguered, is still alive and worthy of allegiance. As G. S. Fraser has said, Lowell's national elegy ultimately becomes a "song of praise"—praise for the enduring forms and values of human civilization.[45]

If on one level "For the Union Dead" is national history, on another complementary level it is inner autobiography. At the same time as the poem contrasts America's past with its present, it also contrasts the poet's personal past with his personal present. Lowell, who as a boy leaned eagerly upon aquarium glass to watch the fish, has grown into a figure of anguish pressing against a barbed fence to watch landmarks being defaced, or crouching to his television set to watch children threatened by violence. "For the Union Dead" reveals the decline of Lowell's morale and the correlated growth of his moral consciousness. His hand which once "tingled" to touch his surroundings now "draws back" from them in horror (st. 2-3).

Further, the very landscape that Lowell observes with horror may be taken as an allegory of his own spiritual condition. He once wrote of *Paterson* that the city "is Williams' life"; in a similar way Boston is his own life. A disembodied eye and voice, he renders eloquent judgment on what his life has meant through his historical and sociological images. The symbolic opposition he perceives between the Union soldiers' lean, almost inhuman idealism and the modern Bostonians' greasy, too-human self-indulgence reflects a similar division within his own character. Recall that in "Memories of West Street and Lepke" he contrasted the "fire-breathing" idealism of his youth with the middle-aged sloth of his present life on "hardly passionate Marlborough Street." Like Boston (America) itself, Lowell feels torn between conflicting impulses of heroic (but possibly deathly) self-sacrifice and knavish self-gratification. Thus, in his meditation on the latent "violence and idealism" in the American character, he taps his own deepest emotional sources, exposes the tensions at his own psychic center. "For the Union Dead" does not resolve this moral conflict; it enables us to experience the turmoil in its full complexity and to recognize the conflict as one with deeply personal as well as broadly cultural resonances. Lowell's private confession coincides with and reinforces his public meditation. Conflating his individual past with the national past, he treats each as a metaphor for the other.[46]

In "For the Union Dead" Lowell weaves his apparently dissimilar strands—the private and public, the historical and contemporary—into a seamless verbal fabric. He achieves unity by meticulously describing personal happenings and national history in analogical language. Apart from unifying the poem, the linguistic parallels have several important functions. Perhaps most importantly, they elucidate moral relationships.

Through its brilliant art of analogy, the poem focuses our attention on the moral contrast between Lowell's childish hand which once "tingled" innocently on aquarium glass and the Massachusetts Statehouse now "tingling" ominously from the blasts of a garage excavation (st. 2, 5). The poem invites us to note the ironic disparity between "Ser-vare" and "servility." It makes us aware of the implicit spiritual connection between the "ditch" where the bodies of Shaw and his men were thrown and the "excavations" for a modern-day garage (st. 13, 6); between Hiroshima "boiling" in 1945 and Boston's commercial "Boylston" Street today (st. 14); between the garage's "earthquake" and the Hiroshima "blast" (st. 6, 15); between the dry "Sahara" of the abandoned aquarium and the "civic sandpiles" of Boston's heart (st. 1, 5); between the "bubbles" which once drifted from the fish in the aquarium and the "bubble" of idealism Colonel Shaw still rides upon— and between both of those bubbles and the transformation of Hiroshima into boiling bubbles by the heat of atomic blast (st. 2, 16, 14). In place of the "noses" of the compliant aquarium "fish" of Lowell's memory, the poem portrays giant finned cars that "nose" forward "like fish," and Colonel Shaw's monument sticking like a "fishbone" in the city's throat (st. 2, 17, 8). By the end of the poem, as Josephine Jacobsen has suggested, we are all in an aquarium similar to that of Lowell's childhood memory. But this one is inhabited by morally grotesque creatures. Rather than an innocent "vegetating kingdom / of the fish and reptile," we occupy a world of caged and grunting "yellow dinosaur steamshovels," of strangely animated "parking spaces" which "luxuriate" like reptiles in the sand, of savage "finned cars" swimming aggressively forward in their own grease (st. 3-5, 17).[47]

Every image in the poem echoes against other images, creating in us a kind of knowledge that is not paraphrasable, a knowledge of feeling and perception. This is another important function of Lowell's analogical language: to suggest the esemplastic power of the consciousness to connect even the most disparate-seeming of phenomena. Although many of Lowell's images serve the immediate function of ironic contrast (the cowed, compliant fish as opposed to the savage and servile fish-like cars, for example), the more lasting effect is synthetic, holistic. "For the Union Dead" is as densely textured as any of Lowell's poems in *Lord Weary's Castle*, but the method and aim of his density has altered. In place of the bifurcating ironies and puns of "The Quaker Graveyard in Nantucket," which communicate a sense of inner discord, "For the Union Dead" is composed of analogies, which communicate a sense of concord. "The Quaker Graveyard" explodes from the force of its irreconcilable conflicts; "For the Union Dead" implodes, its potentially conflicting elements fused in a central imaginative vision.

The subject of Lowell's unifying vision in "For the Union Dead" resembles the subject of "The Quaker Graveyard" and indeed of all Lowell's major poems. It is the subject of life against death. This theme has its ramifications in the public world, a world in which (as Lowell has said) "genocide has stunned us." And it has its ramifications in the private world of the poet's own psyche, which has always been balanced between impulses of annihilating violence and impulses of continuance and endurance.[48]

Everyone and everything in "For the Union Dead" moves toward a confrontation with death: Colonel Shaw leading his "black soldiers to death"; the schoolchildren battling for their civil rights; Colonel Shaw on his "bubble" awaiting its "break" (like Sintram in Fouqué's tale); Boston and Lowell himself, both once young but now aged and ravaged. Images of atrocity deepen the apocalyptic mood. The "barbed and galvanized fence" on Boston Common and the "ditch" that "is nearer" are surely images of the Nazi death camps. Like the brutal skunks of "Skunk Hour," the savage finned cars of "For the Union Dead" represent the triumph of the fascist will. Lowell, like Plath's character in "Three Women," dreams of massacres. The poem abounds in suggestions of suffocation: the dry fish tanks, William James's inability quite to hear the Negroes breathe, the monument sticking in the city's throat, Colonel Shaw wincing and suffocating, and the airless vacuums of the Hiroshima "blast" and outer "space." The poem itself seems to choke in a mass grave.

At the same time it evinces an even more powerful urge

175

for life. Poised between life and death like Colonel Shaw, Lowell discovers his own peculiar power not to "choose life and die" but to do the reverse, to acknowledge death and live. "For the Union Dead" suggests his tripartite development from simple innocence through adult experience to a stage of renewed, complex innocence; innocence that has paid the price of experience; tragic innocence. Lowell has grown from childhood ignorance to adult knowledge of aggressive evil—an evil inside as well as outside himself, as is suggested by his childish but aggressive urge to burst the fish's bubbles. Burdened by this knowledge, he has retreated to an almost deathlike passivity, cut off from what he observes by fences, boundaries, television screens. In his poem itself, however, he actively rages against the forces of the inhuman. He transcends his feelings of self-abasement and renunciation by placing himself firmly in the public sphere and committing himself to a traditional politics of melioration. Attaining moral authority and commitment in his art, Lowell rises above the tortured voyeur of "Skunk Hour" to become at last a visionary hero, as ambiguous and necessary as Colonel Shaw himself. Out of the wreckage of his life and his nation's life, he brings forth the healing wholeness of his prophetic art.

Near the Ocean

> The poet thrusts his body
> like a tolling bell
> against the dome of insults.
> It hurts. But it resounds.
> —*Andrei Voznesensky,* "Poem with a
> Footnote (To Robert Lowell)"

Beginning in 1965 Lowell entered a new phase of his life and career, writing a poetry more explicitly political than he had ever written before. For the first time since the mid-1940s he sought to become a Carlylean-Emersonian hero of deed as well as thought. As in the period of *Lord Weary's Castle*, he thrust his body against a war he considered unjust. He actively opposed the Vietnam war by engaging in various forms of protest, the most subtle and daring being his poems of *Near the Ocean* and *Notebook*. Lowell's characteristic poems have a remarkable power to evoke the historical moment in which they were conceived. They speak to us not of eternity but of time, of an enduring consciousness encountering the "inevitable accidents" of history and being altered and enlarged by the encounter. *Lord Weary's Castle* reflects the atrocity and moral confusion of the 1940s, *Life Studies* suggests the numbed introspection of the Eisenhower era, and the poems of the 1960s record the rising political anger and hope of those years. In the early part of the decade, in such poems as "For the Union Dead" and "Fall 1961," Lowell started to work again with public materials for the first time since he marked Eisenhower's election in "Inauguration Day: 1953" (*LS*, 7). Beginning with "Waking Early Sunday Morning," written in early summer 1965, he became a public poet in earnest.

In part Lowell's movement to political poetry resulted from a need to discover a new subject matter. Like his incarceration in 1943 and his mental breakdown in 1954, the Vietnam war was a disaster that could be converted into artistic inspiration. After *Life Studies* Lowell had found that he had little left to say in the purely personal mode. In the *For the Union Dead* sequence he explored his artistic drouth and transformed even that into a kind of poetry "on suffrance"; but by 1965 he had reduced himself to silence. He wrote in early drafts of "Waking Early Sunday Morning" that when he looked into his heart he discovered "none of the great subjects, death, friendship, love or hate." Unable to find "purpose" in his writing and "sick of reaching for the rhetoric," he resolved to "explore the bottom of the barrel for its dregs and dreck that seem profound." Yet even there he found nothing but "headless arrows of the

177

imagination, junk." Surveying a "year's output" of his verse he discerned only "things done before and better done": "dim confession, coy revelation, liftings, listless self-imitation." As happened so often in Lowell's career, he found himself unable to wear his old skin and in need of a new one.[49]

An equally fundamental reason for his decision to write poems about contemporary affairs lay in the overwhelming nature of the political events themselves. In mid-1965 Lowell, like the nation as a whole, became caught up by the developing war in Vietnam. He found that "when your private experience converges on the nation's experience you feel you have to do something." This new political phase of his life and art was nothing he could have planned or expected. It came to him as a "surprise," a "heavy burden" that he felt he must try to bear.[50]

When Lyndon Johnson, for whom Lowell had voted, was inaugurated for a full term as president in January of 1965, the United States still had no combat soldiers in Vietnam. But the position of the anti-Communist Saigon regime was rapidly deteriorating, and Johnson was strongly advised by his chief foreign policy aide McGeorge Bundy to commit American forces to battle. (Bundy, incidentally, is Lowell's cousin, as if to prove once again that national history is a familial affair for Lowell.) On February 7, President Johnson initiated American bombing raids on Communist targets, and on March 8 he began sending increasing numbers of American troops to Vietnam to fight. Although opinion polls showed that an overwhelming majority of Americans supported the president's policy, an antiwar minority began to stage public protests. On April 17, 15,000 people demonstrated in Washington against involvement in Vietnam; on May 15-16, the first national teach-in was held, accompanied by nationwide college demonstrations; on April 2 and again on June 15, Senator William J. Fulbright made the first of his major statements in opposition to the president's Vietnam policy.

During these months Lowell fully shared the liberal intellectual community's growing doubts and fears concerning the nation's course. In his interview with A. Alvarez in February 1965, he described an America "doomed and ready, for [its] idealism, to face any amount of violence." He was most disturbed by the specter of American attacks on defenseless civilians: "I have never gotten over the horrors of American bombing. For me anti-Stalinism led logically—oh, perhaps not so logically—to my being against our suppression of the Vietnamese." The technologically primitive Vietnamese, perhaps even more than the German and Japanese civilians in the latter phases of World War II, resembled in Lowell's eye the first victims of American ambition and power, the Indians. Once again he thought he saw "the death-dance of King Philip" and heard "his scream / Whose echo girdled this imperfect globe" (*LWC*, 27). At the end of the 1968 version of his play about Puritan-Indian warfare, "Endecott and the Red Cross," Lowell has a conscience-stricken Endecott propose a day of mourning for both his own soldiers and the defeated "Indians, all those who are fighting with unequalled ferocity, and probably hopeless courage, because they prefer annihilation to the despair of our conquest" (*OG*, 77). In that same year he wrote a public letter proposing a national day of mourning "for our own soldiers" and "for the anti-American Vietnamese, those who have fought with unequaled ferocity, and probably hopeless courage, because they preferred annihilation to the despair of an American conquest." As the Vietnam war went on, he once again began to dream of massacres, began to dread that genocide would be repeated. A hundred years after the Civil War, the ditch in which Colonel Shaw and his men had been thrown was nearer than ever. As Lowell was to exclaim after the mass murder of Vietnamese peasants by American soldiers at My Lai, "No stumbling on the downward plunge from Hiroshima. . . . In a century perhaps no one will widen an eye at massacre, and only scattered corpses express a last histrionic concern for death."[51]

Even before the American participation in the war was officially acknowledged, Lowell received and accepted an opportunity to make his fears public—and to make himself an object of controversy. In May 1965, he was invited to recite his poetry at President Johnson's first (and last) "Festival of the Arts" at the White House. He tentatively accepted the invitation by telephone, but soon reconsidered and sent the president a telegram of refusal. The telegram appeared on the front page of the June 3 *New York Times*, and caused a scandal. Lowell had written:

Dear President Johnson:

When I was telephoned last week and asked to read at the White House Festival of the Arts on June fourteenth, I am afraid I accepted somewhat rapidly and greedily. I thought of such an occasion as a purely artistic flourish, even though every serious artist knows that he cannot enjoy public celebration without making subtle public commitments. After a week's wondering, I have decided that I am conscience-bound to refuse your courteous invitation. I do so now in a public letter because my acceptance has been announced in the newspapers, and because of the strangeness of the Administration's recent actions.

Although I am very enthusiastic about most of your domestic legislation and intentions, I nevertheless can only follow our present foreign policy with the greatest dismay and distrust. What we will do and what we ought to do as a sovereign nation facing other sovereign nations seem now to hang in the balance between the better and the worse possibilities. We are in danger of imperceptibly becoming an explosive and suddenly chauvinistic nation, and may even be drifting on our way to the last nuclear ruin. I know it is hard for the responsible man to act; it is also painful for the private and irresolute man to dare criticism. At this anguished, delicate and perhaps determining moment, I feel I am serving you and our country best by not taking part in the White House Festival of the Arts.

Respectfully yours,
Robert Lowell

By means of this statement Lowell joined Lewis Mumford, who had made a strongly antiwar speech several weeks before at the American Academy of Arts and Letters, as a literary spokesman for those opposed to the war. When Johnson learned of Lowell's refusal, according to Eric Goldman, "the roar in the Oval Office could be heard all the way into the East Wing"; within days Arthur Schlesinger and other Administration defenders began to criticize Lowell publicly. On the other hand, the refusal was publicly endorsed by twenty prominent writers and artists.* Murray Kempton praised Lowell for demonstrating that "courtesy is a form of eloquence," and Dwight Macdonald wrote that "rarely has one person's statement of his moral unease about his government's behavior had such public resonance. I think it was because the letter was

---

* The twenty were Hannah Arendt, John Berryman, Alan Dugan, Jules Feiffer, Philip Guston, Lillian Hellman, Alfred Kazin, Stanley Kunitz, Dwight Macdonald, Mary McCarthy, Bernard Malamud, Larry Rivers, Philip Roth, Mark Rothko, Louis Simpson, W. D. Snodgrass, William Styron, Peter Taylor, Edgar Varese, and Robert Penn Warren. Of these only Macdonald, Rivers, and Rothko had actually been invited to the Festival; most of the invited were not artists themselves but financial backers of the arts. Among the few important literary figures who did attend were John Hersey (who read from *Hiroshima* as a protest against the war), Saul Bellow (who distrusted the war but attended to show respect for the presidency), and Ralph Ellison (who supported the war). The Festival itself was dominated by the man who was not there. Macdonald circulated a petition in support of Lowell, Mark Van Doren publicly regretted his absence, and Phillis McGinley, the Festival's representative for light verse, condescendingly ad-libbed a new couplet while reading her poem "In Praise of Diversity": "And while the pot of culture's bubblesome, / Praise poets even when they're troublesome." According to Goldman, a furious President Johnson put in only a token appearance, convinced by now that Lowell and all other intellectuals "were not only 'sonsofbitches' but they were 'fools,' and they were close to traitors."

so personal, so unexpected and yet so expressive of a wide-spread mood of 'dismay and distrust.' " For the second time in his life Lowell had made a "manic statement / telling off the state and president" (*LS*, 85), and for much the same reason as for the first. Several months before receiving President Johnson's invitation he had recalled Robert Frost's remark about poetry and power, "We must have more of both," and had commented: "Well, he seemed to rejoice in that. But in a way I feel it is our curse that we can't disentangle those two things." By publicly refusing to participate in the "Festival of the Arts," Lowell sought to disentangle poetry from misused power.[52]

W. H. Auden observed that "poetry makes nothing happen," and it seems at least as true that to decline to recite poetry makes nothing happen. On July 28, President Johnson announced in a televised address that U.S. troop strength in Vietnam would be soon increased to 125,000, and within days he asked Congress for an additional appropriation of $1.7 billion for the war. He concluded his nationwide address with precisely the kind of "ghost-written rhetoric" Lowell found chilling:

> We must have the courage to resist or we'll see it all—all that we have built, all that we hope to build, all of our dreams for freedom, all, all—will be swept away on the flood of conquest. This shall not happen. We will stand in Vietnam.

Less than two months after Lowell's refusal to visit the White House, President Johnson committed the nation to war.

Following his decision not to attend the White House Festival, Lowell retreated to his summer home in Castine, Maine, where he began work on "Waking Early Sunday Morning" and "Fourth of July in Maine." By spring of the following year all five poems of the "Near the Ocean" sequence had appeared in magazines. "The Opposite House," composed during the Harlem race riot of July

1964, preceded Lowell's White House refusal, but the four major poems of the sequence clearly resulted from his unexpected plunge into national politics. In his own words: *"Near the Ocean* starts as public. I had turned down an invitation to an Arts Festival at the White House because of Vietnam . . . and I felt miscast, felt burdened to write on the great theme, private, and almost 'global.' " Yet he was hardly miscast; he was born for the role. His poems may start as "public" and "almost 'global' " but they never cease being "private" as well. They show him bearing the twin burdens that Ralph Ellison has said are imposed upon us by the American experiment: consciousness and conscience.[53]

"Waking Early Sunday Morning" begins as an intensely inward meditation on spiritual crisis and becomes progressively more external, more political, as it continues (*NO*, 15-25). The poet immediately indicates his tormenting inner conflicts in an initial cluster of radically ambiguous images. The very first line, "O to break loose," suggests that he feels himself to be in chains. Yet the freedom he seeks is curiously restricted: the freedom of chinook salmon and rainbow trout to obey nature's inexorable demands. Seemingly self-affirmative, Lowell's opening stanzas possess a strong suicidal content. The salmon are "alive enough" only "to spawn and die" (st. 1). The trout's freedom consists in their "smashing a dry fly," a seizing of their own demise (st. 2). In "Waking Early Sunday Morning," as in "The Quaker Graveyard in Nantucket" and "For the Union Dead," Lowell collocates within a single image paired opposites: freedom and constraint, life and death. Like the drowned sailor with his "hurdling muscles," the fish exude a seeming vitality but they in fact perish; like Colonel Shaw awaiting the "blessèd break," they "break loose" only to die. Thus Lowell envies these

183

fish not for their freedom, for they are no more free than he, nor for their vitality, for they are no less death-bound than he. He envies their unconsciousness. Unlike himself they know nothing of their unfreedom, nothing of death, nothing of injustice, remorse, cruelty, anguish. Throughout the rest of the poem Lowell prays for a condition of simplicity, for relief from mental pain: "O that the spirit could remain / tinged but untarnished by its strain!" Yet short of death such surcease of pain is not possible. The poet is condemned to consciousness and conscience, and it is precisely his bearing of this burden that constitutes his present poem.

The poem centers first on the apparent departure of the Christian God from the human scene, and then on the political violence occupying the empty space that remains. Lowell has awakened this Sunday morning to a world grown old and dark—a world where a "remorseful" sun can produce only enough light to equal a "blackout," where "vermin" confidently continue their obsessive night activities unaware that day has even dawned (st. 3). Imaged by the world it perceives as waning, Lowell's mind itself is "fierce, fireless," "running downhill," "tarnished by its strain" (st. 4-6). "Waking Early Sunday Morning" is a grim reply to Wallace Stevens's "Sunday Morning," a poem that had haunted Lowell's imagination ever since he repeatedly copied it into his notebooks at Kenyon College. Unlike the woman of Stevens's poem, who learns to be "content" with a Godless world, Lowell feels only benumbed with pain. He shares Stevens's belief that Christianity is the "Faith of our Fathers" and not of ourselves, but he views this development with no sense of self-congratulation: he actually envies the deluded "Faithful" at their Church (st. 6). The mirror image of Stevens's woman, Lowell has wakened *early* Sunday morning, glimpsing reality coldly and clearly. For all its errors, Christianity at least "gave darkness some control, / and left a loophole for the soul" (st. 7). Whereas Stevens's poem

184

celebrates human life without God as "unsponsored, free," Lowell experiences such a life as utter constraint, bound round by violence and death. No alternative moral force now exists to counter the "darkness" of the human spirit, which manifests itself (as the poem's last five stanzas make clear) in a rising tide of oppression, atrocity, and war. The disappearance of God has brought neither pagan joy nor a divinity of the imagination, but anguish.[54]

In his desolation Lowell skeptically questions St. Paul's prophecy of the kingdom to come, "Now we see through a glass darkly, but then face to face":

> When will we see Him face to face?
> Each day, He shines through darker glass.
> In this small town where everything
> is known, I see His vanishing
> emblems, His white spire and flag-
> pole sticking out above the fog,
> like old white china doorknobs, sad,
> slight, useless things to calm the mad.
>
> (st. 9)

God, like everything else in Lowell's purview, grows ever darker and more remote. Exactly as in "After the Surprising Conversions," his early poem about the failure of Puritanism, he perceives God's "sensible withdrawal from this land" (*LWC*, 61). The spire of the chalk-dry Trinitarian Church looms now for him as only an "old white china doorknob," a trivial object pregnant with a symbolic, dreamlike significance that his mind can no longer fathom. In early drafts of the poem he wrote of lying "apart from life and thinking of a blue china doorknob that I could do nothing with, turn, or make it mine." When writing "Skunk Hour" he had been similarly "haunted by the image of a blue china doorknob"; he "never . . . knew what it meant." The image means the meaningless—the thing still deeply felt but no longer understood. Painfully separated now from God, Lowell resembles both his own "forlornly fatherless" father in "91 Revere Street" and the scavenging skunks of "Skunk Hour." He explores the realm left to him, the realm of the "tinkling cymbal" (st. 8), St. Paul's term indicating the inner emptiness of one without God's love in his heart (1 Corinthians). Alone in his darkness, Lowell finds no "loophole" of light, air, or escape.[55]

In the final five stanzas of the poem, Lowell combines his "private" feelings of abandonment and decay with a corresponding "global" vision of disaster. As in *Lord Weary's Castle*, he introduces political events as elements in an essentially metaphysical drama, though a harshly agnostic rather than Christian one. In stanza ten he allegorically portrays Lyndon Johnson and America as Goliath and the Philistines—a tyranny of awesome might ("hammering military splendor") and moral horror ("little redemption in the mass / liquidations"). Top-heavy Goliath, who made war in defiance of God, was of course killed by David, and the kingdom of the Philistines was then destroyed by the Israelites (1 Samuel). By analogy, a similar "crash" now awaits the Americans. Indeed, the entire world now teeters on the edge of time, courting extinction:

> Wars
> flicker, earth licks its open sores,
> fresh breakage, fresh promotions, chance
> assassinations, no advance.
>
> (st. 13)

Human progress has been turned back; we experience "promotions," the illusion of forward movement, but "no advance." The planet, a diseased beast, licks its "open sores" by the flickering light of battle, amid sounds of destruction. If for Stevens the earth seemed "all of Paradise that we shall know," for Lowell it seems all of Hell. Human history in a Godless vacuum devolves to castration and annihilation.

Only man thinning out his kind
sounds through the Sabbath noon, the blind
swipe of the pruner and his knife
busy about the tree of life . . .

(st. 13)

The human symbol and architect of this woe is "the President," Lyndon Johnson—who on close examination proves as lost and troubled as Lowell himself. Like the poet, the president is caught between forces of freedom and constraint, life and death. "Swimming nude" as a fish in his White House pool, "unbuttoned," "free," the president is nonetheless "girdled" by his establishment (st. 12). An image of apparent vitality and joy—"elated" and cuffing his subordinates in bearlike fashion—he nonetheless is "sick": sick of his role as spokesman for death, as reciter of "ghost-written" lies. Although Johnson, Lowell's adversary in life and art, ironically resembles Lowell himself, he has far more atrocious crimes to haunt his dreams. For unlike Lowell's poetic rhetoric, Johnson's "ghost-written rhetoric" has the terrible potential of turning the entire planet into a "ghost" (st. 14).

Lowell concludes "Waking Early Sunday Morning" with this elegy for the Earth:

Pity the planet, all joy gone
from this sweet volcanic cone;
peace to our children when they fall
in small war on the heels of small
war—until the end of time
to police the earth, a ghost
orbiting forever lost
in our monotonous sublime.

The poem, which began before daybreak with its author "squatting . . . on time's hoard," has progressed by its conclusion to "the end of time." Lowell's own joyless constriction and estrangement have been assumed by the world, "orbiting forever lost." Speaking from his own condition of death-in-life, Lowell exhorts us to "pity" the whole human race as it inexorably falls into a death-in-life more appalling even than his, one devoid of consciousness and of yearnings for freedom and life.

Lowell fashions his peroration, tender and bitter at the same time, out of a combination of the journalistic diction of the day and language with consciously literary overtones. This combination provides for both immediacy and tragic perspective. For example, in May 1965, Walter Lippmann wrote in *Newsweek* that "we could, if we take the President's words seriously and literally, become engaged in an *endless series of interventions*. . . . Our official doctrine is that we must be prepared to *police the world*." Lowell echoes such political commonplaces in his phrases "war—until the end of time" and "police the earth." But he reveals the true terror of these phrases by placing them in a context rich with poetic and Biblical half-echoes: his prophecy of "war—until the end of time" recalls Milton's Abyss in which Night and Chaos "hold / Eternal Anarchy, amidst the noise of endless wars"; his image of the earth in "monotonous" orbit recalls Baudelaire's description of the earth as "monotone et petit, . . . / Une oasis d'horreur dans un désert d'ennui"; and his word "sublime," though it merely signifies the empty expanse of outer space, comes ironically freighted with eighteenth-century connotations of religious awe. Finally, Lowell's entire stanza, his farewell to an embattled, joyless, and Godless planet, may be seen as an ironic revision of St. Paul's farewell to the Corinthians, "Be of one mind, live in peace; and the God of love and peace shall be with you" (2 Corinthians). Thus Lowell joins the political experience of spring and summer 1965 to his essentially religious sensibility. The international lawlessness of that time leads him to a vision of the inherent lawlessness of the universe. He foresees the human race and the whole hurtling globe itself "forever lost" in the limitless vacancies of God-empty space.[56]

Despite its approach to thematic unity and its suggestion of the analogic nature of poet / president / planet, "Waking Early Sunday Morning" does not fully resolve its inner conflicts. Its concluding oxymorons—peaceful war, monotonous sublime—emphasize the fragmented vision of the poem. Such contradictions reflect Lowell's experience of the discords of the present and his "gloomy premonition" of an even more discordant and authoritarian future. Although all of Lowell's major elegies bear certain structural resemblances to each other, one can distinguish between the irony and fragmentation of "The Quaker Graveyard in Nantucket" and the analogical cohesion of "For the Union Dead," and say that structurally "Waking Early Sunday Morning" stands closer to the former. The poem testifies to Lowell's sense of helplessness in the face of inner and outer disunity. Although it protests eloquently and compassionately, it cannot imaginatively counter the forces of entropic destruction it perceives to be at work within self, history, and cosmos.[57]

The next three poems of Lowell's sequence continue his confrontation of private mind with public world. "Fourth of July in Maine" was begun as a section of "Waking Early Sunday Morning" and echoes that poem's basic concerns, first in tones of serious light verse and then as a combined elegy for his cousin Harriet, Yeatsian prayer for his young daughter, and lament for a world facing nuclear war. Following this poem Lowell moves from Maine to New York, and turns his attention from cosmic disaster to the dilemmas of domestic politics. He views an urban scene defined by class inequity, racial violence, and an ambiance of repression that calls to mind Marshal Astray's infamous fascist rallying cry, "Viva la muerte!" (long live death!) (*NO*, 38). "Central Park," the second of these New York City poems, shows Lowell at the height of his powers as a public poet (*NO*, 39-41). It is an urban elegy that bears comparison to the best of his earlier works in this vein, "At the Indian Killer's Grave" and "For the Union Dead."

Counterpointing the translations in the second half of *Near the Ocean*, which reveal "the greatness and horror" of Rome, "Central Park" corrosively satirizes the greatness and horror of America. For as Lowell wrote in his review of Williams's *Paterson*, "America *is* something immense, crass, and Roman." With occasional echoes of Juvenal's Tenth Satire, Dante's *Inferno*, and the "Sunday in the Park" section of *Paterson*, Lowell decries a cityscape of poverty and violence. As he crosses New York's desperate refuge of green, he encounters a "drugged and humbled" lion prowling a "slummy cell," and a kitten "dying with its deserter's rich / Welfare lying out of reach" (20-34). These animals image the brutalized urban poor, drugged and humbled in cell-like slums, dying on "welfare" while the nation's incredible richness lies out of their reach. Lowell proceeds to show that the city's rich are hardly better off, trapped in their "slit-windowed" high-rise "foxholes," fearful of the violence their "plunder and gold leaf" inevitably invite (43-51). Like all of *Near the Ocean*, "Central Park" has a "private" as well as "public" resonance. As the recurrence of images from earlier poems of the sequence suggests, the city and its suffering citizens mirror Lowell's own psychic "strain" and "darkness," his own "cindering soul":

> The stain of fear and poverty
> spread through each trapped anatomy,
> and darkened every mote of dust.
> All wished to leave this drying crust. . . .
>
> (14-17)

The park, as Lowell wrote explicitly in an early draft of the poem, symbolizes the "dark wood of my life." Everywhere he perceives images of a despair that is at once his nation's and his own: grounded kite and snagged balloon, spreading stain and failing sun, savages armed with "knife" and "club," creatures "deprived, weak, ignorant and blind, / squeaking, tubular, left behind." Yet within this urban apocalypse (to borrow Hugh Kenner's term), this tableau of brutishness and death, he characteristically detects yearnings, however balked and pathetic, for freedom, connection, and endurance. Lowell and his trapped and threatened compatriots "beg . . . for our life."[58]

"Near the Ocean," the last poem of the sequence, seems at first a strangely out-of-key conclusion to the whole, for it abandons the public themes of the preceding poems in favor of a subjective and private reverie (*NO*, 42-49). Lowell has termed it "a 'Dover Beach,' an obscure marriage-poem set in our small eastern seaboard America." Its only really public aspect is extraliterary. Several months after Lowell's boycott of the White House Festival of the Arts, President Johnson intended to make a magnanimous gesture by reciting and praising a line of poetry he identified as being by Robert Lowell—but which in fact was from Arnold's "Dover Beach" (as the *New York Times* pointed out the next day).* In "Near the Ocean" Lowell sought in a sense to correct the error, to become the author of "Dover Beach" after all.[59]

---

* Even had Johnson not mistaken the authorship of his quotation, the recitation would have proven an embarrassment to him. He approvingly quoted the line, "The world which seems / To lie before us like a land of dreams," and applied it to present-day America, unaware of Arnold's intended point that the world which seems like a land of dreams "hath really neither joy, nor love, nor light, / Nor certitude, nor peace, nor help for pain." All things considered, Johnson could not have chosen a more inopportune text than this one, with its concluding vision of ignorant armies clashing by night. To complete the circle of ironies, Lowell, when reached for comment, at first identified Johnson's quotation as being from the end of *Paradise Lost*. He then recalled that the line was Arnold's and that he had used it as an epigraph for "The Mills of the Kavanaughs," where Johnson or his speechwriter had most likely seen it.

Yet the obscurity and introspection of the poem derived from more purely personal circumstance. By the time he came to write the conclusion to his sequence he had buckled under various kinds of strain. To the usual strain of feverish composition were added the accumulating tensions of his difficult marriage, the psychic toll exacted by America's increasingly bloody descent into war, and finally the terrible shock of Randall Jarrell's death in October 1965. Hospitalized for severe depression, Lowell worked on "Near the Ocean," the "most ambitious and least public" poem in his sequence, an intended answer to the constriction, isolation, violence, faithlessness, suffering, and death of the preceding poems. His answer resembles Matthew Arnold's own: the unsaving salvation of individual human love.

"Near the Ocean" begins with a scene of marital discord (a microcosm, perhaps, of all earthly violence), described in hyperbolic metaphors of Perseus' beheading of Medusa and Orestes' murder of Clytemnestra. In the third stanza Lowell abandons these impersonal trappings of myth to reveal himself and Elizabeth Hardwick as bruised individuals lying in bed together, their argument now over. In stanzas four through seven he recalls their life together, pinpointing significant episodes of love and betrayal: their "first night" (st. 4); the early days of their marriage in a New York "coldwater flat" (st. 5); a reconciliation after separation, seemingly on the grounds of a mental institution (st. 6); and finally the present place and time (Castine, summer of 1965), an ultimate "hitting bottom" in their relationship (st. 7).

Until the last stanza, "Near the Ocean" strikes me as disjointed and opaque, nearly as abstracted from the experience it attempts to reveal and complete as "The Mills of the Kavanaughs." I find the poem's final stanza, however, completely beautiful, one of the supreme moments in American poetry. His bitter and painful reverie done, Lowell forgives his wife and himself everything:

Sleep, sleep. The ocean, grinding stones,
can only speak the present tense;
nothing will age, nothing will last,
or take corruption from the past.
A hand, your hand then! I'm afraid
to touch the crisp hair on your head—
Monster loved for what you are,
till time, that buries us, lay bare.

Lowell here has achieved something of "the toleration, hope and intuition of Matthew Arnold's tragic liberalism." Discarding the past for the present tense (and punningly for the present tenseness as well), he reaches for his wife's "hand," despite her essential human monstrosity. She is to him a tyrant, a Medusa, a moral monster—as all human beings are moral monsters. Further, she is an epistemological monster—as the other must always appear monstrous to the self encountering it, not being that self but another. She is, then, as strange and threatening to him as he is to her, as each of us must be to all others. In addressing his wife as "Monster loved for what you are," Lowell declares his love for her not as idealization or self-projection but *as she really is*, in all her foreignness. Moving from Martin Buber's I-it to I-Thou, Lowell discovers or creates in human communion the value, the reason for living, that a God-empty cosmos does not otherwise provide. He finds the relief from pain he has been seeking throughout the sequence. It comes not by breaking loose but by reconnecting, not by escaping from the human but by immersing in it. In earthly love with all its imperfection, Lowell finds his "loophole," and wins his release from the realm of the "tinkling cymbal."[60]

The muscular public prophet protesting a violent, cipherlike universe in "Waking Early Sunday Morning" has at the last reduced himself to a fragile individual person, settling for the personal easing of pain afforded by love. However ironic and unheroic, this outcome represents a victory in spirit. The vision of the "end of time," which has haunted Lowell from the outset of his sequence, has now retreated from the immanence of the indicative to the remoteness of the subjunctive: "till time . . . lay bare." Apocalypse, if not called off, has been postponed. In the process of the *Near the Ocean* sequence, Lowell's fears in solitude have yielded to a spirit of relatedness, a spirit of tenderness, that makes life possible.

The Imperfect Poem

In 1967 and 1968 Lowell continued his active political involvement and continued to write poetry that was politically engaged. Feeling the need to capture his own war-obsessed existence in his art, he began to experiment with a new poetic style that would replace the denunciatory Marvellian stanzas of *Near the Ocean* with a language and form better able to suggest the vicissitudes of his day-to-day existence. The form he invented for the occasion was an open-ended, improvisational series of fourteen-line units written in "rough blank verse." This sonnet-like stanza form, Lowell explained, "can say almost anything conversation or correspondence can; . . . it can stride on stilts, or talk." In his series of "independent yet dependent" sections of rough blank verse, he sought to achieve the balance of freedom and order, discontinuity and continuity, that he observed in Stevens's late long poems and in John Berryman's *Dream Songs*, then nearing completion. He hoped that his form, "inspired by impulse" but "armed with purpose," would enable him "to describe the immediate instant," an instant in which political and personal happenings interacted with a lifetime's accumulation of memories, dreams, and knowledge. In his "jagged" yet unified poem Lowell sought to create nothing less than an epic of his own consciousness. It was to be his ultimate work, the masterpiece toward which his evolving esthetic had always pointed.[61]

The Imperfect Poem

And yet the poem Lowell created proved not to be a masterpiece. A project taking six years of steady work, it comes in three separate versions: *Notebook 1967-68* (published in 1969); a rewritten and expanded edition called simply *Notebook* (published in 1970); and a rewritten and radically rearranged set of individual volumes called *History* and *For Lizzie and Harriet* (both published in 1973). The story of the six years Lowell spent on this project, the most mammoth undertaking of his career, is the story of two artistic developments which tended to work against one another. First, he slowly had to teach himself to make effective use of a new improvisational language and form. But secondly, as he worked to achieve technical mastery, he found that his attitude toward his material was altering. With the passage of even a few years, his "notebook" of 1967 and 1968 had moved into the realm of "history": the present had become past, and as part of the past it possessed neither more nor less interest than all other historical periods. As he continued to write new sections for his still-expanding poem, the political events that had been the original impetus for it began to loom less and less large in the total design. His subject having lost its experiential immediacy, he felt compelled to abandon his notebooklike structure, initially devised to convey a sense of the here-and-now, but now grown unwieldy. *History*, the culmination of the project, is ordered according to impersonal historical chronology, taking its shape not from the poet's consciousness but from an objective world that has successfully resisted his attempts to internalize and reorder it. Lowell's poem, then, must be viewed an ultimate failure as a pure poem of consciousness. Yet if it fails, it is not stillborn like *The Mills of the Kavanaughs*, but a vital, new beginning for the imagination. In tracing Lowell's progress from *Notebook 1967-68* through *Notebook* to *History* we observe him perfecting his major new poetic style, his "language of imperfection" (*H*, 194).

195

Lowell's political activism became the motive and thematic center for *Notebook 1967-68*, and to a significantly lesser degree for the revised *Notebook*. As the dates placed at the back of both books (but not of *History*) remind us, the world depicted in the poem is framed by "The Vietnam War, 1967" and "The Vietnam War, 1968." During these years Lowell opposed the war through letters, speeches, petitions, and political campaigning, through participation in poetry readings, committees, symposia, and protest marches. *Notebook 1967-68* records this assault on political power in all its immediacy and ambiguity: "If I saw something one day I wrote it that day, or the next, or the next. Things I felt or saw, or read were drift in the whirlpool." Although it interweaves many subjects, the poem begins as an inner narrative of the Vietnam war on its American front—the war against the war.[62]

Lowell's chief antiwar activity in 1967 was his participation in the October march on the Pentagon, along with perhaps 100,000 people including such "notables" as Denise Levertov, Allen Ginsberg, Paul Goodman, and Norman Mailer. In his book on this event, *The Armies of the Night*, Mailer graphically depicts Lowell first reading "Waking Early Sunday Morning" to an audience of demonstrators "stirred by the deep sorrows of the man," and later rebelliously declaring his moral and legal complicity with youthful draft-card burners. Mailer's social portrait of Lowell as a genteel Boston artistocrat is more a projection of his own insecurities than a relevant description of Lowell; nothing could be less intuitive or true than Mailer's rhetorical questions, "You, Lowell, beloved poet of many, what do you know of the dirt and the dark deliveries of the necessary? What do you know of dignity hard achieved, and dignity lost through innocence, and dignity lost by sacrifice for a cause one cannot name?" On the basis of such questions it is impossible to believe Mailer's claim to have read Lowell's autobiographical prose. Nevertheless, his psychological portrait of Lowell as a "disconcerting mixture of strength and weakness," of potential aggression and detestation of that very capacity for aggression, provides authentic insight into the ambiguous temper of Lowell's moral activism. Lowell's politics, no less than his art, exemplifies the dominant role played by irony in his mind's life.[63]

Mailer reports that immediately following the Pentagon march Lowell went home inspired "to begin a long poem." The sections of the poem subtitled "The March" appeared in the *New York Review of Books* a month later. Thus was *Notebook 1967-68* born. Lowell's political vision in the completed poem is essentially inward. He aims neither to score partisan points nor to advertise himself, but to explore moral ambiguity in himself and, implicitly, in his culture. Whereas Mailer in *The Armies of the Night* uses the Pentagon march as an arena for his own heroics, Lowell uses the event to probe his "cowardly, / foolhardy heart" (*N 1967-68*, 27 [*N*, 54; *H*, 149]). When soldiers attack the protesters, Lowell flees in fear—unlike Mailer who stands and is arrested. "Is it worse," Lowell askes himself a page before (in thinking about Munich), "to choke on the vomit of cowardice, / or blow the world up on a point of honor?" Immediately after "The March," he pays ambivalent tribute to the military bravery of his ancestor Charles Russell Lowell. Thus the poet allows his political activities to enter into his interior testing of his own feelings, ideas, beliefs, and character. In his interview with V. S. Naipaul, Lowell explained that his point in "The March" "was mainly the fragility of a person caught in this situation." He then went on to subject even this ironic stance to irony, to exculpate types like Mailer and Charles Russell Lowell: "But I believe in heroic action too."[64]

Lowell's irony appears also in his major political act of 1968, his support of Eugene McCarthy for the Democratic nomination for president. Upon meeting the candidate in 1967, Lowell immediately discovered that they had a "temperamental affinity"; they "talked and told stories."

During the Democratic primary elections of 1968, he accompanied McCarthy on his campaign appearances and officially endorsed him in *The New Republic.** In the Indiana, Oregon, and California primaries, Lowell made speeches on McCarthy's behalf and, more importantly, provided him with intellectual refuge when he "wanted to get away from the hail and brimstone of the campaign, and talk and relax and talk seriously." Yet he never committed himself fully to McCarthy's cause; McCarthy was merely a friend, "a lost-cause man, and ironical." It did not "strike" Lowell "that McCarthy would be president." Rather it was Robert Kennedy, the other antiwar candidate in the race and McCarthy's hated foe, who appealed to Lowell's emotions and imagination. Personally, Lowell and Kennedy did not get on. When they first met, at Jacqueline Kennedy's urging, Lowell tried to read portions of *The Education of Henry Adams* aloud to him. As one of Kennedy's campaign aides tells the story, "Bobby suddenly got up and excused himself. Lowell followed him right to the door of the bathroom, still reading. Bobby shut the door and said, 'If you don't mind.' Lowell said, 'If you were Louis XIV, you wouldn't mind.' " On the campaign trail Lowell reserved his "invective" for Kennedy, whom he characterized as "shy, calculating" and rude, "tarnished with former power and thirsting to return to that power."[65]

The motive behind Lowell's campaign "invective," clearly, was his own strongly ambivalent feelings toward Kennedy, the only candidate apart from McCarthy whom he considered "morally serious." In the closing weeks of

* "I feel no competence or longing to take on the burden of a political logician or polemicist. Of the announced or seriously offered Democratic or Republican candidates, only Senators Kennedy and McCarthy seem morally or intellectually allowable. Of these McCarthy is preferable, first for his negative qualities: lack of excessive charisma, driving ambition, machinelike drive, and the too great wish to be President. But I am for him most for what he possesses, his variable, tolerant and courageous mind, lungs that breathe the air. When the race against President Johnson was hopeless and intractable, he alone hoped, entered and won."

the campaign and of Kennedy's life, Lowell told an interviewer that Kennedy "is a lot better than he seems to a lot of people," and he tried hard to effect a *rapprochement* between the two candidates.* Unlike McCarthy, Kennedy seemed to Lowell a "Plutarchan hero," representing both "the nobility and danger of pride and fate." Repelled by Kennedy's "too great wish to be President," Lowell was nonetheless drawn to him as a figure heroically vital yet fated for destruction: "He felt he was doomed, and you knew that. The course he took, it was black, and that gave a kind of tragedy to it all." For Lowell, Kennedy was the latest link in a chain of ambiguous American heroes "doomed and ready for their idealism to face any amount of violence"—another Endecott, another Edwards, another Charles Russell Lowell, another Shaw. "That's an image," he once said, "one could treasure and it stirs one." Lowell was stirred by Robert Kennedy because he embodied conflicts at the center of American history, and at the center of Robert Lowell himself.[66]

The section of Lowell's poem subtitled "For Eugene McCarthy" expresses affection and limited admiration, but little real confidence in McCarthy's capacity for leadership: "Who will swear you wouldn't / have done good to the country?" (*N 1967-68*, 123 [*N*, 204; *H*, 175]). Lowell ironically describes a McCarthy taking charge not in affairs of the globe but only "in the hollow bowling-alley; / crack of the globe." In contrast, he portrays Kennedy in a haunting

* Feeling that Kennedy and McCarthy "should harmonize somehow" after the California primary, Lowell wrote a note to Kennedy saying, "I think things are very gloomy. Could I call on you for a few minutes? It might be of some use to you, or it might not be of some use to you, God knows." The meeting, however, proved a disaster. Kennedy argued that McCarthy should withdraw from the race immediately. Lowell replied, "These are just debater's arguments. You mustn't talk to me this way." Kennedy: "Well, I guess we have nothing more to say." Lowell: "I wish I could think up some joke that would cheer you, but it won't do any good." Lowell later told McCarthy, "I felt like Rudolph Hess parachuting into Scotland."

tripartite elegy as an authentic tragic hero, larger than life, leaping for the sublime. This Kennedy was a hero of consciousness as well as of action, for he entered the political arena "very conscious of the nobility and the danger."

> Doom was woven in your nerves, your shirt,
> woven in the great clan; they too were loyal,
> and you too more than loyal to them, to death.
> For them like a prince, you daily left your tower
> to walk through dirt in your best cloth.
>
> (N 1967-68, 118 [N, 197; H, 174])

In his "best cloth"—woven of doom—Kennedy walks through dirt "to death." Like Colonel Shaw, he leaves Lowell with just a "bubble": an artist's image of a stilled young man,

> out of Plutarch, made by hand—
> forever approaching our maturity.

In his first draft Lowell wrote that Kennedy forever approached his own maturity, thereby suggesting both his quality of youth and the fact of his untimely death. By substituting "*our* maturity" Lowell makes two additional points. First, Kennedy in some way stands for the poet's own youthful idealism ("his death seemed like the death of one's own adolescence"). And second, Kennedy the epic hero stands for America's idealism, seemingly fated never to attain mature fulfillment. Equally devoted to his "clan," to the wretched of the earth, and to life itself, Robert Kennedy consciously approached death bearing a torch of hope.

> Is night only your torchlight wards gone black,
> wake written on the waves, pyre set for the fire that
> fell?[67]

In addition to the Pentagon march and McCarthy and Kennedy, *Notebook 1967-68* treats numerous political subjects: the deaths of Che Guevara and Martin Luther King,

The Imperfect Poem

the Columbia University demonstrations of spring 1968, the Democratic and Republican nominating conventions, the election of Nixon, and many lesser events. Perhaps a quarter of the fourteen-line segments in the volume are explicitly political in nature, and many of the others are political by implication or allusion. Yet Lowell writes no political propaganda, gives no "marching orders" (*PB*, vi). He intends, rather, to impart a sense of his own fallible self ambiguously enmeshed in society and its dilemmas, responding dishonorably and honorably to an immoral age. The poem exposes the interplay within his consciousness of personal autobiography and the public events he has experienced firsthand.

An equally important and less personal intention of Lowell's political writing is to provide a consistent humanitarian perspective on the use and misuse of power. On this level *Notebook 1967-68* is indeed politically engaged, though its interest in politics is moral rather than pragmatic. Speaking to Dudley Young, Lowell denied having written a "New Left poster" and explained, "I think if anyone read my book, a little slowly, his eyes might smart, and he would be sad for our culture." In *Bech: A Book*, John Updike derides "Lowellian ruminations" that indict "our bombing of thatched villages," but this kind of derision misses its mark, for Lowell does not ruminate on Vietnam. Nor does he even mention Presidents Johnson and Nixon by name (except for an unimportant anti-Johnson remark in "Obit"). Lowell treats the Vietnam war implicitly rather than explicitly. He obsessively exposes the violent acts of "the great," among them Caligula, Mohammed, Henry VIII, Marie Antoinette, Napoleon, Frederick the Great, the Russian Czars, Lenin, Stalin, Mao, the Indian killers, Andrew Jackson, Truman, an unnamed "leader of the left," and the book's darkest villain, Adolf Hitler. He shouts "j'accuse" even at the seemingly gentlest of leaders, Abraham Lincoln. The real subject of this poem is the human lust for violence and the moral horror of violence, a polarity Lowell has long detected in his own character and which he now discerns on a massive scale throughout human history. While he acknowledges the disturbing paradox that good may come out of the evil of violence, he nonetheless provides us with a wry but passionate moral judgment: "I wouldn't / be murdered, or even murder, for my soul" (*N 1967-68*, 101 [*N*, 172]).* Although Johnson and Nixon go unnamed, they are judged and condemned on almost every page.[68]

The revised and expanded edition of *Notebook* is a much more inclusive volume than *Notebook 1967-68* and comes a good deal closer to capturing the fullness of Lowell's conscious existence. In the process of expanding his poem he somewhat muted its political tone: while some few of the ninety-nine new fourteen-liners have significant political content, none describes a specific political activity engaged in by Lowell. His emphasis has shifted away from politics considered as immediate event to politics considered in the tranquility of retrospect. Removed now from the events of 1967-1968, the poem no longer centers around the political scene that dominated his awareness during those years. Rather, a secondary theme of the first edition now comes to the fore, having lost none of its painful immediacy in the intervening year. This is the theme of Lowell's increasingly troubled domestic life. *Notebook* recounts and contemplates three years of conversations, quarrels, and reconciliations with wife and daughter ("Harriet"; "Long Summer"; parts of "February and March" and "Circles"; "Summer"; "Half a Century Gone"; "Obit"), and at least two and perhaps four separate love affairs ("Through the Night," "Charles River," and "Harvard"; "Mexico" and "Eight Months

* In *History* this judgment becomes less wry and even more passionate: "I wouldn't murder and be murdered for my soul." For Lowell, to murder is to murder oneself (*H*, 134).

Later"; and in fuzzier focus "Searchings" and "April"). About fifteen of *Notebook*'s new sections concern marital stresses and strains:

> We jangle like fishwives. Our hopes are more disputed
> than our quarrels. Love lives on trial. . . .
> Lizzie, we wake up to the blood of loneliness,
> we would cry out *Love, Love,* if we had letters.
>
> (*N,* 136 [*FLH,* 25])

Apart from the sections on his domestic life, almost all of the new sections Lowell added to *Notebook* concern no firsthand event but rather meditate almost randomly upon a lifetime's store of memories and acquired knowledge. In some measure the volume shows him attempting to duplicate the success of *Life Studies.* Like the earlier work, *Notebook* reflects his long-held belief that "poetry must escape from its glass." He explained to Dudley Young that "the spine of the book is my own life, more or less like an early book of mine, *Life Studies.*" Yet in even larger measure *Notebook* shows Lowell attempting to circumvent what he now viewed as the inherent limitations of *Life Studies.* If poetry must escape from its glass in the sense of not being removed from life, it must also escape from its glass in the sense of not merely reproducing life as through a camera lens. In much of *Life Studies* Lowell simply "photographed" scenes from his past; "it's a decent book," he said while writing *Notebook,* "but I don't want to write another *Life Studies.*" Rather, he designed *Notebook* as a "hybrid poem, largely invention and largely record," an extended meditation in which the actual is effectively interiorized. The emphasis is not on what happened but on how what happened enters and affects thought. Lowell later explained that though *Notebook* is as "personal" as *Life Studies,* he tried "to make it more difficult and complicated because more can perhaps be said thrusting through complication. . . . What I wanted to get away from was the photograph of reality." Rather than a detached, outer view

203

of his past self, *Notebook* gives us Lowell's present self viewed from the inside.[69]

Stylistically, *Notebook*'s revisions and additions make it a more rhythmic and generally more elegant poem than its predecessor; they also make it more abstract, and at times opaque. In order to perfect a style adequate to the rich complication of his mental life, Lowell turned increasingly to Wallace Stevens as his "guiding angel." Dazzled by what he thought of as Stevens's "obscurity, his love of generalization, his occasional simplicity, his improvisation, and his Tennysonian sweetness so far from my own bent," he sought to adapt these qualities for his own blank verse. He wanted *Notebook* to be the kind of poem Stevens termed "the poem of the act of the mind." Turning his back on the hard-won lucidity of *Life Studies*, Lowell risked obscurity in order to convey what he considered "actual" (phenomenological) truth as opposed to "literal" (empirical) truth. His motive for *Notebook* is suggested by his evaluation of Stevens in an unpublished essay of 1968. He wrote that Stevens "speaks a language refined to the point of unintelligibility. . . . It doesn't matter. He is a large poet because he had Shakespeare's ear and could express nuance and the inexpressible, and pushed back the barriers of language." In *Notebook* too, Lowell refined his language in order to break through the glass of literary art, in order to express the inexpressible nuances of his own mind.[70]

Yet if *Notebook* is a richer and more subtly articulated poem than *Notebook 1967-68*, it also suffers from a structure that is debilitatingly deficient. Even *Notebook 1967-68* was formally "discontinuous," as Lowell several times acknowledged in manuscript, but it achieved at least a measure of coherence through its fiction of being a "Notebook of a Year" (its original title).* Although the simulated

---

* The poem, of course, is not *literally* a "notebook" or, as one critic has called it, a "scrapbook." Lowell wrote and revised the individual sections with painstaking care and arranged them with little reference to their ac-

chronology was frequently interrupted by flashbacks and occasionally by flashforwards, the whole found form "within its loose frame of the seasons." In *Notebook*, however, Lowell cast aside even this rudimentary principle of order. After *Notebook 1967-68* was published, he continued to write new fourteen-liners which he then "scattered" into the poem "where they caught" (*N*, 264). The new additions were "intended to fulflesh [the] poem, not sprawl into chronicle," but sprawl they do. *Notebook* consists of numerous flashforwards and innumerable flashbacks. In his "Afterthought" Lowell continues to claim that his "plot rolls with the seasons," but now adds that "one year is confused with another" (*N*, 262). Within his initial structure roughly corresponding to the change of seasons in 1967-1968, he has simply interspersed ninety-nine additional sections according to their thematic associations. Thus "1970 New Year" appears directly after a section called "New Year's Eve 1968," though both are part of an extended digression from Lowell's treatment of April 1968. *Notebook*, then, has elements of both chronological order and thematic order, but is essentially a disorder. Lacking structural necessity, or even plausibility, the poem makes no figure capable of suggesting an essential *shape* to Lowell's consciousness.[71]

In the years following the publication of *Notebook*, Lowell came painfully to recognize the formal failure of his enterprise. In 1973 he reorganized and rewrote the poem for the third time in six years. In a "Note" to the new version he confessed, "My old title, *Notebook*, was more accurate than I wished, i.e. the composition was jumbled. I hope that this jumble or jungle is cleared—that I have cut the waste marble from the figure" (*H*, 7). By "waste marble" he had

tual order of composition. He chose his title for its tentative, improvisatory air, similar to Stevens's "Notes toward a Supreme Fiction."

in mind those parts of *Notebook* dealing with his troubled domestic life, most of which he now detached and arranged as a separate sequence entitled *For Lizzie and Harriet*. His stormy quarter-century-long marriage to Elizabeth Hardwick finally ended in divorce in 1972, and Lowell sought to transform his passages in praise of difficult love into a self-sustained elegy for a tragic failure of love, on the order of Meredith's *Modern Love*. The transformation does not fully succeed. *For Lizzie and Harriet* is often quite touching in its depiction of human frailty and desire, and yet it possesses nothing like the emotional power and essential seriousness of Meredith's great sequence. Alternating between Lowell's tense family relations and two of his love affairs, *For Lizzie and Harriet* has a static and fragmentary quality, as if the poem were indeed but "waste marble." Further, Lowell bathes his potentially conflict-ridden poem in the tranquilizing waters of nostalgia—nostalgia especially for married love that through no one's fault "will not come back on fortune's wheel" (*FLH*, 48). After such forgiveness, what knowledge? For the only time in Lowell's career since *The Mills of the Kavanaughs*, one senses him evading and disguising the complex truth of his own deepest feelings.

History, the "figure" Lowell cut from the waste, is a far more compelling piece of work. It seems to me the best of the three versions of this long poem. First, there is a practical reason for preferring it over either *Notebook 1967-68* or *Notebook*. Lowell's innumerable revisions of words and lines in *History* are almost all to the good, and his eighty new fourteen-liners show him at the top of his form. By the time he came to rewrite his poem as *History*, he had mastered his new quasi-Stevensian style, his abstract and exploratory language of "imperfection" (*H*, 194). Regardless of ostensible subject, the real subject of every line of *History* is the poet's questing consciousness itself. Stevens once wrote that because the mind's "imperfect is our paradise," delight "lies in flawed words and stubborn sounds." In a similar spirit, Lowell appears in *History* as a clown-prince of consciousness, a *"hero demens,"* exposing in his "incurably imperfect" lines the infinite inflections of his mind (*H*, 194, 198, 207).[72]

A second reason fo preferring *History* to its predecessors is that it possesses a coherent form, though it is one that implicitly signals the failure of Lowell's original intentions. Unlike *Notebook 1967-68* and *Notebook*, which took their form from the inside of his consciousness, from his actual experiencing of his world, *History* takes its form from the outside, from the world structured in terms of linear clock-time. *History* proceeds, more or less regularly, from the beginning of human history to the present moment. Whereas *Notebook 1967-68* gave us a gestalt of Lowell's consciousness framed within the circle of a year's seasonal change, and whereas *Notebook* sought to "confuse" linear chronology even further by making it submit to the spatial organization of the human mind, *History* acknowledges the authority of linear time to give shape to our conceptions of the world. Thus *History* moves Lowell from the center of his experience, in Allen Tate's phrase, toward the periphery. What once was undergone has now been judged, placed, and understood. Whereas the two *Notebook*s mixed "the day-to-day with the history," *History* gives us the history pure and simple, for the day to day of 1967-1970 had by 1973 become pure history. By giving shape to his unshapely, ever-lengthening poem, by providing a close for his open-ended form, Lowell completed his experience of the poem, and freed himself from it. The poem too was freed to be itself, not perhaps the self its author had hoped it would be—the utter revelation, the transcendent confession of what he *himself* most truly was—but a self of value and purpose nonetheless. *History* gives us Lowell's mind interacting with human history, framed within the fictional "plot" of historical chronology.[73]

History falls into two parts of roughly equal length. The

kind of historical interaction in each part varies. In the first part of the poem Lowell meditates on the distant past, the past that occurred before his birth and that he can know only at secondhand. His meditations in this part of the poem take several significant forms. In some of the sections Lowell seeks to actualize the past; he brings significant historical figures like Sir Thomas More, Margaret Fuller, Emerson, and Thoreau to life in their own quoted words and allows his sensibility to enter into dialogue with them. His translations or "imitations" of poems by Homer, Sappho, Juvenal, Dante, and numerous nineteenth-century poets might be seen as a variation on this mode of retrieving an earlier period by interacting with its literal words. Somewhat more subjective are his imaginative re-creations of the past. Here he focuses more openly on himself in the process of inventing, and the characters that he re-creates are often versions or foils of himself: Solomon, Caligula, Milton in separation. A similarly subjective use of the past are his occasional essays at making historical or literary characters into surrogates for characters out of his own life: his mother speaking as Clytemnestra, his own childhood self as Orestes, his new wife as Mary Stuart. Whatever form his historical imagination takes, Lowell in this part of *History* infuses recorded or invented past with a sense of his present self, thereby insisting that the past is not dead object but living act of the mind.

In the second part of *History*, beginning with the boyhood memories of "Wolverine, 1927" and "Two Farmers," Lowell defines himself more explicitly, for here he enters into his poem as historical object as well as historian. He ponders events in his own life as well as events in the history of Western civilization. In this second part, *History* becomes literal as well as spiritual autobiography, gaining a sense of direction and human reality that the first part perhaps lacks. For all their intelligence and variety, the initial 157 sections of the poem occur in the strongroom of the mind, a locale not entirely hospitable to Lowell's genius. In the latter 211 sections, the poem opens itself to the world he has encountered firsthand. It thereby attains moments of real power: the sequence concerning his youthful rebellion against his parents (*H*, 112-117), the sequences on the politics of the 1960s (*H*, 145-160, 173-79), and the numerous tributes to poets he has known (such as Tate, Williams, Pound, Eliot, Jarrell, Bishop, and Berryman) and to art itself. Interweaving impersonal and personal chronologies in this latter part of the work, Lowell achieves that dynamic union of public and private voices so characteristic of his poetic maturity.

History differs from the two *Notebooks* in theme as well as arrangement. With the passage of years, Lowell's concerns changed, and his ongoing poem reflects that change. Having become politically disengaged, he relegates his once-dominant theme of political revolt to two relatively brief sequences in the second half of *History*. Divorced from Elizabeth Hardwick, he expunges the theme of married love from the poem entirely. Instead, he expands upon two of the minor themes of the preceding volumes, making them central to his new conception.

The first of these themes is the fear of death. Always before in Lowell's poetry, death appeared as both moral choice and heroic occasion of violence (whether homicidal or suicidal). Death was typically presented as locked in dubious battle with life, often within a single individual: the drowned sailor in "The Quaker Graveyard in Nantucket," Colonel Shaw in "For the Union Dead," or Lowell himself in "Skunk Hour" and "Waking Early Sunday Morning." Death in *History*, however, is neither chosen nor heroic. It is the unwilled, inevitable "decay" of old age (*H*, 28). "Aging downstream faster than a scepter can check," "palate-sprung for the worm, senility," "sour with age," Lowell begins to contemplate for the first time, and with terror, his own involuntary movement toward death (*H*, 37, 38, 189). In the very first section of the poem he comments, "it is so dull and gruesome how we die," and in one of the most striking passages, near the end, he dreams that he discovers himself already dead.

> I opened an old closet door, and found myself
> covered with quicklime, my face deliquescent . . .
> by oversight still recognizable.
> Thank God, I was the first to find myself.

                                                    (*H*, 204)

A mundane and faintly comic condition, death itself occasions only embarrassment and relief. It is not the end as such that terrifies Lowell, but his constant *awareness* of its inexorable approach, his discerning of death's signs in the self: gray hair, lapses of memory, fatigue. For Lowell, "dying" is "harder than already being dead" (*H*, 204); not the physical fact but the consciousness of the fact terrifies.

The second major theme of *History* appears almost entirely in the latter half of the poem, and works to assuage Lowell's fears that he may cease to be. This is the theme of art. Art, the triumph of consciousness, counters death, the cessation of consciousness. Lowell suffers from no illusion that art affords immortality; rather he views art as proof of existence and means of creating identity. Throughout his career he has struggled to close the gap between life and artwork, and in *History* the two have finally joined: "If I stop writing I stop breathing" (*H*, 169). In a repeated punning image, he claims that for the great artist, art "enlarges the heart"—it fully humanizes, and it kills like a disease. Yet the risk must be taken, for Lowell, like Henry James, has come to believe that art *makes* life. Lowell's revision of his tribute to John Berryman makes the point. In the *Notebook* version he wrote, "I feel I know what you have worked through, you / know what I have worked through—these are words" (*N*, 255). In *History* he alters the last phrase to read *"we* are words" (*H*, 203). The poet, a sensuous being containing a consciousness, and his poem, a sensuous entity in which that same consciousness culminates, are one. As both Tate and Williams taught Lowell long ago in their different vocabularies, the artist realizes himself most fully in the act of writing, and the writing therefore is a living record of his own self-realization.

Art achieves its final victory over death in "End of the Year," the brilliant last section of *History*. This section climaxes the poem's highly elegiac close with images of death and night, yet counters these with the saving possibilities of written language. After Lowell ambiguously acknowledges the failure of his own writing—scorning his sentences as "bad," "stamped," "trampled," "branded," "nailed" (and redemptive, like Christ on the cross?)—he delivers a veiled self-justification that makes good his every artistic shortcoming. His typescript seems to him "a Rosetta stone," a seemingly incomprehensible hieroglyphic inscription which on close inspection furnishes clues to its own decipherment, and to the decipherment of universal hieroglyphs. His words, for all their flaws, illuminate. In the final, wonderful line of the poem, Lowell superimposes the image of his art—his marked-up carbon paper (his Rosetta stone)—upon the image of deepening night: "bright sky, bright sky, carbon scarred with ciphers." In the joining of inexplicable world and language, in the transformation of his world into language, Lowell finds his sustaining though ambiguous value. His words become stars, "scarred" but "bright."

When *History* was published it received a number of hostile reviews by critics grown impatient with Lowell's seemingly endless recastings of his poem. In the most savage review of all, Peter Dale assailed the "fortuitous form" Lowell had chosen: "The poems salvaged from *Notebook* are drastically rearranged in sequence to provide a chronological order from Biblical times through Greek, Roman, Mediaeval, to modern times where it culminates, with the obvious delusions of grandeur created by this pattern, in the life and times of Lowell." Dale's criticism, though entertaining in a facile way, misses the point of Lowell's project, for the true subject throughout the poem

is Lowell's own life and times. The poem seeks to reveal
not the truth of the past but the truth of Lowell's mind as it
meditates upon the past in terms of its inmost concerns.
This antipositivist conception of the historian's task recalls
R. G. Collingwood's argument in *The Idea of History* that
"historical inquiry reveals to the historian the powers of
his own mind. . . . The historian himself, together with the
here-and-now which forms the total body of evidence
available to him, is a part of the process he is studying."
Lowell similarly maintains that "history is an art, not a science." He tests the interactions of imagination with the actual in his poem: "History has to live with what was here, /
clutching and close to fumbling all we had" (*H*, 24). Out of
such clutchings and fumblings does his mind create
itself. [74]

Lowell's poem, in all its forms, represents his effort to
write what Roy Harvey Pearce has defined as "an American epic": "a poem which will create rather than celebrate
a hero and which will make rather than recall the history
that surrounds him." Like other such epic enterprises—
"Song of Myself," *The Bridge*, "Notes toward a Supreme
Fiction," *Paterson*, *The Cantos*, and the work Lowell in his
manuscript called "closest to home," *The Dream Songs*—
Lowell's *History* centers on his own sensibility, on his inner
struggle for "self-identification and self-preservation." Yet
his creation does not entirely succeed in the manner of its
great precursors. Unlike the other poets, Lowell holds
something of himself back. *History*, replete with intellectual power, lacks emotional power. Except in brilliant
flashes which occur mostly in the poem's latter half, one
feels neither that these verses cost Lowell his life (to borrow Emerson's phrase), nor that they take on a life of their
own. As he worked to complete *History*, Lowell himself
sensed its failings. In a 1973 *Encounter* essay, he made am-

bivalent sport of American poems "long as novels, aping immensity." Possibly remembering his admission to Stanley Kunitz years before that his gift was for short pieces, he had already begun to work on his small, magnificent poem of consciousness called *The Dolphin*. The epic urge subsided. Lowell came to see that all of his poems "are in a sense one poem"—that the true epic of his sensibility is not any one of his single volumes, but all of his volumes. [75]

❧ V ❧
The Book of Life

The Dolphin

This is a vital affair, not an affair of the heart (as it may be in one's first
poems), but an affair of the whole being (as in one's last poems).
—*Stevens*, "John Crowe Ransom: Tennessean"

In 1970 Robert Lowell departed America for England,
leaving everything behind. Now in his early fifties, he
made the move to accept posts as Professor of English at
the University of Essex and honorary Visiting Fellow at All
Soul's College, Oxford, but the deeper reason for the move
was self-renewal. "It's an American theme," he commented, "the discovery, the pioneer going into the wilderness. After a while the wilderness changes into the Europe
of Henry James and Eliot—a freehold almost barbaric in its
newness." In England's green and (for him) virgin land, he
hoped to recover his freedom, both personal and artistic.
He was "on vacation from [his] Furies"—from a Vietnam
war that raged on and on, from a New York City bristling
with physical threat and intellectual fierceness, from a failing marriage. Perhaps he also sought freedom from
Notebook, his poem precisely about those Furies, his poem
that refused to click shut. (The revised *Notebook* was finished in January of 1970 and published later that year to
generally negative reviews.) Troubled in mind and spirit,
Lowell needed once more to create himself and his art
anew.[1]

Soon after arriving in London he met Caroline Blackwood, thirty-nine years old, a gifted writer and a mother of
three young girls. The progress of their love—her giving
birth to a son, his tormenting decision to divorce Elizabeth
Hardwick and marry her—became the basis for *The Dolphin*, published in 1973. In this complex, beautiful, and

214

deeply original poem, Lowell achieved the artistic renewal he sought. *The Dolphin*, he told Christopher Ricks, is "the story of changing marriages, not a malice or sensation, far from it, but necessarily, according to my peculiar talent, very personal." Yet it is not only a "story of changing marriages"; it is also, more deeply, a poem of and about the mind. Lowell's marital affairs are more pretext (pre-text) than text; the real text is his mind in the act of grasping at the bare events and turning back upon itself, converting them and itself to fiction—the necessary fiction of consciousness and the closely related fiction of poetry. *The Dolphin* thus owes less to such "marriage-torture, marriage-strife" poems as Meredith's *Modern Love* and Snodgrass's *Heart's Needle* than to Stevens's and Williams's late philosophic poems. It is ultimately a poem about consciousness and art, and about how to live in the world.[2]

In beginning to work on *The Dolphin* Lowell found that "my problem, more than in any of my other books, was that I had something I had to find a way to write. That something is its raison d'etre, and what, if achieved, is the bone of its merit." That something, as I have suggested, is the manner in which consciousness grapples with experience. In this, *The Dolphin* is very different from *Life Studies*, the other personal sequence which it superficially resembles. The earlier volume focused "out there," on selected people and events from the past; Lowell's consciousness, both as experiencing child and remembering adult, was for the most part kept hidden, revealed only through silences and implication until it exploded in the conclusion of the sequence ("I myself am hell"). *The Dolphin* is a far more introspective work. It focuses "in here," on Lowell's consciousness in its daily existence. Perhaps it would be better to say that *The Dolphin* differs from *Life Studies* precisely in that it does not focus at all; it abstracts the world of facts and events into interior reverie. Thus the sharp-edged facticity of *Life Studies*, which required Lowell to supply accurate names and dates in almost every poem, gives way to a verbal opacity that even obscures (as Stephen Yenser has complained) when and if the poet and Caroline marry. Yet the abstraction of *The Dolphin* is perfectly suited to its purposes: not to photograph surfaces but to enact the motions of the mind, not to retrieve the lost past but to express the living present, not to use personal experience as cause for confession but as material for meditation.[3]

Lowell found a "way to write" *The Dolphin*, most problematical of his books, by interweaving two separate but related subjects and uniting them in the central symbol of the dolphin. His first subject is his "changing marriages." Here he seeks to expand the resources of poetry by giving his poem "a plot and action like a novel." Half memoir and half fiction, Lowell's story develops dynamically. It is a book of changes, not only of "changing marriages" but of changing minds (Lowell's, Caroline's, Lizzie's) and changing lives. On this level *The Dolphin* is about human freedom and growth. And it is supremely a poem about love, love that makes freedom meaningful, love that allows for human growth. The figure of love in the poem is Caroline, the dolphin and mermaid, symbol of Eros and agape. In the largest sense Caroline as dolphin stands for Lowell's loving relationship to the universe. His opening himself to her represents his opening to the world outside himself; his physical and spiritual union with her represents his union with his world. His love for the dolphin brings him to earth and rescues his life. It is the "love," to borrow a phrase from Saul Bellow, "that makes reality reality."[4]

The second subject of *The Dolphin* is the process of the poem itself. As Lowell tells his love story, he simultaneously meditates upon his own consciousness, which through invention and intense perception becomes imagination, which in turn through inspired craft becomes art. On this level the poem explores the interrelationship of being, consciousness, and art. This subject, unlike the first, has no "plot and action like a novel," and shows no sequential development. It is a series of mental probes on a theme, an extended effort to get at and surround that theme. It is fixed in time, just as the first subject is changing. Further, as a series of almost didactic formulations about consciousness and art, it seeks to concentrate poetry into abstract statement, just as the first subject seeks to expand poetry to include the resources of prose narrative. It may be, as some have thought about Wallace Stevens's late poems, that Lowell's extended meditation about poetry is itself not poetry at all. Yet his meditation remains linked to the world of forms through its relations to his love story and through its metaphoric embodiment in the dolphin. The dolphin-mermaid on this plane symbolizes consciousness and artistic form: she is the muse.

The dolphin as muse elaborates upon and fulfills the meaning of the dolphin as Eros. For in both aspects, she represents a form of love and creation, as well as a heightened perception, miraculous perception, of the world around and within. In both of her aspects the dolphin acts as redeemer, a divine presence in a world without Divinity.

As the inclusive symbolism of the dolphin suggests, Lowell's two subjects cannot be entirely separated. Indeed, his whole poetic effort is directed toward making his two subjects one. This union enacts the essential metaphor of the poem: the metaphor of marriage. In *The Dolphin* Lowell marries a real woman named Caroline, and he also marries his life to his art. Founded on mutuality, the poem concerns events in his life and the way they become his art, and it also concerns art itself and the way art gives meaning (even existence) to his life. A wedding of life experience and artistic experience, *The Dolphin* is thus the culmination of Lowell's entire poetic endeavor. This is not to say that it is his best poem, but rather to suggest that it is the poem toward which his poetics had long been pointing.

The Dolphin begins with a prologue, "Fishnet," which stands apart from the poem that follows, apart from what Lowell has elsewhere called "the bulk, confusion, and de-

217

feat of mortal flesh . . . all that blithe and blood-torn dolor!'' "Fishnet" includes the poem's important ideas and images in epitome, but expresses them with a calm lucidity almost unprecedented in Lowell's poetry. This same lucidity recurs in the epilogue, "Dolphin," which responds to and completes the prologue. Prologue and epilogue are in a sense autonomous, though given flesh by the poem that resides between; they contain the poem, both in the sense of enclosing it and in the sense of encapsulating its transcendent meaning. Luminous, they bespeak the achieved wisdom of a lifetime, the wisdom to accept that life. They express Lowell's passion for yes which underlay his every mortal no.[5]

"Fishnet" celebrates Lowell's love for the dolphin:

Any clear thing that blinds us with surprise,
your wandering silences and bright trouvailles,
dolphin let loose to catch the flashing fish. . . .
Poets die adolescents, their beat embalms them,
the archetypal voices sing offkey;
the old actor cannot read his friends,
and nevertheless he reads himself aloud,
genius hums the auditorium dead.
The line must terminate.
Yet my heart rises, I know I've gladdened a lifetime
knotting, undoing a fishnet of tarred rope;
the net will hang on the wall when the fish are eaten,
nailed like illegible bronze on the futureless future.

In the first three lines he defines his symbol as a creature of blinding clarity, of "surprise" and "trouvailles." The wit of this initial rhyme—one of the few rhymes in *The Dolphin*—focuses attention and pleasure on the lines. The surprising "trouvailles" are windfalls, moments of grace that occur in life (Lowell is surprised by joy often in the ensuing pages) and that occur in art (Stevens similarly thought that "the acquisitions of poetry are fortuitous; *trouvailles*.") Lowell here is acknowledging, with newfound humility, a force outside the self which provides occasions of self-tran-

218

scendence. In one sense the force is human love, represented by Caroline, who gladdens his life and inspires this poem. In another sense it is language itself conceived as a divinity. There is no contradiction in his positing both Caroline and language within the single numinous symbol of the dolphin, for as Williams wrote in "Asphodel," "love and the imagination are of a piece." As Lowell's poem progresses, we come to see that this is so for him too; each is a form of the other.[6]

The image in these initial lines is complex. Literally, dolphins do assist fishermen in catching schools of albacore that swim alongside them. Metaphorically, the dolphin is Eros and muse, a majestic creature providing "flashing fish," or moments of beauty and perfection. As metaphor she is paradoxically divine yet dangerous: her "clear," "bright," "flashing" brilliance "blinds." Further ambiguities proliferate in the syntax. To call attention only to the most crucial of these, does "let loose" modify "dolphin" adjectivally, so that the sentence is a verbless fragment in praise of her power? Or does "let loose" function as a verb, so that the sentence is a command to the dolphin (muse, Eros) to act? Perhaps the syntax must be read in both ways, a suggestion of the doubleness underlying the poem. The dolphin herself is entirely double: clear (or transparent) yet blinding; clear (or free from doubt) yet surprising; clear (or unmistakable) yet silent; wandering (lost) yet provider of trouvailles (finds); free ("loose") yet ordered (she is "let") and ordering (she catches). An instrument of life, she causes fish to die.* Lowell's paradoxi-

* It is worth noting here that whereas in "Waking Early Sunday Morning" Lowell himself wished to "break loose" and die like a fish, he now watches the dolphin "let loose" to catch fish. That is, he has replaced an image of inner torment with an image of joyous mastery. A similar significance is revealed when one contrasts his Hopkins-like vision of "flashing fish" and "dolphin" with such earlier images of fish and sea mammals as the dying "blood-mouthed rainbow trout" of "The Drunken Fisherman," the preying sharks of "The Quaker Graveyard in Nantucket," the pathetic seal and whales of "Waking in the Blue," and the aquarium fish and giant finned cars of "For the Union Dead."

cal dolphin is kin to the dolphin of Yeats's "Byzantium,"
and even closer kin to the unknowable and holy white
whale of the final chapters of *Moby-Dick* and to Oberon's
vision in *A Midsummer's Night Dream* of a "mermaid on a
dolphin's back" who uttered

> such dulcet and harmonious breath
> That the rude sea grew civil at her song
> And certain stars shot madly from their spheres,
> To hear the sea-maid's music.[7]

The remaining ten lines of "Fishnet" comprise a troubled commentary on poets and poetry. Lowell contends
that poets "die adolescents," meaning either that they
cease being poets young or that they remain immature
even in their old age (or both). Their poetry merely "embalms" them, certifies that they are dead. There are hints
of praise hidden in Lowell's words: poets, by remaining
adolescent or youthfully passionate, may create an art
which "embalms" in the sense of restoring, healing, and
preserving. But his treatment of poetry is largely negative.
The poet sings "offkey"—his art inevitably fails. His "line"
must "terminate"—the line of poetry must end, must even
eventually die in time, and the descended "line" of poets
too must cease. Elaborating his fishing line / poetic line
metaphor, Lowell prophesies that just as his flashing fish
(life's moments of sensual beauty) will pass away, so his
very fishnet (the art that captures that beauty) will perish,
will cease in time to be admired or understood. Yet despite
this despairing vision of the fate of poetry, he continues to
affirm the artistic quest. In the "knotting, undoing" of his
fishnet, in the continual annihilation and renewal of his
art, he has "gladdened a lifetime," his own and ours. He
understands art to be solely an existential gesture of self-
creation and passion for life, a Sisyphian labor. As Camus
wrote of Sisyphus, one must imagine Lowell happy.

Following "Fishnet," the novel-like plot of *The Dolphin*
formally commences. Lowell arrives in England in early

1970 and takes up residence on Redcliffe Square in the Earl's Court section of London. The mid-Victorian buildings take getting used to, for they are foreign and ugly. But they are also curiously familiar. They are the image of Lowell himself. Trembling, "aboriginal," "sour," unappeased by time, and "condemned by age, rebuilt by desolation," they signal both his pain and his potential for renewal (*D*, 16). This architectural metaphor is filled out later in the poem, when he reveals himself in the image of the revarnished floor of his restored country home, aged but newly bright (*D*, 59). There is a sense in which *The Dolphin* is a Jamesian novel about an American's discovery of English culture, but in a deeper sense the book concerns a quest for self-rediscovery. In this sense Lowell's London is perhaps closer to Thoreau's Walden, a symbol of the author's essential self, than to James's London, Paris, or Rome. Lowell makes the true meaning of his voyage clear later on in the poem: "Change I earth or sky I am the same" (*D*, 66).

On a stormy night soon after arriving in London, Lowell becomes reacquainted with Caroline, whom he first met four years before in New York. The two begin an affair which is at first sensually pleasing but emotionally "estranged," so estranged that he contemplates Aztec rites of human sacrifice, so estranged that he thinks he "might be home" (*D*, 17). His emotional divorce is complicated by other forms of divorce—the American "lancing" of Cambodia in early May, his impending divorce from Lizzie, a brief separation from Caroline while she tours Scotland—and he feels the onset of madness, his "old infection" (*D*, 18). The figure of the dolphin, potentially a mystical presence and a symbol of illumination, now appears to him only as a tawdry ornament on his toilet stand, rebuking and "crazy," a sign of his emotional and imaginative breakdown.

"Hospital," "Hospital II," and "Caroline" recount Lowell's hospitalization in July and August of 1970. The institution closely resembles those images of confinement and alienation present in nearly all his previous books, from the "cage" in *Lord Weary's Castle* to the "slummy cell" and "foxholes" in *Near the Ocean*. The hospital sections represent the nadir of *The Dolphin* as sequence. Medicated and confused, Lowell is unfree, unable to perceive correctly, unable to imagine, out of his mind and his world. He is as far from the dolphin as he could possibly be. Separated from the muse, he thinks his poems "tapeworms" or a "knife," a threat to his life (*D*, 20). Alienated from Eros, he does not even recognize Caroline when she visits (*D*, 22). When Lizzie visits and later when she writes, he recognizes *her* tone of voice all too well; he shouts into the air but cannot "reach" her hurt, accusing "black silhouette" (*D*, 23). Clinging "foolishly alone," Lowell transforms all phenomena—even a phrase from Caroline's letter from Scotland (*D*, 26, 21), a postcard given him by Lizzie (*D*, 23, 22)—into his own private chamber of horrors. Divorce is the sign of his only knowledge now. Then slowly he begins to recover his interest in the power of art, begins to remember his old love for Lizzie and acknowledge his new love for Caroline (*D*, 24-26); and "hope grows less malign or thinks it might." He recovers sufficiently to leave the hospital, though still depressed, frightened, and withdrawn. "It's safer outside," he reflects, "the car flying forward to hit us, has room to swerve" (*D*, 27).

As the novelistic plot of *The Dolphin* unfolds, Lowell gradually achieves health and ultimately joy. He spends the autumn with Caroline at Milgate, his country house in Kent. Unlike Lizzie, who reveals herself in her quoted letters to be all common sense and decency, all realism, Caroline does not develop as a recognizable person but becomes ever more symbolic—shimmering and ambiguous. As delineated in "Mermaid" (*D*, 35-37), she is beautiful ("Alice-in-Wonderland straight gold hair, / fair-featured, curve and bone") and she is grotesquely ugly ("bulge eyes bigger then your man's closed fist, / slick with humiliation when dismissed"). She is protective and dangerous, fleshly and spiritual, "bright as the morning star or a blond starlet" and monstrous as a "baby killer whale." While Lizzie and Harriet have come to appear, primarily through Lizzie's letters, as ever more human in their strengths and weaknesses, Caroline appears as both less and more than human—half-human, a mermaid, a "singeing conjunction of tail and grace." By the end of the "Mermaid" section, she has momentarily turned wholly symbolic. In one sense she is consuming love and in another, consuming art. Lowell, who has "searched the rough black ocean" for her, draws back from her finally, "glad to escape beguilement and the storm."

Lowell ends the fall season torn between Lizzie and Caroline, between "the dismay of my old world" and "the blank new" (*D*, 42). Winter is worse. Spending weekends alone in London while Caroline and her children are at Milgate, he feels exiled and homesick. "My family," he calls out to Lizzie and Harriet, "why are we so far?" (*D*, 46). Lizzie answers only in rebuke: *"Don't you dare mail us the love your life denies"* (*D*, 48). Then comes a change. In "Before Woman," Lowell and Caroline acknowledge to each other the intensity of their love. They unite in a sexual and spiritual ecstasy, an eternal "Godborne instant":

Darling, the cork, though fat and black, still pulls,
new wine floods our prehistoric veins—
the day breaks, impossible, in our bed.

(*D*, 51)

Thanks to the power of Eros, Lowell is reborn as Adam, poised at the start of a new life—an authentic American quester-hero. Again envisioning his dolphin-mermaid in "Mermaid Emerging" and "Marriage," he now comes boldly to where she is, she who spouts the "smarting waters of joy" in his face, she who "cuts" his "nets and chains" (D, 54). Instead of escaping her "beguilement" as before, he now approaches ever closer:

> I am waiting like an angler with practice and courage;
> the time to cast is now, and the mouth open,
> the huge smile, head and shoulders of the dolphin—
> I am swallowed up alive . . . I am.
>
> (D, 55)

Seeking to catch her, he is caught by her instead. Like Jonah's whale, she acts as an agent of redemption. She swallows him alive and thereby gives him life: swallowed up, he *is*.

"Marriage" contains the climax of Lowell's story: his union with the dolphin. Caroline has become pregnant and in August of 1971 gives birth to his son, Robert Sheridan. His new love has thus borne a miraculous fruit; his new life has given life to a child, an event he compares to the birth of the Christ-Child (D, 61-62). Characteristic of his style and intent in this poem, Lowell leaves the literal facts of this crucial episode unclear. Indeed, it seems that despite the title of this section, a legal marriage to Caroline does not take place at this time. The Dominican Republic divorce from Lizzie has yet to occur (D, 64). But Lowell is not interested in the facts of the case, as he would have been if he were updating *Life Studies*. He is interested only in emotional and imaginative truth. Emotionally and imaginatively he does marry Caroline now. Although forbidden from living with her "under a common name" (D, 56), he begins, in "Late Summer at *Milgate*," to call her "my wife" (D, 59). In his heart he has made a marriage with her, and through her with love, with happiness, with life itself. He wakes each morning "glad," "without old fears," feeling "a happiness so slow burning, it is lasting" (D, 62, 61, 60).

The final sections of *The Dolphin*, its dénouement, occur a year later. With subdued happiness, Lowell tells of a summer spent adapting to a new wife, a year-old son and three stepdaughters. His almost elegiac tone suggests a descent to darkness on extended wings. Their time, he writes, grows "shorter and brighter like the summer"— brightened by an intensity of love that must die (*D*, 63). In December of 1972 he returns to New York to dispose his old life and to spend a last Christmas with Lizzie and Harriet. The elegiac tone deepens; his wings contract. His new life has come to feel rather uncomfortable as he falls away from joy: "the shine and stiffness of a new suit, a feeling, / not wholly happy, of having been reborn" (*D*, 72). Back in the comfortable "déjà-vu" of his old world, he finds himself uncertain what to do with his "stormy life blown towards evening," finds himself waking up at night in tears (*D*, 74-77). He imagines his return to Caroline in ironic antidolphin images: "gaping jaws," "a submarine, / nuclear and protective like a mother," a "shark." The moment of erotic transcendence is over.[8]

At the same time that Lowell chronicles his attainment of joy and his falling away from joy, he layers that chronicle with meditations on the relations between his life story and the artwork that expresses it. His meditations comprise at once a running commentary on the story and a poetics. Thus *The Dolphin* is both a narrative of love's progress and a series of poetic statements about itself, an unfolding story and the story of its own unfolding. Lowell's point is that these two are so thoroughly interwoven as to be inseparable. His love for Caroline has been an affair of consciousness just as is his writing of the poem. And conversely, his writing of the poem is an act of love, as were the events that precipitated it. Lowell sees that his life and art have a coextensive existence. The life gives birth to the art, and the art completes the life, for it culminates his consciousness of that life.

Lowell helps to define the relationship between his life and art by frequently commenting upon his words as he writes them. He begins one fourteen-liner by calling attention to the blank page about to become "defiled / by my inspiration running black in type" (*D*, 46). Throughout, he

225

contemplates the nature and value of his poem. These self-reflexive comments serve a double function. First, they prevent any confusion that the poem is simply equivalent to the life by calling attention to the obvious fact that it *is* being written or invented. But second, they show how, in another way, art is intimately connected to life. Lowell makes us aware that the poem's composition is an act occurring within his life by bringing that composition into the life of the poem. By revealing its own processes of composition, the poem is able to suggest the place that composition occupies in the life of the poet who is at once its subject and its author.

Echoing D. H. Lawrence on the novel, Lowell calls his poetry "a book of life" (*D*, 72), thus implying both that it affirms life and that it contains his own truest life. He muses upon such propositions continuously, but tentatively, willing always to change his way of putting things. At one point, for example, he addresses to Caroline these words about the art-life relationship:

> fiction should serve us with a slice of life;
> but you and I actually lived what I have written.
>
> (*D*, 52)

This is first of all a corrective to his earlier complaint, made while mentally ill, that art is a knife that "slices," or a tapeworm that feeds parasitically off his life (*D*, 20). He now sees art as more life-sustaining than life-threatening. (He even states a few lines earlier, Stevens fashion, that art "should support" [*D*, 52].) Yet in the second quoted line, Lowell suggests a simple identity between what was "actually lived" and what "written." This cannot be entirely true. It ascribes to art a power of representational fidelity it does not in fact possess, and it denies art's very real power to heighten and clarify, to give form, to provide moral illumination.[9]

Later on, Lowell readdresses himself to this question and answers it more carefully:

The Dolphin

Conscience incurable
convinces me I am not writing my life;
life never assures which part of ourself is life.
(D, 59)

He now realizes that he can never be guilty of "writing his
life," for he can never truly know what his life is. Day-to-
day existence is a continuing fiction of the mind; *The Dolphin* is a similar but inevitably different fiction. Although
they are related since both are part of himself, neither fiction is a pale reflection or mimesis of the other. The two are
overlapping but not identical circles. Lowell continues: his
"life" with Caroline

was never a book, though sparks of it
spotted the page with superficial burns;
the fiction I colored with first-hand evidence,
letters and talk I marketed as fiction.
(D, 59)

The Dolphin, then, is not synonymous with what happened
"first-hand," but is sparked and spotted, burned and colored, by the "first-hand." It is indeed a book of life, not
precisely the life Lowell lived but that life as it ignites his
poetic imagination. He frames his dialectic as paradox: the
poem is a fiction with only "superficial" resemblances to
truth or it is truth "marketed as fiction." Finally he turns
the paradox back upon itself, in a concluding question,
"but what is true or false . . . ?" (D, 59). Truth is not bare
facts, empty of human meaning, but the mind that experiences the facts and knows itself in the experiencing, the
mind capable of giving that knowledge form and meaning
in art. It is this truth, of consciousness and imagination,
that *The Dolphin* embodies.

To achieve *The Dolphin*'s particular kind of poetic truth,
Lowell commingles art and life within the very texture of
his language. He does this in two ways. First, he admits
actual conversations and letters into his poem unaltered,

227

except insofar as being selected, put in line form, and placed in the context of the poem inevitably alters them. By allowing into his poem voices other than his own—real voices speaking unaware that their words would eventually appear in a poem—Lowell attempts to replace the "clangorous rhetoric" that he thinks mars Meredith's *Modern Love* with a language torn from life instead. His practice here most directly recalls *Paterson* (and indirectly "Song of Myself"). Like Williams's poem, *The Dolphin* is a collage, but it integrates its foreign materials into its poetic medium and narrative rather than having them stand apart as prose. Lizzie's letters, Caroline's conversations, are *objets trouvés* or "trouvailles" provided by actuality to the poem. In their suffering and humor and contingency they give *The Dolphin* human reality, a ground from which the lyric symbolism of mermaid-dolphin can grow. They also at times reveal an astonishing beauty of their own: Lizzie writing,

> I got the letter
> this morning, the letter you wrote me Saturday.
> I thought my heart would break a thousand times,
> but I would rather have read it a thousand times
> than the detached unreal ones you wrote before.
>
> (D, 31)

Or Caroline saying, "Darling, / we have escaped our death-struggle with our lives" (D, 61). Such passages suggest that everyday life and poetry cannot be divorced, for life becomes poetry all the time, however unexpectedly and unacknowledged.[10]

Lowell's second way of commingling art and life is to regard his life consistently through the metaphor of art. This practice testifies again to his Jamesian notion that one's life, like art, is essentially a form of fiction, a structure of moral and esthetic perception. He introduces this motif at the very outset, when he and Caroline regard a storm through the window of his flat on Redcliffe Square. The stormy scene momentarily becomes a canvas, "the limited window of the easel painter"—a circumscribed but accurate representation of their own emotional turbulence (*D*, 16). Later in the poem he says of himself, "I cannot hang my heavy picture straight. / I can't see myself" (*D*, 28), and later still he compares himself both to Manet and Manet's model (*D*, 52). For Lowell, his life has all the resonances of art, and he himself plays all the roles: artist, model, viewer, depicted character. If his life is not a painting, it is a "movie," a "melodrama," a verse "tragedy," a "common novel" or even *War and Peace* (*D*, 48-51). He interweaves his life with references to all artistic genres, from literature and the plastic arts to achitecture, photography, music, film. Manet's bar-girls, Degas' dancers, Feininger's skyscrapers, a portrait of Dante, Ford's *Good Soldier*, Shakespeare's *Hamlet* and *Macbeth*, Raleigh, Racine, Hölderlin, Carpaccio, even contemporary doggerel (Muhammed Ali's "Float Like a Butterfly and Sting Like a Bee")—all these and more parade through Lowell's pages. They all image in some way the life story unfolding in *The Dolphin*, a story like Shakespeare's of doubt and guilt, like Ford's of passion.

Lowell has several points to make by this overlapping of art and life. First and most simply, we imagine and understand our lives in terms provided by art. Life does indeed, as Wilde contended, imitate art. Second, Lowell's depiction of himself as both the determined character and determining artist captures his inner sense of being both fated and free. As character, he has only a limited "choice of endings" and none at all as to the ultimate ending of death (*D*, 72); as artist, though, he is free, able with the dolphin's help to cut his "net and chains" (*D*, 54). Finally, the artistic references suggest the manner in which conscious life aspires to the condition of art, the superior structure of perception. In showing that his life is already a variety of artwork, a sequence of fictionlike moments, Lowell further diminishes the space between art and life.

The Dolphin does not transform his life into art so much as it takes what was already art in fragment and allows it to become the form of unified artwork it always sought to be.

The Dolphin, then, begins with the dualism of life and art and tries in every possible way to fuse it into a monism. This welding, or wedding, is exemplified by the poem's proliferating verbal ambiguities, most of which involve the life-art dichotomy. *The Dolphin*'s puns are "trouvailles"— lovely hidden meanings waiting to reveal themselves to the observant eye, Thoreauvian invitations to see more deeply. What they invite us to see ultimately is not inner discord, as did the puns of *Lord Weary's Castle*, but wholeness. The puns in *The Dolphin* yoke similarities rather than dissimilarities. They surprise us with two meanings where we had expected only one, and then further surprise us by showing that the two are really one after all. For instance, Lowell claims to "go on typing to go on living" (*D*, 28). This may mean that art alone can give him the purpose necessary to sustain his life, and it may also mean that he truly lives only on his typed page. These two possible meanings reinforce rather than contradict each other. Both point to the interdependency of life and art. The most extended such conceit occurs in "Exorcism" and "Plotted," in which Lowell envisages his life in quick succession as movie, melodrama, novel, and revenge play. He describes his situation as "one man, two women, the common novel plot" (*D*, 48). The double meanings of the last three words allow two different interpretations: his life centers around a plot (conspiracy) which is common (vulgar) and novel (new to him), and his life resembles the plot (story line) of a common (typical) novel (work of fiction). Both readings are true.

Most of the puns in *The Dolphin* are variations on the central pun of its title: the dolphin as double symbol of life-force (Eros) and artistic form (muse). The poem on every page seeks with miraculous inventiveness to unify its doubleness. Its glory lies not in any prolonged attainment of unity, but in the heroic imagination of the quest itself.

In "Dolphin," the final section of the poem, Lowell returns for one last time to his centralizing symbol and achieves its momentary apotheosis.

My·Dolphin, you only guide me by surprise,
forgetful as Racine, the man of craft,
drawn through his maze of iron composition
by the incomparable wandering voice of Phèdre.
When I was troubled in mind, you made for my body
caught in its hangman's-knot of sinking lines,
the glassy bowing and scraping of my will. . . .
I have sat and listened to too many
words of the collaborating muse,
and plotted perhaps too freely with my life,
not avoiding injury to others,
not avoiding injury to myself—
to ask compassion . . . this book, half fiction,
an eelnet made by man for the eel fighting—

my eyes have seen what my hand did.

"Dolphin," the poem's epilogue, rhymes in its language and ideas with "Fishnet," the prologue. Its fifteen lines supply what the thirteen-line prologue lacks. The two "sonnet" structures, like their subjects life and art, are imperfect individually but potentially perfect together. When fitted together, they suggest what *The Dolphin* has been all about, what Lowell's poetic career has been all about. They arc over the poem like a rainbow, a sign of peace.

In "Fishnet" Lowell could only praise the dolphin from afar, as a shimmering and transforming presence, baffling intimacy. Indeed "Fishnet" contains hints of futility, even of terror. In "Dolphin," however, he has achieved a union with her. Where once she blinded him with surprise, now she only guides him by surprise. Where once her "wandering silences" drew him, now it is her "wandering voice."

Where once she eluded his grasp, now she swims toward
him unbidden. The "fishnet," catcher of life, has turned
"eelnet," fighter of time. The "dolphin" has become holy
"Dolphin." Lowell now sees to the bottom of his being.
Brilliantly resurrecting the pun in the word "plot," he
apologizes for "collaborating" with the muse too often, at
times without inspiration. He similarly apologizes for a life
in which he has injured himself and others. In profound
humility he accepts responsibility for all his art and life, for
all that his eye has seen and his hand has done. After a
lifetime of kicking against the pricks, Lowell, in a moment
of spiritual insight, unconditionally accepts his world and
himself. The "dolphin" now, at the last, transcends both
Eros and the muse, though she contains both. She is
earthly grace.

"We are poor passing facts"

By early 1977 his marriage to Caroline Blackwood had
seemingly reached its end, and Lowell was back in Manhattan living with Elizabeth Hardwick. After a strenuous State Department-sponsored tour of the Soviet Union
in late June, and before the scheduled beginning of his fall
teaching semester at Harvard, he flew to Dublin for a
week's visit with Caroline and Sheridan. Returning from
this trip on September 12, he seemed tired. He was in a
"dry or vacation moment" in which writing poems was
difficult. Further, he was suffering from continuing
physical ailments in the aftermath of congestive heart fail-
ure.the previous year. Riding in a taxicab from Kennedy
Airport toward home, he slumped over in his seat, and
when the cab arrived at his door, the driver could not
rouse him. The poet's enlarged heart had finally failed
him. Lowell died as he lived and wrote, in the midst of a
journey through a world of lost connections, moving toward a destination he would never reach. In the book he

"We are poor passing facts"

had published just days before, called *Day by Day*, he had prophesied:

> I will leave earth
> with my shoes tied,
> as if the walk
> could cut bare feet.
> (*DBD*, 62)[11]

The funeral was held four days after his death, in the baroque splendor of the Church of the Advent in Boston's Beacon Hill. There was both poignancy and irony in such a funeral. "It was," said a friend, "like a poem by Cal—only he's not here to write it." The Episcopalian solemn requiem mass was attended by Elizabeth Hardwick and Caroline Blackwood (both distraught with grief), his two children, and hundreds of friends and fellow writers, including Peter Taylor, Elizabeth Bishop, Frank Parker, and Saul Bellow. Allen Tate was too ill to attend; and William Carlos Williams was dead, as were so many others— Ransom, Pound, Eliot, Roethke, Berryman, Schwartz, Plath, Jarrell. Lowell was buried, in accordance with his wishes, in the Dunbarton cemetery where as a child he had helped rake leaves from the graves of his forebears. "The immortal" was thus "scraped unconsenting from the mortal" (*DBD*, 50): Lowell became, as Auden said of Yeats, his admirers. [12]

After he finished *The Dolphin* in 1973, Lowell wrote to a friend, "the barrel is empty," but as so often before, the barrel was refilled. The result was *Day by Day*, a volume that both "carries on the old story" and begins something new. If *The Dolphin* was Lowell's ultimate poem, *Day by Day* is a postultimate work, almost a postpoetic work. His experience is not "worked up" as in all his previous books, but boiled down to its essence. Although the title sequence continues the story begun in *The Dolphin*, he abandons his complex dolphin-mermaid symbology and tries simply to "say what happened" (*DBD*, 127). Most of the poems would suffer by being anthologized; isolated from their context, they would seem mere associative jotting. But taken together, they add up to a major new advance in what Helen Vendler has termed Lowell's effort "to break the icon—to dismember and reconstitute the English lyric." If Lowell does break the icon in *Day by Day*, he does so not merely to be breaking icons (however much he might enjoy that activity), but also to be making a new artistic freedom—the freedom to focus, without artifice, on his daily moments as they really are.[13]

The book begins and ends strongly with poems in a public mode, "Ulysses and Circe" and "George III," in which personal concerns and even implicit self-depiction are contained in impersonal structures. In the long title sequence of the book, however, Lowell reveals himself without disguise, a text denuded of context. The "Day by Day" sequence is probably the most completely personal work Lowell ever wrote, as if like Emerson in "Experience" he had for once "set [his] heart on honesty." "What I write about" in "Day by Day," he remarked, "almost always comes out of the pressure of some inner concern, temptation or obsessive puzzle." It is his most deliberately Freudian work. The poems, developing through a process close to free association, bring content from his unconscious into the light of consciousness. At the same time they also look intensely at the outer, factual world, as Lowell rejects the abstractness of *History* and *The Dolphin*. The poet's great autobiographical venture thus concludes quietly, in fragments of free verse that are at once private and transparent. The circus animals have not exactly deserted, they have been put back in the cage, and the ringmaster stands alone in the ring, leaning for support, speaking softly as himself.[14]

"We are poor passing facts"

In "Day by Day" Lowell exposes moments of his life between 1973 and 1976, during which his marriage to
Caroline decays and he himself approaches old age. "I fear
it comes close to tragic," he explained, "though that's not
clear either in the book or life." The end of the marriage
does not appear in the sequence itself, but in several of the
poems in the first part of the volume: obliquely in "Ulysses
and Circe" and more openly in "Last Walk?," "Suicide,"
and "Departure." These last three may be read as poems
within a poem, since Lowell depicts himself composing
one of them at the end of "Day by Day" (*DBD*, 118). The
sequence does not conclude with an explicit description of
marital dissolution because its overriding theme is not
union, as in *The Dolphin*, but the power of the individual,
despite age and illness, to bear his life, to learn to understand and even prize it. [15]

The first section of "Day by Day" takes place in summer
and early autumn of 1973 at Milgate, Lowell and Caroline's
home in Kent. The introductory poem, "The Day," indicates Lowell's themes (which are familiar) and his methods
(which are new):

> It's amazing
> the day is still here
> like lightning on an open field. . . .
>
> (*DBD*, 53)

He joyously celebrates his intense perception of life, but
also suggests, through his astonished tone, his foreboding
sense of death. (Later in the poem he writes, "we lived
momently," implying both "momentously" and "momentarily.") Things seem to him as "fresh as when man first
broke"—"broke" in the prelapsarian sense of *broke out*
(came into being) but also in the postlapsarian sense of
broke up (destroyed, died). Hoping to understand this inner
conflict by raiding his unconscious, he lets his mind wan-
der. The sight of cows in the noonday sun reminds him of
"child's daubs in a book / I read before I could read." As-

sociating natural joy and peace with infancy, he must now account somehow for his present happiness in an adult life he inherently associates with danger and pain. He accomplishes this through use of the subjunctive:

> as if in the end
> in the marriage with nothingness,
> we could ever escape
> being absolutely safe.
>
> (*DBD*, 53)

This conclusion suggests that even the Sartrean self, constructed of nothingness and destined only for conflict, is really as "safe" as a child in its parents' house, as Adam in paradise. Yet children soon grow to terror, just as Adam fell from grace; despite flash-in-the-pan moments of joy there is danger everywhere, and the only absolute safety the poet can point to is that of "the end" or death. Lowell's method of apparent randomness in this poem is in fact a way for him to probe both his feelings of happiness, which he unconsciously associates with early childhood, and his equally real feelings of dread which underlie that happiness. He reveals his psyche to us, and we as readers feel, if not the shock of recognition, then at least the pleasure of empathy.

As summer turns to autumn, Lowell continues to experience his pastoral surroundings and to contemplate that experience. Repeatedly he sees and thinks in images of change, decline, arrest and loss: "neglected" houses, "crumbling" trees, "lost" spirits and toys, "things gone" (*DBD*, 54, 59, 60, 68, 57). And repeatedly he returns to himself as a younger man or child, on the implicit premise that past experience can explain present feelings, that memory may contain a needful clue. This section concludes in "The Withdrawal," in which the images of loss and the obsessive interest in the past come together. The seasonal decline mirrors the decline of Lowell's marriage: love like summer's warmth has withdrawn, leaving him

alone, chilled, old, "despondent chaff" in a harvested field
(*DBD*, 72). Instinctively he free-associates to childhood's
moment of joyous freedom (*DBD*, 73); and then to his early
manhood in which childish "license" became rootlessness
and loneliness; and then inevitably to his present isolation
which, like that of "Skunk Hour," seems to him like hell.
The poem, and this section of the sequence, ends in contemplation of death, the ultimate isolation. Lowell is rush-
ing headlong toward a psychic chaos he senses but cannot
yet comprehend.

In the second section of the sequence the isolation and
distress increase. Lowell returns to Boston to teach at Harvard, leaving Caroline behind. Being alone in the locale of
his childhood accelerates his process of associating backward into the painful past, where he discerns prefigure-
ments of his present condition, but not the essential key.
In "Robert T. S. Lowell" he fantasizes a meeting between
his father and himself, who resemble one another. The
father, articulate in fantasy as never in life, charges his un-
protesting son with failures identical to his own: "It's your
life, and dated like mine" (*DBD*, 81). In "To Mother" Lowell allows his wandering mind to pass from a similar sense
of self-identification with his mother to more sublimated
feelings—erotic attachment (the "seductive" stem of her
lily makes him "wish I were there with you"), which instantly becomes rejection ("but not forever"), which in
turn becomes guilty acceptance of her ("you are as human
as I am . . .") and self-hatred ("if I am") (*DBD*, 78-79).
Buried enigmatically within this psychic twisting and turning is a clue to his turmoil: "Becoming ourselves, / we lose
our nerve for children." In this bent epigram we catch a
glimpse of the wound at his core, a wound he can expose
to light only at the end of the sequence.

The final section of "Day by Day" takes place back in
England, after a lapse of two years. The time is early 1976,
and Lowell is nearing fifty-nine. In a series of non-
Coleridgean conversation poems, he addresses the flow of

his thoughts to Caroline, who now is no symbolic dolphin at all but merely human—self-centered, reproachful, vulnerable, striking out against him as their love inexorably recedes. These are "days of poems and depression" for Lowell (*DBD*, 118), who is composing the very sequence we are now reading. It remains unclear whether he writes in order to divert himself from his mounting depression or whether the intensity of writing itself precipitates the crisis. Whatever the exact causal relationship, he has embarked on a quest for psychological truth even as his psyche collapses. He fears that his quest will fail, that his "lies" will triumph, that he will find "no truth" in "this processing of words" (as if his poetic process were a mere mechanical processing) (*DBD*, 108). Yet he persists. In harrowing poems he tells of his removal to a mental hospital. The police who deliver him prove correct: he doesn't need his Dante here, for he himself has entered purgatory, "committed" both to a hospital and to his own madness (*DBD*, 111, 113). His stiffened and numbed feelings find their catharsis in a humor that expresses human tragedy as incongruous comedy, a saving humor that pays tribute to sanity in the midst of insanity. Lowell's doctors love him and wish he would stay always:

> "A model guest . . . we would welcome
> Robert back to Northampton any time,
> the place suits him."
>
> (*DBD*, 114)

Caroline, however, does not love him any longer, understanding his illness "only as desertion" (*DBD*, 114).

Lowell recovers by forcing himself to notice "what I cannot bear to look at," the phenomenal world and his own unconscious (*DBD*, 118). In the pivotal poem of the sequence, "Unwanted," he looks unblinkingly at an unbearable psychic wound, which his marital estrangement has evidently reopened: he was unwanted, not only by his distant father but by his beloved mother as well, unwanted at the start just as he is unwanted and unwantable now. Thus

was born the poet of alienation, the poet who began his
first book with the word "exile" (*LWC*, 3) and his last with
"fugitive" (*DBD*, 4), the poet whose struggle to overcome
his sense of estrangement shaped everything he ever
wrote.

> Is the one unpardonable sin
> our fear of being unwanted?
> For this will mother go on cleaning house
> for eternity, and making it unlivable?
> Is getting well ever an art,
> or art a way to get well?
>
> (*DBD*, 124)

Lowell's art of psychological truth does prove a way for
him to get well, because it diminishes his heart's isolation—for him, as for Hawthorne, the one "unpardonable
sin." Able to name his wound for the first time in forty
years, he begins his cure. He completes his sequence "free
of the terror that made me write" (*DBD*, 126).

In "Epilogue," a last testament, Lowell affirms the artistic ideal of *Day by Day*, and implicitly of all his poetry, even
while denigrating his actual achievement. He ends his
career paying equal homage to the created world and the
human eye that apprehends the world creatively. The vision of the artist, he believes, "trembles to caress the light"
(*DBD*, 127); it tries to possess life, not merely passively, in
the manner of naive empirical realism, but actively, imaginatively, lovingly. Art, then, is ultimately passion for existence. The artist, an inspired namer, strives for the
"grace of accuracy" that makes consciousness momentarily coextensive with reality. He seeks to restore the lost
connections between human beings and the world they
inhabit so fleetingly.

> We are poor passing facts,
> warned by that to give
> each figure in the photograph
> his living name.

Chronology

1917   Robert Traill Spence Lowell, Jr. born March 1 in Boston, the only child of Robert Traill Spence Lowell, USN, and Charlotte Winslow Lowell. Descendant of Pilgrim father Edward Winslow (1595-1655), Plymouth colony governor Josiah Winslow (1629-1680), and Revolutionary War soldier John Stark (1728-1822); great-grandnephew of Episcopal clergyman Robert Traill Spence Lowell (1816-1891) and poet James Russell Lowell (1819-1891); distant cousin of astronomer Percival Lowell (1855-1916), president of Harvard Abbott Lawrence Lowell (1856-1943), and poet Amy Lowell (1874-1925).

1924   Lowell family settles in Boston after periods in Washington, D.C. and Philadelphia.

1924-30   Brimmer School (Boston).

1930-35   St. Mark's School (Southborough, Mass.). Studies with Richard Eberhart; befriends Frank Parker.

1935-37   Harvard University.

1937   Spring and summer with Allen Tate at Clarksville, Tenn. Decides to transfer to Kenyon College in the fall.

1937-40   Kenyon College. Studies under John Crowe Ransom; befriends Randall Jarrell and Peter Taylor. Graduates summa cum laude in Classics.

1940   Converts to Roman Catholicism. Marries Jean Stafford on April 2.

1940-41   Teaches English at Kenyon College. Graduate study in English at LSU.

1941-42   Editorial assistant at Sheed & Ward Publishers in New York.

1942-43   Works on *Land of Unlikeness* manuscript during year's stay with Allen Tate and Caroline Gordon at Monteagle, Tenn.

Chronology

1943 Refuses induction into armed service. Sentenced in October to a year and a day for violation of Selective Service Act; serves five months in federal prison at Danbury, Conn. and West Street jail in New York. Parole in Black Rock, Conn.

1944 *Land of Unlikeness*. Jean Stafford's novel *Boston Adventure*. Move to Damariscotta Mills, Maine; then residence in New York.

1946 *Lord Weary's Castle* (Pulitzer Prize for poetry).

1947 Guggenheim Fellowship.

1947-48 Poetry Consultant to the Library of Congress in Washington, D.C.

1948 Divorce from Jean Stafford.

1948-49 Yaddo Writers' Colony.

1949 Returns to New York. Member of committee awarding the first Bollingen Prize (for 1948) to Pound's *Pisan Cantos*. Hospitalized for mental disturbance in March. Marries Elizabeth Hardwick on July 28.

1950 *Poems 1938-49*. Teaches creative writing at the University of Iowa, spring term. Teaches at Kenyon College School of English, summer. Father dies.

1950-53 Extended European sojourn.

1951 *The Mills of the Kavanaughs* (Harriet Monroe Prize).

1952 Supports Stevenson for president. Teaches at the Seminar in American Studies at Salzburg.

1953 Teaches at the University of Iowa. Colleagues include Paul Engle and John Berryman; students include W. D. Snodgrass. Teaches at the summer workshop at the University of Indiana.

1954 Lectures at the University of Cincinnati. Mother dies in February. Returns to New York, then moves to Boston. Mental disturbance and recovery.

1954-60 Lowell and Hardwick live on Marlborough Street, in Back Bay, Boston.

Chronology

1955-60 Teaches at Boston University. Students include Sylvia Plath, Anne Sexton, and George Starbuck.

1957 Daughter Harriet Winslow Lowell born on Jan. 4. West Coast speaking tour, March 20-April 7. Begins to write "Skunk Hour" and other "Life Studies" poems at summer home in Castine, Maine.

1958 Hospitalization for mental disturbance in Jan. Continues work in Boston on "Life Studies" sequence.

1959 *Life Studies* (National Book Award for poetry). Shares Guiness Poetry Award with W. H. Auden and Edith Sitwell.

1960 Reads "For the Union Dead" at Boston Festival of the Arts on June 5. Moves to New York. Supports Kennedy for president.

1960-70 Lowell and Hardwick live on upper west side in Manhattan.

1961 *Imitations* (Harriet Monroe Prize and shares Bollingen Translation Prize). *Phaedra*.

1963-77 Teaches at Harvard (with leave 1970-71; commutes from England for one semester a year, 1973-76). Students include Frank Bidart.

1964 *For the Union Dead. The Old Glory.* "My Kinsman, Major Molineux" and "Benito Cereno" premiere at the American Place Theatre in New York on Nov. 1 (Obie Award). Ford grant for drama.

1965 Publicly declines President Johnson's invitation to the White House Festival of the Arts in protest against the Vietnam war. *Phaedra* premieres at Wesleyan University.

1966 Defeated for Oxford Chair of Poetry by English neo-Georgian poet Edmund Blunden. Wins Sarah Josepha Hale Award for distinguished contribution to New England literature.

1967 *Near the Ocean.* Participates in anti-Vietnam war march on Pentagon. Writer-in-residence at Yale School of Drama. *Prometheus Bound* premieres at Yale on May 9.

Chronology

1968   *The Old Glory*, revised edition. "Endecott and the Red Cross" premieres at the American Place Theatre in New York on April 18. Campaigns for Eugene McCarthy in Democratic primaries; refuses to vote for president in November.

1969   *Notebook 1967-68*. *Prometheus Bound*.

1970   *Notebook*. Visiting Fellow, All Souls' College, Oxford.

1970-76 Residence in England.

1970-72 Teaches at Essex University.

1971   Son Robert Sheridan Lowell born to Lowell and Caroline Blackwood.

1972   Divorce from Elizabeth Hardwick, marriage to Caroline Blackwood in October.

1973   *The Dolphin* (Pulitzer Prize for poetry). *History*. *For Lizzie and Harriet*.

1974   *Robert Lowell's Poems: A Selection* (ed. Jonathan Raban). Copernicus Award for lifetime achievement in poetry.

1976   *Selected Poems*.

1977   *Day by Day* (National Book Critics Circle Award). *Selected Poems*, rev. ed. American Academy and Institute of Arts and Letters National Medal for Literature. Returns to residence in the United States without Caroline Blackwood. Summer in Castine, Maine with Elizabeth Hardwick. Dies of heart failure in New York, Sept. 12. Funeral in Boston, Sept. 16; burial in family plot at Dunbarton, N.H.

1978   *The Oresteia of Aeschylus* published posthumously.

Appendix A

Poems Lowell Copied into His Notebooks, 1939-1943

Non-English

Dante: Canto V of *The Purgatorio*
Horace: Book II of *Carminium*

Renaissance

Thomas Carew: "Elegy on Maria Wentworth"
Richard Crashaw: "Hymn to St. Theresa"
Samuel Daniel: "Ulysses," "The Siren"
John Donne: "The Apparition," "Holy Sonnets" VII, XIII, XIV, "A Valediction: Forbidding Mourning," "A Nocturnal upon St. Lucy's Day," "The Relique"
George Herbert: "Hope," "Church Monuments," "Pilgrimage," "Redemption," "Death," "Employment," "Frailty," "Trinity Sunday," "The Collar" (twice), "The Pulley"
Robert Herrick: "To Blossoms," "Upon Ben Jonson," "An Ode for Him," "Cherry-Ripe"
Ben Jonson: "Epitaph on Elizabeth, L. H."
Christopher Marlowe: passage from *Dr. Faustus*
Andrew Marvell: "The Definition of Love"
John Milton: "On Shakespeare," "On Time," "An Epitaph on the Marchioness of Winchester," opening lines of Book 1 and passage from Book 3 of *Paradise Lost*, "When the Assault Was Intended to the City" (Sonnet VIII), "To the Lord General Fairfax" (Sonnet XV), passage from *Samson Agonistes*
Sir Walter Raleigh: "The Lie," "On the Life of Man"
William Shakespeare: passages from *Measure for Measure*, *King Lear*, *Othello*, *Hamlet*, and *Macbeth*

245

Appendix A

Eighteenth and Early Nineteenth Century

William Blake: "Ah! Sun-flower"
Alexander Pope: passages from "Epistle to Dr. Arbuthnot," "An Essay on Criticism," and "The Rape of the Lock"
William Wordsworth: "She Dwelt Among the Untrodden Ways," "On the Frozen Lake," passage from "Tintern Abbey"

Late Nineteenth and Twentieth Century

W. H. Auden: "Dover" (first six stanzas)
R. P. Blackmur: sections eight, nine ("Mirage"), and thirteen ("Seas Incarnadine") of "Sea Island Miscellany"
Robert Bridges: "Low Barometer"
Hart Crane: "Repose of Rivers," "Voyages" II, "For the Marriage of Faustus and Helen" II
Emily Dickinson: "Because I Could Not Stop for Death," "If You Were Coming," "I Found the Words to Every Thought," "A Thought Went Up My Mind Today," "The Last Night that She Lived"
T. S. Eliot: passage from "Ash Wednesday"
Gerard Manley Hopkins: "No Worst, There is None," "Spring and Fall," "Spring," "The Blessed Virgin Compared to the Air We Breathe"
Louis MacNeice: "Bagpipe Music"
John Crowe Ransom: "Painted Head" (twice)
Karl Shapiro: "Necropolis"
Wallace Stevens: passages from "Sunday Morning" (thrice), "Le Monocle de Mon Oncle" (third stanza), "On the Manner of Addressing Clouds," "Of Heaven Considered as a Tomb," "The Death of a Soldier"
Allen Tate: "The Cross"
Dylan Thomas: "Altar-wise by Owl-light," "Poem for Caitlin"
William Butler Yeats: "All Souls' Night," "The Second Coming"

Appendix B

Three Versions of Section Three of "My Last Afternoon with Uncle Devereux Winslow" and a Draft of "Skunk Hour"

1.

Up in the air,
by the sunset window in the billiards-room,
my Great Aunt Sarah
was learning the *Overture to the Flying Dutchman*,
and thundered on the keyboard of her dummy piano.
With gauze skirts like a boudoir table,
accordion-like, yet soundless,
it had been bought to spare the nerves
of my Grandmother Winslow,
tone-deaf, quick as a cricket—
now grousing through a paper-bound *Zola*, and saying:
"Why does Sally thump forever
on a toy no one can hear?"

Forty years earlier,
twenty, auburn-headed, a virtuoso
wept over by Liszt,
Aunt Sarah, the Winslows' only "genius,"
had lifted her archaic Athenian nose,
and jilted an Astor.
Each morning she had practiced
on the grand piano at Symphony Hall,
deathlike in the off-season summer—
its naked Greek statues draped with purple
like the saints during Holy Week . . .
On concert day, Miss Winslow could not appear.

Now her investments were made by her Brother.
Her career
was a danger-signal for the nieces.

Appendix B

High above us,
Aunt Sarah lifted a hand
from the dead keys of the dummy piano,
and declaimed grandly:
"Barbarism lies behind me;
mannerism is ahead."

(Yale and SUNY, Buffalo)

2.

Up in the the air
by the lakeview window in the billiards-room,
lurid in the doldrums of the sunset hour,
my Great Aunt Laura
was learning *Samson and Delilah*.
She thundered on the keyboard of her dummy piano
with gauze skirts like her boudoir table,
accordionlike yet soundless.
It had been bought to spare the nerves
of my grandmother,
tone-deaf, quick as a cricket,
now needing a fourth for *Auction*,
and casting a thirsty eye
on Aunt Laura, risen like the Phoenix
from her bed of troublesome snacks and Tauchnitz classics.

Forty years earlier,
twenty, auburn-headed,
the Winslows' only *genius*!
Family gossip says
she tilted her archaic Athenian nose
and jilted an Astor.
Each morning she practiced
on the grand piano at Symphony Hall,
deathlike in the off-season summer—
its naked Greek statues draped with purple
like the saints in Holy Week . . .
On the concert day, she failed to appear.

Child-like, childless
Nothing atones
for failure in Boston.
Gone Aunt Laura's

Appendix B

grasshopper notes of genius,
corrupted by the overcordial fingering
of *Liszt*, her master,
those afternoons, when high above us,
she lifted a hand from the piano
and put away worldly things
for *Parsival* and *Samson*.
Barbarism lay behind her,
the Philistines were in the wings.

(SUNY, Buffalo)

3.

Up in the air
by the lakeview window in the billiards-room,
lurid in the doldrums of the sunset hour,
my Great Aunt Sarah
was learning *Samson and Delilah*.
She thundered on the keyboard of her dummy piano,
with gauze curtains like a boudoir table,
accordionlike yet soundless.
It had been bought to spare the nerves
of my Grandmother,
tone-deaf, quick as a cricket,
now needing a fourth for "Auction,"
and casting a thirsty eye
on Aunt Sarah, risen like the phoenix
from her bed of troublesome snacks and Tauchnitz classics.

Forty years earlier,
twenty, auburn headed,
grasshopper notes of genius!
Family gossip says Aunt Sarah
tilted her archaic Athenian nose
and jilted an Astor.
Each morning she practiced
on the grand piano at Symphony Hall,
deathlike in the off-season summer—
its naked Greek statues draped with purple
like the saints in Holy Week. . . .
On the recital day, she failed to appear.

(*LS*)

249

Appendix B

"Inspiration" (a draft of "Skunk Hour")

The season's ill;
Yesterday Deer Isle fishermen
Threw Captain Greenwright's wreaths into the channel
And wooed his genius for their race
In the yachtsmen's yawls. A red fox stain
Covers Blue Hill.

Beaten by summer,
I hear a hollow, sucking moan
Inside my wild heart's prison cell;
The slow wave loosens stone from stone
By bleeding. I myself am hell;
I hate the summer,

But cannot move it.
My shades are drawn, my daylight bulb is on;
Writing verses like a Turk,
I lie in bed from sun to sun—
There is no money in this work,
You have to love it.

On a dark night,
My old Ford climbs the hill's bald skull;
I look for love-cars. Lights turned down,
They lie together, hull to hull,
Where the graveyard shelves on the town;
My mind's not right—

It's the moon's search,
All elbows, crashing on a tree,
Downhill and homeward. My home-fire
Whitens deadly and royally
Under the chalk-dry and pure spire
Of a Trinitarian church.

My headlights glare
On a galvanized bucket crumpling up—
A skunk glares in a garbage pail.
It jabs its trowel-head in a cup
Of sour cream, drops its ostrich tail,
And cannot scare.

(SUNY, Buffalo)

Notes

Where no author is given, the item is by Lowell. References to Lowell's volumes are abbreviated as in the text. References to Lowell's interviews have been abbreviated as follows:

McCormick: John McCormick, "Falling Alseep over Grillparzer," *Poetry*, Jan. 1953, pp. 269-79.

Brooks & Warren: Cleanth Brooks and Robert Penn Warren, *Conversations on the Craft of Poetry* (New York: Holt, Rinehart, 1961), pp. 32-47.

Seidel: Frederick Seidel, "Interview with Robert Lowell," *Paris Review*, 25 (1961); rpt. *Writers at Work: The Paris Review Interviews*, 2nd series, ed. George Plimpton (New York: Viking, 1963), pp. 337-68.

Alvarez, *Observer*: A. Alvarez, "Robert Lowell in Conversation," *London Observer*, July 21, 1963, p. 19.

Alvarez, *Review*: A. Alvarez, "Robert Lowell in Conversation," *The Review*, No. 8 (Aug. 1963), 36-40.

Kunitz: Stanley Kunitz, "Talk with Robert Lowell," *New York Times Book Review*, Oct. 4, 1964, pp. 34-39.

Alvarez, *Encounter*: A. Alvarez, "Talk with Robert Lowell," *Encounter*, Feb. 1965, pp. 39-43.

Gilman: Richard Gilman, "Life Offers No Neat Conclusions," *New York Times*, May 5, 1968, section 2, pp. 1, 5.

Naipaul: V. S. Naipaul, "Et in America ego," *The Listener*, Sept. 4, 1969, pp. 302-304.

Young: Dudley Young, "Talk with Robert Lowell," *New York Times Book Review*, April 4, 1971, pp. 31-32.

Hamilton: Ian Hamilton, "Conversation with Robert Lowell," *The Review*, No. 26 (1971); rpt. *Modern Occasions*, 2 (Winter 1972), 28-48.

Chapter I

1 *DBD*, 8. Naipaul, 304. Young, 32.

2 Pearce, *The Continuity of American Poetry* (1961; rev. ed., Princeton: Princeton Univ. Press, 1965), p. 10. Lowell, "Digressions from Larkin's 20th-Century Verse," *Encounter*, May 1973, p. 66.

3 "After Enjoying Six or Seven Essays On Me," *Salmagundi*, No. 37 (Spring 1977), p. 113. Seidel, 352.

4 Review of *Maule's Curse*, *Hika*, April 1939, p. 18.

Notes to Pages 6-11

5 Seidel, 342-46, 368. Eliot, "Tradition and the Individual Talent." Naipaul, 304.

6 Alvarez, *Review*, 34. Emerson, "The Poet." James to H. G. Wells, July 10, 1915, *Letters of Henry James*, II, ed. Percy Lubbock (New York: Scribner, 1920), p. 490. Alvarez, *Encounter*, 43.

7 Alvarez, *Encounter*, 43.

8 Waggoner, *American Poets from the Puritans to the Present* (Boston: Houghton Mifflin, 1968), xii. Poirier, *A World Elsewhere: The Place of Style in American Literature* (New York: Oxford Univ. Press, 1966), p. 214. Bloom, *A Map of Misreading* (New York: Oxford Univ. Press, 1975), p. 162. Lowell, "New England," unpublished essay in *N* MS (Harvard).

9 Emerson, "The Poet." "New England," *N* MS (Harvard). "Address of Robert Lowell," National Book Awards, March 23, 1960 (press release, Yale). Alvarez, *Observer*, 19.

10 Rahv, *Image and Idea* (New York: New Directions, 1957), p. 9. Whitman, "Song of Myself." Pound, "The Rest." Stevens, "Esthétique du Mal." Moore, "Poetry." Crane, "For the Marriage of Faustus and Helen." Williams, "The Red Wheelbarrow." Affirmation of individual experience fostered by democratic idealism: Alexis de Tocqueville, in contemplating the likely effects of "equality of conditions as the creative element" in American society, saw clearly that the experience of the individual person would prove the great subject of American poetry:

> There is no need to traverse earth and sky to find a wondrous object full of contrasts of infinite greatness and littleness, of deep gloom and amazing brightness, capable at the same time of arousing piety, wonder, scorn, and terror. I have only to contemplate myself. . . . Among a democratic people poetry will not feed on legends or on traditions and memories of old days. The poet will not try to people the universe again with supernatural beings in whom neither his readers nor he himself any longer believes, nor will he coldly personify virtues and vices better seen in their natural state. All these resources fail him, but man remains, and the poet needs no more.

(*Democracy in America*, I, "Author's Introduction"; II, "On Some Sources of Poetic Inspiration in Democracies.")

11 Emerson, "The Poet." Brooks, *America's Coming-of-Age* (1915); rpt. in *Van Wyck Brooks: The Early Years*, ed. Claire Sprague (New York: Harper, 1968), pp. 82, 86. Fussell, *Frontier: American Literature and the American West* (Princeton: Princeton Univ. Press, 1965), pp. 3-25. Rahv, "Paleface and Redskin," *Image and Idea*, pp. 1-6. Santayana, "The Poetry of Barbarism" (1900) and "The Genteel Tradition in

American Philosophy" (1911), rpt. in *Selected Critical Writings*, ed.
Norman Henfrey (London: Cambridge Univ. Press, 1968), I, pp. 84-
116, and II, pp. 85-107. Lawrence, *Studies in the Classic American Literature* (1924; rpt. New York: Viking, 1964). Pearce, *The Continuity of
American Poetry* (note 2). Lewis, *The American Adam* (Chicago: Univ.
of Chicago Press, 1955). "Address of Robert Lowell," National Book
Awards, March 23, 1960. Richard Chase, *The American Novel and its
Tradition* (Garden City, N.Y.: Doubleday Anchor, 1957), p. 1. Emerson, "The Poet." On "cooked" and "raw" poetry, Lowell went on to
explain: "The cooked, marvelously expert, often seems laboriously
concocted to be tasted and digested by a graduate seminar. The raw,
huge blood-dripping gobbets of unseasoned experience are dished up
for midnight listeners [clearly the Beat poets are in mind here]. There
is a poetry that can only be studied, and a poetry that can only be declaimed, a poetry of pedantry, and a poetry of scandal."

12 Lowell to William Carlos Williams, Jan. 22, 1958, Nov. 29, 1958 (Yale).
Lowell to Axelrod, Feb. 10, 1974. Naipaul, 304. Eliot, *Knowledge and
Experience in the Philosophy of F. H. Bradley* (1916); rpt. (New York: Far-
rar, Straus, 1964), pp. 157, 21.

13 *H*, 203. "New England," *N* MS (Harvard).

14 "After Enjoying Six or Seven Essays On Me" (note 3), p. 112. Alvarez,
Encounter, 43.

Chapter II

1 Matthiessen, *Oxford Book of American Verse* (New York: Oxford Univ.
Press, 1950), xxiv. "Moulding the Golden Spoon," *Hika* (Kenyon Col-
lege), June 1940, pp. 8, 25, 34-35. "William Carlos Williams," *Hudson
Review*, 14 (1961-1962), 530.

2 Ransom, "Robert Lowell," *Concise Encyclopedia of English and American
Poets & Poetry*, ed. Stephen Spender and Donald Hall (London: Hutch-
inson, 1963), p. 191. "The Second Chance," *Time*, June 2, 1967, p. 73.

3 "Moulding the Golden Spoon," p. 35. "The Second Chance," p. 71.
"War: A Justification," *The Vindex*, 59 (1935), 156-58. In the same volume of *The Vindex*, see also "Diego Velasquez," "Dante's Inferno,"
and "Madonna," pp. 130-31, 215.

4 Lowell to Eberhart, Oct. 20, 1937 and letters following (Dartmouth).
Eberhart to Axelrod, July 14, 1977. Lowell to Untermeyer, Feb. 20,
1947 (Indiana). Lowell's early poems dated Oct. 19, 1935 (MS at
Dartmouth). Eberhart, "Four Poets," *Sewanee Review*, 55 (1947), 524.
R.T.S. Lowell, *Fresh Hearts that Failed Three Thousand Years Ago* (Bos-
ton: Ticknor & Fields, 1860). "Madonna," *The Vindex*, 59 (1935), 215.
Lowell did *not* discover free verse, as he seems to suggest in his inter-

view with Seidel, in Elizabeth Drew's *Discovering Poetry* (1933), which contains none to speak of.

5 Lowell to Eberhart, July 10, 1935 (Dartmouth). "Art" (MS at Dartmouth).

6 Eberhart, *Collected Verse Plays* (Chapel Hill: Univ. of North Carolina Press, 1962), pp. 137, 151, 147, 143. Eberhart's note to the MS of *The Mad Musician* at Boston University identifies the protagonist as Lowell.

7 Kunitz, 36. *N* MS (Harvard). Lowell to Axelrod, Feb. 10, 1974. Seidel, 351. Lowell to Tate, April 15, [19?] (Princeton). Lowell to Williams, Jan. 22, 1958 (Yale). *N*, 121.

8 "William Carlos Williams," p. 531. "Robert Frost: 1875-1963," *New York Review of Books*, Aug. 29, 1963, p. 47. Naipaul, 304. Brooks & Warren, 37. Seidel, 358.

9 "William Carlos Williams," pp. 530-36. Laughlin to Axelrod, June 28, 1974. "William Carlos Williams" MS (Harvard). Seidel, 357. *Harvard Advocate Centennial Anthology* (Cambridge: Schenkman, 1966), p. 388. "The Second Chance" (note 2), p. 71.

10 "Visiting the Tates," *Sewanee Review*, 67 (1959), 557, 559.

11 Hamilton, 37. Tate, *Essays of Four Decades* (New York: William Morrow, 1968), pp. 283, 219. Lowell to Eberhart, [1937] (Dartmouth). Radcliffe Squires, *Allen Tate: A Literary Biography* (New York: Pegasus, 1971), p. 124. Tate, "Ford Madox Ford," *New York Review of Books*, 1, no. 2 (1963), 5. Arthur Mizener, *The Saddest Story* (New York: World, 1971), p. 359. Tate quoted in Eberhart to Lowell, [1937] (Dartmouth).

12 "Visiting the Tates," p. 558. "William Carlos Williams," p. 535. Seidel, 359. In his *Autobiography* (New York: New Directions, 1951, p. 312), Williams states that he "had always despised" Tate and that Tate in turn considered him "of the lunatic fringe." Beginning in the late 1940s, however, the two poets finally came (in Williams' words) "to respect, even to like each other."

13 Tate, "Preface to Reactionary Essays," *Essays of Four Decades*, pp. 613-14.

14 "Visiting the Tates," pp. 558-59. Seidel, 343. "William Carlos Williams," p. 535.

15 Tate, "Three Types of Poetry," *Essays of Four Decades*, p. 174.

16 Lowell quoted in "Robert Lowell," *Twentieth-Century Authors, First Supplement*, ed. Stanley Kunitz (New York: H. W. Wilson, 1955), p. 600. For memoirs of this period, see: Ransom, "A Look Backward and a Note of Hope," *Harvard Advocate*, 145 (Nov. 1961), 22; Lowell, "John Crowe Ransom 1888-1974," *New Review*, 1 (Aug. 1974), 3; Lowell, "Randall Jarrell," *Randall Jarrell 1914-1965*, ed. Robert Lowell, Peter Taylor, and Robert Penn Warren (New York: Farrar, Straus, 1967), p.

101; John Thompson, "Robert Lowell 1917-1977," *New York Review of Books*, Oct. 27, 1977, pp. 14-15; and Peter Taylor, "1939," *Collected Stories* (New York: Farrar, Straus, 1969), pp. 326-59. In Taylor's account, Lowell is fictionalized as "Jim Prewitt."

17 Unpublished essay on southern writers, N MS (Harvard). Lowell to Ransom, Dec. 8, 1961; rpt. "Robert Lowell, The Years at Kenyon: A Remembrance," *Kenyon College Alumni Bulletin*, Nov. 1977, p. 22. "John Crowe Ransom 1888-1974," p. 3. Peter Taylor, "1939," pp. 350, 335. Ransom, "A Look Backward and a Note of Hope," p. 22.

18 Hamilton, 38.

19 "John Crowe Ransom 1888-1974," p. 4. "Mr. McCleary and Our Education," *Hika*, Nov. 1939, pp. 15-16. "From Parnassus to Pittsburgh" MS (Buffalo).

20 "John Ransom's Conversation," *Sewanee Review*, 56 (1948), 375. "John Crowe Ransom 1888-1974," p. 4. Lowell to Eberhart, Oct. 20, 1937 (Dartmouth). "Randall Jarrell," pp. 101-102.

21 "Yvor Winters: A Tribute," *Poetry*, 98 (April 1961), 40-41. Winters, *Primitivism and Decadence*, in *In Defense of Reason* (Denver: Alan Swallow, 1947), pp. 28, 87. "William Carlos Williams" (note 1), p. 535. Review of *Maule's Curse* by Yvor Winters, *Hika*, April 1939, pp. 18, 21.

22 Tate, "A Note on Donne," *Essays of Four Decades* (note 11), p. 242. Nine of Lowell's notebooks are now at Harvard and one is at Indiana.

23 *LU* MS (Harvard). Tate, "Emily Dickinson," *Essays of Four Decades*, pp. 281-98. Blackmur, "Emily Dickinson: Notes on Prejudice and Fact," *Southern Review*, 3 (1937), 323-47. Winters, "Emily Dickinson and the Limits of Judgment" and "Wallace Stevens, or the Hedonist's Progress," rpt. in *In Defense of Reason*, pp. 283-99, 431-59.

24 Review of *Maule's Curse*, *Hika*, p. 18. MS of unpublished essay on John Crowe Ransom's *World's Body* (Indiana). Review of *The World I Breathe* by Dylan Thomas, *Hika*, March 1940, p. 21. *LU* MS (Harvard). "The Cities' Summer Death" and "The Dandelion Girls" appeared in *Kenyon Review*, 1 (1939), 32-33. See Jerome Mazzaro, *Poetic Themes of Robert Lowell* (Ann Arbor: Univ. of Michigan Press, 1965), pp. 4-6, 9-10, for a negative comparison of "The Cities' Summer Death" to the poem it eventually became, "Death from Cancer" (part one of "In Memory of Arthur Winslow" in *LWC*). The six poems Lowell published in *Hika* between Dec. 1938 and Feb. 1940 are called "Lake View," "A Suicidal Fantasy," "A Prelude to Summer," "Clouds," "Cloisters" and "Sublime Feriam Sidera Vertice." None has been republished except "A Suicidal Fantasy" which, revised as "A Suicidal Nightmare," appears in *LU*. "Sublime Feriam" contains several lines later included in "Leviathan" (*LU*).

25 *LU* MS (Harvard). Ransom quoted in Lowell to Tate, July 31, [1944] (Princeton). Empson, *Seven Types of Ambiguity* (1930; rpt. London: Chatto and Windus, 1956), p. 115. Winters, *In Defense of Reason*, p. 31. "Prayer for the Jews" was eventually published in *Sewanee Review*, 51 (1943), 395, but never republished.

26 *Hika*, Feb. 1940, p. 17. Horace, Ode I.1, trans. Helen Rowe Henze, *The Odes of Horace* (Norman: Univ. of Oklahoma Press, 1961). Seidel, 341.

27 Seidel, 342-43. Squires, *Allen Tate* (note 11), pp. 157, 174.

28 Brooks and Warren, 38. Hamilton, 38. Lowell to Axelrod, Feb. 10, 1974.

29 "William Carlos Williams" (note 1), p. 535.

30 Tate, *Essays of Four Decades* (note 11), pp. 613, 289, 56-71. Ellmann and O'Clair, eds., *Norton Anthology of Modern Poetry* (New York: W. W. Norton, 1973), p. 928n. Jarrell's remark on "The Quaker Graveyard" appears among his marginal annotations on the manuscripts of a number of poems which eventually went into *LWC* (MS at Harvard).

31 Tate, "Narcissus as Narcissus," *Essays of Four Decades*, p. 598; "Aeneas in Washington," *Poems* (Chicago: Swallow, 1961), p. 5; Introduction to Lowell's *LU*. Lowell quoted in "In Bounds," *Newsweek*, Oct. 12, 1964, p. 122. "Liberalism and Activism," *Commentary*, April 1969, p. 19. Meiners, *Everything to be Endured* (Columbia: Univ. of Missouri Press, 1970), p. 23.

32 "William Carlos Williams," p. 535. Alvarez, *Encounter*, 43.

33 Boston *Post*, Sept. 9, 1943, p. 15; Oct. 2, 1943. "Homage to T. S. Eliot," *Harvard Advocate*, 125 (Dec. 1938), 20. Peter Taylor, "1939" (note 16). Mazzaro, "Robert Lowell's Early Politics of Apocalypse," *Modern American Poetry*, ed. Jerome Mazzaro (New York: David McKay, 1970), pp. 321-50.

34 Seidel, 342.

35 Seidel, 350, 342, 352.

36 Staples, *Robert Lowell: the First Twenty Years* (London: Faber, 1962), p. 26. Cf. Tate's wartime poems "More Sonnets at Christmas" and "Ode to Our Young Pro-Consuls of the Air."

37 Seidel, 29. Hugh Staples (*Robert Lowell*, p. 22) has pointed out that St. Augustine's term *"regio dissimilitudinis"* was expatiated upon by Etienne Gilson in *The Mystical Theology of Saint Bernard* (London: Sheed & Ward, 1940, p. 58), a book Lowell much admired: "Such is the condition of those who live in the *Land of Unlikeness*. They are not happy there. Wandering, hopelessly revolving, in the 'circuit of the impious,' those who tread this weary round suffer not only the loss of God but also the loss of themselves. They dare no longer look their own souls in the face; could they do it they would no longer recognize

themselves. For when the soul has lost its likeness to God it is no longer like itself." The phrase "Land of Unlikeness" also appears in the final chorus of Auden's Christmas oratorio *For the Time Being*, but Lowell had not yet seen it there when he chose the phrase for his title. Auden's oratorio, though composed in 1941-1942, was first published in September 1944, two months after the publication of Lowell's book.

38 "A Note" (later retitled "Hopkins' Sanctity"), *Kenyon Review*, 6 (1944), 583-86. "Four Quartets," *Sewanee Review*, 51 (1943), 432-35. Eliot, *Four Quartets*.

39 Blackmur, "Notes on Seven Poets," *Form and Value in Modern Poetry* (Garden City: Doubleday-Anchor, 1957), p. 335.

40 Kunitz, 38, 36. Seidel, 347.

41 Eliot to Robert Giroux, Sept. 24, 1946 (Harvard). Williams, *I Wanted to Write a Poem* (London: Jonathan Cape, 1967), p. 106. Hall, "Lord Weary in 1947," *Harvard Advocate*, 145 (Nov. 1961), 20. Berryman, "Lowell, Thomas, &c.," *Partisan Review*, 14 (1947), 74-78. Viereck, "Facts versus Readers," *Atlantic*, July 1947, p. 110. Jarrell, "From the Kingdom of Necessity," *Nation* (1947); rpt. *Poetry and the Age* (New York: Knopf, 1953), p. 219. The only cool review *LWC* received was by Leslie Fiedler who questioned its Roman Catholic orientation ("The Believing Poet and the Infidel Reader," *New Leader*, May 10, 1947, p. 12).

42 Lowell, "Randall Jarrell," (note 16), pp. 103, 111-12. Mary Jarrell, "The Group of Two," *Randall Jarrell 1914-1965*, pp. 292-93. *LWC* MS (Harvard).

43 Jarrell, "Poetry in War and Peace," *Partisan Review*, 12 (1945), 125. Jarrell, "Fifty Years of American Poetry," *Prairie Schooner* (1963); rpt. *The Third Book of Criticism* (New York: Farrar, Straus, 1969), p. 332.

44 Jarrell, "Poetry in War and Peace," p. 126; *Poetry and the Age*, pp. 197-98.

45 Berryman, "Lowell, Thomas, &c.," p. 76. *LWC* MS (Harvard). Alvarez, *Observer*, 19. Lowell's Latin epigraph may be translated "Receive, O Lord, these gifts for the commemoration of thy saints, that just as their passion made them glorious, so may our devotion free us of sin."

46 Lowell to Untermeyer (concerning 1950 ed. of *Modern American Poetry*), Feb. 28, 1947 (Indiana). Hamilton, 48. *Robert Lowell's Poems: A Selection*, ed. Jonathan Raban (London: Faber, 1974). Seidel, 368. Alvarez, *Encounter*, 43.

47 Staples, p. 46. The facts concerning Warren Winslow's death are documented in Alan Williamson, *Pity the Monsters* (New Haven: Yale Univ. Press, 1974), p. 35n, and in greater detail in Stephen Fender, "What Really Happened to Warren Winslow?," *Journal of American Studies*, 7, 187-90. "The Quaker Graveyard" has generally been taken

to be the masterpiece of *LWC*. See, for example, the discussions of the poem in Staples, *Robert Lowell: the First Twenty Years* (note 36); Mazzaro, *Poetic Themes of Robert Lowell* (note 24); Jay Martin, *Robert Lowell* (Minneapolis: Univ. of Minnesota Press, 1970); Richard Fein, *Robert Lowell* (New York: Twayne, 1970); and Patrick Cosgrave, *Public Poetry of Robert Lowell* (New York: Taplinger, 1972). Among the few critics to raise serious objections are Irvin Ehrenpreis ("Age of Lowell," *American Poetry*, London, 1965) and Stephen Yenser (*Circle to Circle*, Berkeley and Los Angeles, 1975) who fault the poem for its baroque rhetoric; and Marjorie Perloff (*Poetic Art of Robert Lowell*, Ithaca, 1973) who argues that Lowell "has great difficulty in articulating the total structure of the elegy" (p. 140). As my analysis of the poem suggests, I believe that there is merit in these objections, but that the poem achieves greatness despite its flaws—as an embodiment of the unreconciled, irreconcilable conflicts of consciousness.

48 "Four Quartets" (note 38), p. 435. *LU* MS (Harvard). Tate, *Essays of Four Decades* (note 11), p. 174.

49 Thoreau, *Cape Cod* (New York: AMS Press, 1968), pp. 6-7. "Four Quartets," p. 434.

50 *LWC* MS (Harvard).

51 Milton, "Lycidas," 77; *Paradise Lost*, 2.788. Alvarez, *Encounter*, 42.

52 Jarrell, *Poetry and the Age* (note 41), p. 192. Edwards, "Future Punishment of the Wicked" and "Sinners in the Hands of an Angry God." Exodus 3:14. Hopkins, "That Nature is a Heraclitean Fire": "what Christ is, / . . . IS immortal diamond."

53 Watkin, *Catholic Art and Culture* (1942; rev. & rpt. London: Hollis & Carter, 1947), p. 177. Perloff (note 47), p. 144. *LWC* MS (Harvard).

54 Hamilton, 40.

55 "We are poured out like water" is from Psalms 22:14, commonly taken as a prefiguration of Christ's crucifixion, as in the Roman Catholic litany of penance "Water from the side of Christ / Wash us."

56 McCormick, 275. Hamilton, 36.

57 Cassirer, *Essay on Man* (New Haven: Yale Univ. Press, 1944), p. 191. Wiebe, "Mr. Lowell and Mr. Edwards," *Contemporary Literature*, 3 (1962), 23. As has been noted by Wiebe and other critics, Lowell's sources for "Mr. Edwards" were Edwards's "Of Insects," "The Future Punishment of the Wicked," and "Sinners in the Hands of an Angry God," and his source for "After the Surprising Conversions" was the conclusion to Edwards's "Narrative of Surprising Conversions."

58 Alvarez, *Encounter*, 42. Lowell's epigraph is from Hawthorne's "The Gray Champion." The fullest modern account of King Philip's War is D. E. Leach, *Flintlock and Tomahawk: New England in King Philip's War*

(New York: Macmillan, 1958). For a critical discussion of Lowell's handling of historical themes, see Alan Holder, "The Flintlocks of the Fathers," *New England Quarterly*, 44 (1971), 40-65.

59 Hawthorne, "The Dragon's Teeth," *Tanglewood Tales*. Lowell, "Introduction," *Pegasus, the Winged Horse: A Greek Myth Retold by Nathaniel Hawthorne* (New York: Macmillan, 1963). Raban, ed. *Robert Lowell's Poems: A Selection* (note 46), p. 164.

60 *LWC* MS (Harvard).

61 Lowell to Louis Untermeyer, May 15, 1947 (Indiana). *Time*, May 15, 1944, p. 44. *Life*, May 19, 1947, p. 91.

62 Tate to Lowell, Oct. 25, 1946 (Princeton). Eliot to Robert Giroux, Sept. 24, 1946 (Harvard). Lowell to Williams, 1948 (Yale). Allen Tate, quoted in Williams to Lowell, April 25, 1948 (Harvard). Pound to Lowell, n.d. (2 letters) (Harvard). Michael Reck, *Ezra Pound: A Close-up* (New York: McGraw-Hill, 1967), p. 115. Harry Meacham, *Caged Panther* (New York: Twayne, 1967), p. 66. Edward Latham, ed., *Interviews with Robert Frost* (New York: Holt, Rinehart & Winston, 1966), p. 126 (see also p. 140). Lowell to Untermeyer, Feb. 20, 1947 (Indiana).

63 Jarrell, *Poetry and the Age* (note 41), p. 198.

64 "William Carlos Williams" (note 1), p. 535. "Thomas, Bishop, and Williams," *Sewanee Review*, 55 (1947), 503.

65 "Paterson II," *Nation*, June 19, 1948, pp. 693-94.

66 Williams, *I Wanted to Write a Poem* (note 41), p. 106. Williams to Lowell, Nov. 12, 1948 (Harvard). Jarrell, *Poetry and the Age*, p. 212.

67 Jarrell, *Poetry and the Age*, pp. 188, 196. Lowell, "Randall Jarrell" (note 16), p. 103. Schwartz, *Selected Essays* (Chicago: Univ. of Chicago Press, 1970), p. 4. Seidel, 363.

68 Seidel, 366-67.

69 *MK* MS (Harvard). Lowell to Untermeyer, Dec. 28, 1947[?] (Indiana).

70 Jarrell, *Poetry and the Age*, pp. 234-35.

71 Bogan, "Verse," *New Yorker*, June 9, 1951, p. 110.

Chapter III

1 *D*, 18. Hamilton, 44-45.

2 Jarrell, "Three Books," *Poetry and the Age* (New York: Knopf, 1953), p. 260. Alvarez, *Review*, 36. Hamilton, 30. Lowell to Tate (Princeton). Seidel, 368. The seven poems of 1953-1954 are "Beyond the Alps" (*Kenyon Review*, 15, 1953, 398-401); "The Banker's Daughter" (*Partisan Review*, 21, 1954, 272-74); "Inauguration Day: January 1953" (*Partisan Review*, 20, 1953, 631); "Ford Madox Ford" (*Encounter*, April 1954, p. 32); "Santayana's Farewell to His Nurses" (*Perspectives USA*, 3, Spring

Notes to Pages 86-92

1953, 67), which was later combined with portions of "Beyond the Alps" to become "For George Santayana"; and "Epitaph of a Fallen Poet" (*Partisan Review*, 20, 1953, 39), later to become "Words for Hart Crane." The only poem in parts one and three of *LS* not published during the early 1950s was "To Delmore Schwartz"; but a draft of this poem, entitled "The Stuffed Duck," exists in a manuscript dated 1946 (Buffalo). All eight of these poems were, in Lowell's words, "heavily revised, shall I say reinspired?" before their appearance in *LS* (Hamilton, 30).

3 "John Ransom's Conversation," *Sewanee Review*, 56 (1948), 375-76. "Thomas, Bishop, and Williams," *Sewanee Review*, 55 (1947), 498, 495. "Inspiration" MS (Buffalo).

4 Lowell to Axelrod, Feb. 10, 1974. Seidel, 368. Lowell to Williams, Jan. 22, 1958 (Yale).

5 Lowell to Williams, n.d. (Yale). Williams, "The Poem as a Field of Action," *Selected Essays* (New York: New Directions, 1954), pp. 284-88. Williams to Lowell, Nov. 27, 1948 (Harvard). See also Williams, *Selected Letters* (New York: McDowell, Obolensky, 1957), pp. 301-303, 311-13, 324.

6 Williams, "In a Mood of Tragedy," *New York Times Book Review*, April 22, 1951; rpt. *Selected Essays*, pp. 324-25.

7 "William Carlos Williams," *Hudson Review*, 14 (1961-1962), 534. Lowell to Williams, April 21, 1951; March 11, 1952 (Yale).

8 Williams, *Selected Letters*, pp. 302, 324. Williams to Lowell, March 16, 1954 (Harvard). Lowell to Williams, March 19, 1954 (Yale).

9 Lowell to Williams, March 13, 1954; Dec. 2, 1955 (Yale).

10 Williams, *I Wanted to Write a Poem* (London: Jonathan Cape, 1967), p. 104. Lowell to Williams, Sept. 5, 1956 (Harvard). "William Carlos Williams" (note 7), p. 536.

11 Williams, Notes for lecture at Brandeis Univ., 1957 (Yale). Williams, "On Measure," *Selected Essays*, pp. 337-40.

12 Lowell to Williams, June 19, 1957 (Yale). Williams, Notes for lecture at Brandeis Univ., 1957 (Yale). *In the Money* (Norfolk, Ct.: New Directions, 1940) is a novel based on the childhood of Williams's wife Flossie; Williams's Preface to his translation of Quevedo's *The Dog and the Fever* (Hamden, Ct.: Shoe String Press, 1954) is an ambivalent biographical sketch of Williams's mother.

13 Lowell to Williams, Sept. 30, 1957; Dec. 3, 1957; Jan. 22, 1958; Sept. 26, 1958; Feb. 15, 1959 (Yale).

14 Elizabeth Hardwick to Allen Tate, Dec. 16, 1957; Tate to Hardwick, Dec. 18, 1957; Lowell to Tate, Jan. 24, 1958 (Princeton). Interview with Isabella Gardner, Sept. 20, 1973. Williams to Lowell, Dec. 4, 1957; Nov. 24, 1958 (Harvard).

Notes to Pages 94-100

15 Williams, "On Measure," *Selected Essays* (note 5), pp. 339-40; *I Wanted to Write a Poem*, p. 86. Poetic line based on flexible rhythmic unit: cf. *I Wanted to Write a Poem*, pp. 26-27 and Lowell's interview with Brooks & Warren, 43.

16 Williams, *I Wanted to Write a Poem*, p. 76; "Robert Lowell's Verse Translation into the American Idiom," *Harvard Advocate*, 145 (Dec. 1961), 12; *Autobiography* (New York: New Directions, 1951), p. 311. Alvarez, *Review*, 36. Fussell, *Lucifer in Harness: American Meter, Metaphor and Diction* (Princeton: Princeton Univ. Press, 1973).

17 Williams, *Selected Essays*, 284.

18 Breslin, *William Carlos Williams: An American Artist* (New York: Oxford Univ. Press, 1970), p. 205. Naipaul, 304. Kunitz, 36. "Confessional": Alvarez, *Review*, 38 and "William Carlos Williams" (note 7), p. 536. Williams, *Autobiography*, p. 334. Williams to Lowell, Nov. 27, 1948 (Harvard).

19 Jarrell, *Poetry and the Age* (note 2), pp. 208-209. Lowell to Williams, n.d. (Yale).

20 Interview with Snodgrass, June 1974. Snodgrass, "Finding a Poem," *Partisan Review*, 26 (1959), 283. Snodgrass to Axelrod, July 17, 1977. Examples of Snodgrass's early academic style are "Orpheus" and "MHTIS . . . OU TIS" in *Heart's Needle* (New York: Knopf, 1959).

21 William White, *W. D. Snodgrass: A Bibliography* (Detroit: Wayne State Univ. Press, 1960), p. 16.

22 Interview with Snodgrass, June 1974. Lowell to Gardner, Oct. 27, 1957 (Washington Univ.). Seidel, 347. For Snodgrass's sense of mutual influence between himself and Lowell, see Philip Gerber and Robert Gemmet, "No Voices Talk to Me: A Conversation with W. D. Snodgrass," *Western Humanities Review*, 24 (1970), 67.

23 "The Second Chance," *Time*, June 2, 1967, p. 72. Alvarez, *Review*, 37. Seidel, 19. "On Skunk Hour," *Contemporary Poet as Artist and Critic*, ed. Anthony Ostroff (Boston: Little, Brown, 1964), p. 108. Lowell's view that poetry should be "less cut off from life" parallels Snodgrass's in "Spring Verse Chronicle," *Hudson Review*, 12 (1969), 116. Lowell's admiration for the prose in *Paterson* is expressed in "Thomas, Bishop, and Williams" (note 3), p. 500n, and "Paterson II," *Nation*, June 19, 1948, pp. 692-94.

24 "On Skunk Hour," p. 108. Hamilton, 44-45. Symposium on Beat Poetry, *Wagner*, Spring 1959, p. 24. Thomas Clark, "Interview with Allen Ginsberg," *Writers at Work, Third Series*, ed. George Plimpton (New York: Viking, 1968), p. 288. Charles Molesworth, "Republican Objects and Utopian Moments," *American Poetry Review*, 6 (Sept.-Oct. 1977), 39.

25 Seidel, 347, 361-62.

26 "Thomas, Bishop, and Williams," pp. 497-98. Kunitz, 28. Lowell to Williams, Sept. 26, 1958 (Yale).

27 Lowell to Isabella Gardner, Oct. 27, 1957 (Washington Univ.). MS poems in Lowell to Williams, Dec. 3, 1957 (Yale). In this packet Lowell did not include "The Banker's Daughter," which had been published in 1954. The poem on Crane, still entitled "Epitaph of a Fallen Poet," was little changed from its 1953 magazine appearance. A poem entitled "Saint Ovid" was also included, essentially the fourteen-line stanza Lowell added to the version of "Beyond the Alps" in *For the Union Dead*.

28 Bennett, "Snobbish Memoirs," *Hudson Review*, 12 (1959), 435. Standerwick, "Pieces too Personal," *Renascence*, 13 (1960), 56. Alvarez, "Something New in Verse," *London Observer*, April 12, 1959, p. 22. Kazin, "In Praise of Robert Lowell," *Reporter*, June 25, 1959; rpt. *Contemporaries* (Boston: Little, Brown, 1962), pp. 229-30. Rosenthal, "Poetry as Confession," *Nation*, Sept. 19, 1959. Rosenthal's review formed the basis for his illuminating chapter on *Life Studies* in *The New Poets* (New York: Oxford Univ. Press, 1967). Other distinctive perspectives on *Life Studies* include Marjorie Perloff's valuable stylistic analysis (*Poetic Art of Robert Lowell*, Ithaca, Cornell Univ. Press, 1973, ch. 3), Jerome Mazzaro's treatment of the book as "religiously despairing" (*Poetic Themes of Robert Lowell*, Ann Arbor, Univ. of Michigan Press, 1965, ch. 7-8), and Alan Williamson's analysis of the book as a study in "the socialization of the individual" (*Pity the Monsters*, New Haven, Yale Univ. Press, 1974, ch. 3).

29 St. Augustine, *City of God; Confessions*, ch. 1, 7, 8. Glauco Cambon interestingly compares "Beyond the Alps" to Lowell's earlier "Dea Roma" (*LWC*) in "Dea Roma and Robert Lowell," *Accent*, 20 (1960), 51-61, but because he incorrectly assumes that Lowell remained a Catholic, he misreads the ironies of "Beyond the Alps" as evidence of religious affirmation.

30 "Prose Genius in Verse," *Kenyon Review*, 15 (1953), 621. *Letters of Henry James*, I (New York: Scribner's, 1920), p. 232. Lowell's ambivalence toward traditional form is indicated by the fact that this poem rejecting formalism is composed of three quasi-sonnets, albeit unscanned and irregularly rhymed ones. When he reprinted it in *FUD* he further disordered his form by dropping one line from one of the stanzas.

31 James, *Autobiography* (New York: Criterion, 1956), p. 4. Besides subverting the Bostonian mode of memoir, "91 Revere Street" contrasts with Williams's anecdotal, spontaneous, cheerful *Autobiography*, a volume Lowell read with admiration but did not imitate.

32 James, *Autobiography*, pp. 350, 37, 4, 41, 131.

33 Seidel, 346, 363. "Poetry and Meter," *Hudson Review*, 15 (1962), 318.

Notes to Pages 108-122

Jarrell, *Poetry and the Age* (note 2), p. 260. Williams, *Selected Letters* (note 5), p. 303. Kunitz, 36. For a critical discussion of Lowell's altering prosodies see Harvey Gross, *Sound and Form in Modern Poetry* (Ann Arbor: Univ. of Michigan Press, 1968).

34 "My daddy was chief engineer" MS (Yale). "On Skunk Hour" (note 23), p. 109.

35 Williams, *Selected Letters*, p. 313. Alvarez, 37. "My Last Afternoon" MS (Yale). Brooks & Warren, 41-42. Seidel, 346, 349.

36 "Aunt Laura" version: MS (Buffalo), published in *Botteghe Oscure*, 23 (1959), 205-209. Virtually completed version: MS (Yale).

37 Seidel, 349. Herndl, "Literary Criticism, English Departments, Con III Students," *College English*, Feb. 1974, p. 542. Alvarez, *Observer*, 19. My thinking about autobiography has been influenced by Roy Pascal's excellent *Design and Truth in Autobiography* (London: Routledge & Kegan Paul, 1960).

38 Emerson, "The Poet." James, "Religion and Neurology," *Varieties of Religious Experience*. Laing, *The Divided Self* (1960; rpt. New York: Pantheon, 1969). Alvarez, *Savage God* (New York: Bantam, 1972), pp. 248-52 and throughout. Melville, "Hawthorne and His Mosses." Max Byrd in *Visits to Bedlam* (Columbia, S.C.: Univ. of So. Carolina Press, 1974) finds madness, divine truth, and poetic inspiration to be historically related terms—a view supported by the work of many American writers. Contemporary Confessional poets, however, have a more clinical interest in the subject than their predecessors; Lowell, Ginsberg, Berryman, Plath, and Sexton have all explicitly described their own institutionalization.

39 Meyerhoff, *Time and Literature* (Berkeley: Univ. of California Press, 1965), p. 2. Sartre, *Being and Nothingness* (1943), trans. Hazel Barnes (New York: Citadel, 1956), p. 83.

40 Alvarez, *Encounter*, 41. Berryman, Song 384, *Dream Songs* (New York: Farrar, Straus, 1969), p. 406. Jarrell, "The Lost World," *Complete Poems* (New York: Farrar, Straus, 1969), p. 283. Ginsberg, "Kaddish," *Kaddish and Other Poems* (San Francisco: City Lights, 1961), pp. 7, 31. Roethke, "The Far Field," *Collected Poems* (Garden City: Doubleday, 1966), p. 201.

41 Rosenthal, *The New Poets* (note 28), pp. 54, 60, 79. Alvarez, *Encounter*, 41. Watt, "The First Paragraph of *The Ambassadors*: An Explication," *Essays in Criticism*, 10 (1960), 261.

42 Seidel, 343.

43 "Prose Genius in Verse," p. 619. "Displaced mimetic" mode of iconography: see John Vickery, "Modern Literature and Iconography," *Modernist Studies*, 1 (1974), 48.

44 Seidel, 349.

45 Hamilton, 44.

46 Lowell to Williams, April 19, 1957 (Yale). Compare Lowell's use of "seedtime" to Wordsworth's "fair seed-time had my soul," and his use of "jailbird" to Wordsworth's "free, / Free as a bird to settle where I will" (*Prelude*, I.301, 8-9).

47 Pound, Cantos 74-84 ("Pisan Cantos"), *Cantos* (New York: New Directions, 1970), pp. 423-540. Lowell to Williams, n.d. (Yale). McCormick, 277. Hamilton, 34. See George Lensing, "Memories of West Street and Lepke," *Concerning Poetry*, 3 (1970), 23-26 for an analysis of Lowell's imagery.

48 "On Skunk Hour" (note 23), pp. 109-10. "Inspiration" MS (Buffalo).

49 "On Skunk Hour," p. 107.

50 Alvarez, *Review*, 38. James, "The Sick Soul," *Varieties of Religious Experience*. For Lowell's identification with the decorator see also his comment in *Time* (June 2, 1967, p. 67) that "there's no money in" poetry.

51 Hawthorne, "Sights from a Steeple"; *The Blithedale Romance*, ch. 18; "Ethan Brand: A Chapter from an Abortive Romance." Henry James, "The Beast in the Jungle." "On Skunk Hour," p. 107. Matthew 27:33.

52 William James, "Preface," *The Will to Believe*; "Conclusions" and "The Religion of Healthy-mindedness," *Varieties of Religious Experience*. Seidel, 352. In reference to the "religious" quality of "Skunk Hour," it is instructive to consider William James's idea that the sinner is closer to God than the conventional good person and that through confession, a highly moral act, he exteriorizes his rottenness and thereby purges himself of it ("Other Characteristics," *Varieties*). Lowell's description of the "chalk-dry" church calls to mind James's labeling of doctrinaire Christianity as "chalky" and "dry" ("The Value of Saintliness," *Varieties*).

53 Sartre, *Being and Nothingness* (note 39), pp. 32, 35, 136-37, 416, 455.

54 Camus, *Myth of Sisyphus* (1942), trans. Justin O'Brien (New York: Vintage, 1955), pp. 3, 10, v, 29.

55 "On Skunk Hour" (note 23), pp. 107-108.

56 "On Skunk Hour," p. 109. Bishop, "The Armadillo," *Complete Poems* (New York: Farrar, Straus, 1969), pp. 122-23.

57 Spender, *The Making of a Poem* (London: Hamish Hamilton, 1955), p. 69. "Address of Robert Lowell," National Book Awards, March 23, 1960 (Yale).

58 Kazin, *Contemporaries* (note 28), p. 226.

59 Melville, "Hawthorne and his Mosses." Emerson, "The Poet"; "Fate." Whitman, "A Hand-Mirror." Williams, *Paterson*, books one and two; "Asphodel," book one.

Chapter IV

1 Sexton to Lowell, Feb. 10, 1960 (Harvard); "To a Friend Whose Work Has Come to Triumph" was later published in Sexton, *All My Pretty Ones* (Boston: Houghton Mifflin, 1961). "Address of Robert Lowell," National Book Awards, March 23, 1960 (Yale).

2 Lowell to Charles Abbott, Oct. 12, 1959 (Buffalo). Lowell to Williams, Jan. 22, 1958 (Yale). Alvarez, *Encounter*, 43.

3 Seidel, 348. *Imitations*, xi. Lowell's Drydenesque intention in *Imitations*: His quoted phrase deliberately echoes Dryden, who in his *Preface to Ovid's Epistles* defined imitation as a mode of translation in which the "translator" feels free to write as he thinks his "author would have done had he lived in our age and in our country." *Imitations* as sequence: Soon after the book was published Edmund Wilson suggested that it is "really an original sequence" (*New Yorker*, June 2, 1962, p. 126). I have analyzed *Imitations* briefly in this light in "Baudelaire and the Poetry of Robert Lowell," *Twentieth Century Literature*, 17 (Oct. 1971), 263-67, and at greater length in "The Meaning of Robert Lowell's *Imitations*," *Studies in Language and Literature*, ed. Charles Nelson (Richmond, Ky.: Eastern Kentucky Univ. Press, 1976), pp. 41-47. The most complete study of *Imitations* and Lowell's other volumes as "whole books of poems" is Stephen Yenser's *Circle to Circle* (Berkeley and Los Angeles: Univ. of California Press, 1975).

4 Tate, *Memoirs and Opinions 1926-1974* (Chicago: Swallow, 1975), p. 200. Williams to Lowell, May 23, 1961 (Harvard). Hamilton, 30.

5 Lowell to Tate, May 22, 1961 (Washington Univ.). Lowell to Gardner, Oct. 10, 1961 (Washington Univ.).

6 "Address of Robert Lowell," National Book Awards, March 23, 1960. Hamilton, 45. Ungaretti, "Eterno." For a negative appraisal of the style of *FUD* see Thomas Parkinson, "For the Union Dead," *Salmagundi*, 1 (1966-1967), 87-95.

7 Mary Jarrell, "The Group of Two," *Randall Jarrell 1914-1965*, ed. Robert Lowell, Peter Taylor, and Robert Penn Warren (New York: Farrar, Straus, 1967), pp. 288-89.

8 Alvarez, *Encounter*, 43, 40. "Address of Robert Lowell," National Book Awards, March 23, 1960. Lowell to Gardner, Sept. 19, 1956 (Washington Univ.). Kunitz, 37.

9 Kunitz, 36. Lowell to Williams, Jan. 22, 1958 (Yale). Voznesensky, "Poem with a Footnote (for Robert Lowell)." Although our critical intentions differ, Stephen Yenser perceives an overall structure in *FUD* quite similar to the structure I outline below. See *Circle to Circle*, ch. 6.

10 Lowell to Tate, Oct. 9, 1964 (Princeton).

11 Roethke to Lowell, Dec. 20, 1958 (Harvard). Hamilton, 44. Lowell's eye/I pun also appears in "Eye and Tooth" and was probably suggested by Allen Tate's "The Eye" and "Two Concerts for the Eye to Sing, if Possible."

12 "Yvor Winters: A Tribute," *Poetry*, April 1961, pp. 40-43.

13 Ricks, "Three Lives of Robert Lowell," *New Statesman*, March 26, 1965, p. 496.

14 Alvarez, *Observer*, 19. Hamilton, 40.

15 Kunitz, 36. *FUD* MS (Harvard). In writing this poem Lowell surely remembered Williams's similarly symbolic use of the same landscape in Corydon's song in book four of *Paterson*:

> At the entrance to the
> 45th Street tunnel   .   Let's see
>   .   houses placarded:
>   Unfit for human habitation   etc   etc
> Oh yes   .
>   Condemned   .
> But who has been condemned   .   where the tunnel
> under the river starts? *Voi ch'entrate*
> revisited! Under ground, under rock, under river
> under gulls   .   under the insane   .

16 Alvarez, *Review*, 39. *Time*, Sept. 15, 1961, p. 21. Halle, "On War in Gestation," *New Republic*, Nov. 20, 1961, p. 10. For detailed analyses of the political crisis of fall 1961 together with bibliographies of relevant materials, see Louise Fitz Simons, *Kennedy Doctrine* (New York: Random House, 1972) and Richard Walton, *Cold War and Counterrevolution* (New York: Viking, 1972).

17 Auden, "September 1, 1939." "Cold War and the West," *Partisan Review*, 29 (Winter 1962), 47.

18 *FUD* MS (Harvard). Kennedy, *To Turn the Tide* (New York: Harper, 1962), p. 210.

19 *Time*, Sept. 29, 1961, p. 13. Apocalyptic phrases: quoted from *New York Times*, Sept. 28, 22, Oct. 1, and 5, and *To Turn the Tide*, p. 222. Fallout shelters: Cover stories on shelters appeared in *Time* in September and *Life* in October ("How You Can Survive Fallout. Ninety-seven out of 100 People Can Be Saved. Detail Plans for Building Shelters"), but even before then almost five million Americans had requested a Defense Department pamphlet entitled "The Family Fallout Shelter."

20 James, *Psychology*, "The Sense of Time." Filmed interview with Lowell, National Educational Television (Audio Visual Center, Indiana Univ., Bloomington, Ind. 47410).

21 "In Bounds," *Newsweek*, Oct. 12, 1964, p. 122.

22 "Liberal Anti-Communism Revisited," *Commentary*, Sept. 1967, p. 54. For a more favorable evaluation of "July in Washington," see Thomas R. Edwards' *Imagination and Power* (New York: Oxford Univ. Press, 1971). Edwards finds it one of Lowell's best public poems in the way it intermingles "mind with world" without subjugating either one to the other (pp. 223-25). For myself, I worry that the poem's admirable intellectual balance may have been purchased at the expense of emotional immediacy.

23 Pearson, "Robert Lowell," *Review*, No. 20 (March 1969), 13.

24 Tate, "Robert Lowell," *Harvard Advocate*, 145 (Nov. 1961), 5. *FUD* MS (Harvard). Lowell to Tate, March 15, 1953; Nov. 5, [1952] (Princeton). Radcliffe Squires, *Allen Tate: A Literary Biography* (New York: Pegasus, 1971), pp. 207, 213. Lowell to Axelrod, Feb. 10, 1974.

25 Lowell to Williams, Dec. 23, 1960, Sept. 8, 1961, Dec. 8, 1961 (Yale). Williams, "Robert Lowell's Verse Translation into the American Idiom," *Harvard Advocate*, 145 (Nov. 1961), 12. Florence Williams to Lowell, May 23, 1961 (Harvard). "William Carlos Williams," *Hudson Review*, 14 (1961-1962), 536.

26 *FUD* MS (Harvard). "William Carlos Williams," pp. 530-31, 536. Williams, "Robert Lowell's Verse Translation into the American Idiom," p. 12. Williams's description of Hudson: cf. n. 15. Williams's encouragement of Lowell's independence: see Williams's rebuke to Pound in 1954, "Cal Lowell is a man I respect and for whom I feel a strong bond of sympathy, but he don't need either you or me to further him in his career. In fact our presence would only hamper him in what he has to do. Leave him alone" (*Selected Letters*, New York, 1957, p. 324).

27 Annie Fields, *Nathaniel Hawthorne* (Boston: Small, Maynard, 1899), p. 102. Lowell to Williams, Jan. 22, 1958 (Yale). Poirier, "Our Truest Historian," *Book Week*, Oct. 11, 1964, p. 1.

28 Brooks & Warren, 45. Cassirer, *Essay on Man* (New Haven: Yale Univ. Press, 1944), p. 191. *FUD* MS (Harvard).

29 Williams to Lowell, Jan. 14, 1958 (Yale). *FUD* MS (Harvard). *Christian Science Monitor*, June 6, 1960, p. 14 (a slightly different version of Lowell's reading may be found in the *Boston Globe*, June 6, 1960, p. 1). Influence of Tate's "Ode" on "For the Union Dead": Similarities between the two poems in structure, imagery, and theme have been discerned by Jerome Mazzaro in *Poetic Themes of Robert Lowell* (Ann Arbor: Univ. of Michigan Press, 1965), pp. 124-27. E. T. Helmick in "The Civil War Odes of Lowell and Tate" (*Georgia Review*, Spring 1971, pp. 51-55) carries this point much too far, however, in asserting that there is *no* essential difference between Tate and Lowell. Tate, incidentally, approved of "For the Union Dead."

30 *FUD* MS (Harvard).

31 *FUD* MS (Harvard). Hardwick, ed., *Selected Letters of William James* (New York: Farrar, Straus, 1961), pp. 167-68. Hardwick, "Boston: the Lost Ideal," *Harper's*, Dec. 1959, pp. 64-69. Lowell's title "One Gallant Rush" derives from a broadside by Frederick Douglass exhorting blacks to volunteer for the Massachusetts Fifty-fourth: "The iron gate of our prison stands half open. One gallant rush from the North will fling it wide open, while four millions of our brothers and sisters shall march into liberty" ("Men of Color, to Arms!," n. 33 below).

32 *FUD* MS (Harvard).

33 *FUD* MS (Harvard). I discuss in my text below the relationship of "For the Union Dead" to many of the major poems, essays, and addresses about Shaw and his regiment. A full list of such works follows.

POEMS: R. W. Emerson, "Voluntaries" (1863), *Complete Works*, IX (Boston: Houghton Mifflin, 1904); Anna C.L.Q. Waterston, "Together," printed on the flyleaf of *Verses* (Boston, 1863); Anon. and untitled ["They buried him with his niggers!"], *Negro in the American Rebellion* (1867; rpt. New York: Johnson Reprint, 1968), p. 202; Phoebe Cary, "The Hero of Fort Wagner," *Poetical Works of Alice and Phoebe Cary* (Boston: Houghton Mifflin, 1897); James Russell Lowell, "Memoriae Positum R.G.S." (1864) and "Ode Recited at the Harvard Commemoration" (1865), *Complete Poetical Works* (Boston: Houghton Mifflin, 1925); Thomas Bailey Aldrich, "Shaw Memorial Ode" (1897), *Poems*, II (Boston: Houghton Mifflin, 1907); Richard Watson Gilder, "Robert Gould Shaw," *Poems* (Boston: Houghton Mifflin, 1908); Paul Laurence Dunbar, "Robert Gould Shaw" (1900), *Complete Poems* (New York: Dodd, Mead, 1967); Benjamin Brawley, "My Hero, to Robert Gould Shaw," *The Poetry of the Negro, 1746-1970*, ed. Langston Hughes and Arna Bontemps (Garden City, N.Y.: Doubleday, 1970); Robert Underwood Johnson, "Saint-Gaudens: An Ode," *Saint-Gaudens: An Ode, and Other Verse* (New York: Century, 1910); William Vaughn Moody, "Ode in Time of Hesitation" (1900), *Poems* (Boston: Houghton Mifflin, 1901); Percy MacKaye, "Prologue to the Saint-Gaudens Masque," *Poems and Plays*, II (New York: Macmillan, 1916); Charles Ives, "The 'St. Gaudens' in Boston Common," program note for the first performance of "Three New England Places," Boston, January 1931, rpt. Richard Benson and Lincoln Kirstein, *Lay This Laurel* (New York: Eakins, 1973); John Berryman, "Boston Common," *The Dispossessed* (New York: William Sloane, 1948).

ESSAYS AND ADDRESSES: Frederick Douglass, "Men of Color, to Arms!," "Why Should a Colored Man Enlist?," "Another Word to Colored Men," and "To Major G. L. Stearns," *Life and Writings*, III (1861-1865) (New York: International Publishers, 1952); Thomas Wentworth Higginson, *Army Life in a Black Regiment* (1870; rpt. East

Lansing: Michigan State Univ. Press, 1960), ch. 10, and "Colored Troops under Fire," *Century Magazine*, June 1897; Oliver Wendell Holmes Jr., "Harvard College in the War" (1884), *Mind and Faith of Justice Holmes* (Boston: Little, Brown, 1951); Henry Lee Higginson, "Robert Gould Shaw" (1897), *Four Addresses* (Boston: Merrymount Press, 1902); William James, "Robert Gould Shaw" (1897), *Memories and Studies* (New York: Longmans, Green, 1911); Booker T. Washington, "Address" (1897), *Monument to Robert Gould Shaw*, ed. anon. (Boston: Houghton Mifflin, 1897).

In addition to these poems, essays, and addresses, the Shaw tradition in art includes St. Gaudens's Shaw Memorial and, as Chadwick Hansen has pointed out (*Massachusetts Review*, 16, 745-59), the first movement of Charles Ives's *Three Places in New England*, entitled "The 'St. Gaudens' in Boston Common: Col. Shaw and his Colored Regiment" (Mercury MG 50149).

34 See Peter Burchard, *One Gallant Rush: Robert Gould Shaw and his Brave Black Regiment* (New York: St. Martin's, 1965), which includes a bibliography.

35 Thomas Wentworth Higginson, "Colored Troops under Fire" (note 33), p. 196.

36 *FUD* MS (Harvard).

37 J. R. Lowell to Mrs. Francis Shaw, Dec. 4, 1863, *New Letters of James Russell Lowell* (New York: Harper, 1932), p. 115.

38 William Coffin, "Shaw Memorial and the Sculptor St. Gaudens," *Century Magazine*, June 1897, pp. 179, 181. James (note 33), pp. 40, 43. Monument's epigraph: note that in his poem Robert Lowell changes the subject from singular to plural, in order to commemorate the sacrifice of the black soldiers as well as that of the white commanding officer.

39 James (note 33), p. 44. Holmes (note 33), p. 17.

40 James, pp. 42, 40, 60-61.

41 Holmes, pp. 18, 16, 42. Lowell to Axelrod, Feb. 10, 1974. Suicidalism: Phillip Cooper, in *The Autobiographical Myth of Robert Lowell* (Chapel Hill: Univ. of North Carolina Press, 1970) makes much of the "death-wish" in Colonel Shaw and in the poem generally (pp. 73-101). While Cooper has caught an important undertone, I believe that he errs in identifying Shaw with the forces of oppression and chaos (pp. 86, 98-99).

42 Emerson, "The American Scholar." Doherty, "Poet as Historian," *Concerning Poetry*, 1 (Fall 1968), 39. James, p. 57.

43 *FUD* MS (Harvard). Alvarez, *Encounter*, 41.

44 *FUD* MS (Harvard).

45 Rahv, *The Myth and the Powerhouse* (New York: Farrar, Straus, 1965), p. 6. Fraser, "Amid the Horror, A Song of Praise," *New York Times Book Review*, Oct. 4, 1964, p. 1.

46 "Thomas, Bishop, and Williams," *Sewanee Review*, 55 (1947), 501. Alvarez, *Encounter*, 41.

47 Jacobsen, "Poet of the Particular," *Commonweal*, 81 (1964), 251-52.

48 "In Bounds," *Newsweek*, Oct. 12, 1964, p. 122.

49 Hamilton, 45. *NO* MS (Harvard).

50 Gilman, 5. Lowell to Axelrod, Feb. 10, 1974.

51 Alvarez, *Encounter*, 42. "Liberal Anti-Communism Revisited," *Commentary*, Sept. 1967, p. 54. "Day of Mourning," *New York Review of Books*, Feb. 29, 1968, p. 32. "Judgment Deferred on Lieutenant Calley," *New York Review of Books*, May 6, 1971, p. 37.

52 Eric Goldman, *The Tragedy of Lyndon Johnson* (New York: Knopf, 1969), ch. 16. Kempton, "Lessons from Lowell," *Spectator*, June 11, 1965, pp. 745-47. Macdonald, "A Day at the White House," *New York Review of Books*, July 15, 1965, p. 15. Alvarez, *Encounter*, 41.

53 Hamilton, 30. Ellison, *Shadow and Act* (New York: Random House, 1964), xix.

54 *LU* MS (Harvard). "Waking Early Sunday Morning" as Lowell's reply to "Sunday Morning": Lowell's love of Stevens's poem, fostered by Tate, Winters, and Blackmur, could never have been for the poem's neo-pagan affirmations but rather for its verbal and prosodic brilliance and perhaps for its elegiac undertones. In its aspect as an elegy for the Christian idea of God, "Sunday Morning" is an unironic precursor of "Waking Early Sunday Morning"; Stevens's concluding images of chaos and descent into darkness are faithfully reflected in Lowell's own imagery. Another such precursor is MacNeice's poem also entitled "Sunday Morning," which includes a satiric indictment of the failure of modern Christianity:

> But listen, up the road, something gulps, the church spire
> Opens its eight bells out, skulls' mouths which will not tire
> To tell how there is no music or movement which secures
> Escape from the week day time. Which deadens and endures.

A third precursor is Baudelaire's bleak prose-poem "Anywhere Out of the World," which supplies Lowell with his refrain, "Anywhere, but somewhere else!"

55 *NO* MS (Harvard). "On Skunk Hour," *The Contemporary Poet as Artist and Critic*, ed. Anthony Ostroff (Boston: Little, Brown, 1964), p. 110. Lowell perceives God's "sensible withdrawal": the beliefs underlying "Waking Early Sunday Morning" and indeed the entire "Near the

Ocean" sequence are clarified by Lowell's remarks concerning T. S. Eliot's religion in an unpublished essay on Eliot written in 1967 or 1968: "Christianity for ages has had a spindly, undistinguished record. Ever more so, increasingly weak and irrelevant in fact, thought and imagination. Eliot's faith seems almost willfully crooked, dry, narrow and hard in comparison with what I would like to describe as the toleration, hope and intuition of Matthew Arnold's tragic liberalism" (N MS, Harvard).

56 Lippmann, *Newsweek*, May 24, 1965, p. 23. *Paradise Lost*, II, 894-97. Baudelaire, "Le Voyage." Lowell echoes political commonplaces: the phrase "police the earth" (or a close variant) was used not only by Lippmann but also by Irving Howe, *Time*, and the *New York Times* in the months preceding the composition of "Waking Early Sunday Morning."

57 "What's Happening to America," *Partisan Review*, 34 (Winter 1967), 38.

58 "Paterson II," *Nation*, June 19, 1948, p. 693. *NO* MS (Harvard). Kenner, "The Urban Apocalypse," *Eliot in His Time*, ed. A. Walton Litz (Princeton: Princeton Univ. Press, 1973), pp. 23-49. Echoes of Juvenal, Dante, and Williams: One of Lowell's several discernible Juvenalian echoes is his conclusion, "Behind each bush, perhaps a knife, / each landscaped crag, each flowering shrub, / hides a policeman with a club" (*NO*, 41), an adaptation of Juvenal's warning in "The Vanity of Human Wishes": "If you take a walk at night, / carrying a little silver, be prepared / to think each shadow hides a knife or spear" (as translated by Lowell in *NO*, 70). Lowell's Dantesque echoes are more distinct in manuscript than in the poem's final version: his deleted line, "Midway in this dark wood of my life," condenses the beginning of *The Inferno*: "Midway in our life's journey, I went astray / from the straight road and woke to find myself / alone in a dark wood" (*The Inferno*, trans. John Ciardi, New Brunswick, Rutgers Univ. Press, 1954). Even without this clear reference, Lowell's park may perhaps be usefully compared to Dante's wood of error, and his lion and kitten to Dante's leopard, lion, and wolf. Lowell's echoes of William Carlos Williams were first pointed out by Donald Ewart in "Robert Lowell and W. C. Williams: Sterility in 'Central Park,' " *ELN*, 5 (Dec. 1967), 129-35. Like Williams in the first part of "Sunday in the Park," Lowell traverses an urban park on a weekend, witnessing and judging. "Sunday in the Park" begins with Dr. Paterson climbing "stones" and "paced by . . . dogs"; "Central Park" begins with Lowell "scaling small rocks" and gasping "like a dog." Williams's protagonist watches lovers undress "beneath the sun in frank vulgarity," seeking to escape their "waste" and sterility on the "gay wings of sex." Lowell similarly watches nude lovers "sunning openly," seeking to escape their "fear

and poverty" borne on "the delicate wings of lust." Both poems lament the victory in our time of repressive authoritarianism over love, sexuality, and natural joy.

59 Hamilton, 30. *New York Times*, Aug. 5, 1965, p. 13.

60 *N* MS (Harvard). Lowell reaches for his wife's hand: This plea for love resonates not only Arnold's plaintive "love, let us be true / To one another!" but also the peripety of "In Memoriam," in which Tennyson overcomes his sense of isolation while revisiting Hallam's London house: "And in my thoughts with scarce a sigh / I take the pressure of thine hand."

61 Lowell to Axelrod, Feb. 10, 1974. Hamilton, 31. *N* MS (Harvard).

62 Hamilton, 32.

63 Mailer, *The Armies of the Night* (New York: New American Library, 1968), pp. 18-22, 40-46, 63-68, 73-74, 82-84, 89, 109, 124-29, 139.

64 *The Armies of the Night*, p. 265. Naipaul, 303. "The March," the first portion of Lowell's poem to see print, appeared in the *New York Review of Books*, Nov. 23, 1967, p. 3.

65 Gilman, 5. Hamilton, 40-41. *American Journey: The Times of Robert Kennedy*, ed. Jean Stein and George Plimpton (New York: Harcourt Brace Jovanovich, 1970), pp. 192-193, 270. "Why I'm For McCarthy," *New Republic*, April 13, 1968, p. 22. Lowell provided McCarthy with intellectual refuge: Lowell was uniformly resented by McCarthy's more orthodox political advisors, who called him one of McCarthy's "astrologers"—a "circle of sycophants and friends" which also included Shana Alexander and Mary McGrory (*American Journey*, p. 302; Richard Stout, *People*, New York, Harper & Row, 1970, pp. 243-44). Lowell and the other "astrologers" succeeded all too well in providing the candidate with refuge from the campaign. Arthur Herzog remembers Lowell and McCarthy discussing poetry "while speech writers, press aides, and others waited in the hall" (*McCarthy for President*, New York, Viking, 1969, p. 167). Richard Stout recalls that during one political briefing, "Lowell broke in with: 'You know, Senator, this reminds me of the situation that existed between King James I and the Archbishop of Canterbury in 1604.' Spasms of chuckling ensued, and the briefing went down the drain" (*People*, p. 244). A third campaign worker, Andreas Teuber, blames Lowell for McCarthy's weak showing in his televised debate with Kennedy. Although his staff tried to hide McCarthy from Lowell "at very crucial times because we thought he always took the edge off," Lowell found McCarthy just before the debate and joined him for the limousine ride to the television studio. They composed "a twentieth-century version of 'Ode to St. Cecilia's Day' in the back seat. So by the time [McCarthy] got to the studio, yes, he was then like Henry the Fifth at Agincourt" (*American Journey*, pp. 311-12).

66 *American Journey*, pp. 270, 193, 341. Gilman, 5. Alvarez, *Encounter*, 40-42.

67 *American Journey*, pp. 193, 341. *N* MS (Harvard). McCarthy in the bowling alley: Lowell's sporting metaphors here reflect McCarthy's habit of making his way into newspapers during the campaign by bowling and swinging a baseball bat for photographers.

68 Young, 32. Updike, *Bech: A Book* (New York: Fawcett, 1971), p. 142.

69 Hamilton, 35. Young, 32. Naipaul, 304. *N* MS (Harvard).

70 Lowell to Axelrod, Feb. 10, 1974. Stevens, "Of Modern Poetry." Hamilton, 42. Unpublished essay on Stevens, *N* MS (Harvard). Lowell used Stevens: he taught Stevens's poetry at Harvard at this time.

71 *N* MS (Harvard).

72 Stevens, "The Poems of Our Climate."

73 Hamilton, 31. Lowell closes his open-ended form and frees himself from the poem: He thereby distinguishes his poem from several of the poems it otherwise resembles—Williams's *Paterson*, Pound's *Cantos*, Berryman's *Dream Songs*.

74 Dale, "Fortuitous Form," *Agenda*, 11 (1973), 74. Collingwood, *The Idea of History* (1946; rpt. London: Oxford Univ. Press, 1956), pp. 218, 248. McCormick, 269. Negative reaction to *History*: the best-humored critique occurs in Clive James's burlesque, "Peregrine Prykke's Pilgrimage through the London Literary World: A Tragedy in Heroic Couplets" (*New Review*, Aug. 1974, pp. 12-24), in which "Bob Lull, an American poet" describes

> The business I began some years ago
> (And whose results so far I'm sure you know)
> Of smashing up my work in angry fits
> Until it's strewn about in little bits.

75 Pearce, *The Continuity of American Poetry* (1961; rev. ed. Princeton: Princeton Univ. Press, 1965), pp. 61, 130. *N* MS (Harvard). "Digressions from Larkin's Twentieth-Century Verse," *Encounter*, May 1973, p. 67. Cooper (note 41), v.

Chapter V

1 Young, 32. Hamilton, 29.

2 See Blackwood, *For All That I Found There* (New York: Braziller, 1974); and *The Stepdaughter* (New York: Scribner, 1977). Ricks, "The Poet Robert Lowell," *Listener*, June 21, 1973, pp. 830-31. *The Dolphin* was awarded the 1973 Pulitzer Prize for poetry, yet it was received coldly by most critics. Marjorie Perloff, for example, complained that "Lowell no longer quite succeeds in transforming his life into art, and his reve-

lations, sometimes embarrassingly personal, sometimes boring, should indeed have remained 'sealed like private letters' " ("The Blank Now," *New Republic*, July 7 and 14, 1973, p. 24).

3 Lowell to Axelrod, Feb. 10, 1974. Yenser, *Circle to Circle* (Berkeley and Los Angeles: Univ. of California Press, 1975), p. 318.

4 Lowell to Axelrod, Feb. 10, 1974. Bellow, *Henderson the Rain King* (New York: Viking, 1959), p. 286.

5 Lowell, "Randall Jarrell," *Randall Jarrell 1914-1965*, ed. Robert Lowell, Peter Taylor, Robert Penn Warren (New York: Farrar, Straus, 1967), p. 102.

6 Stevens, "Adagia," *Opus Posthumous* (New York: Knopf, 1957), p. 169. Williams, "Asphodel, That Greeny Flower," *Pictures from Brueghel* (New York: New Directions, 1962), p. 179. Many of Williams's late poems associate sexual love with art, perhaps most conspicuously book five of *Paterson*.

7 Yeats, "Byzantium," stanza 5: his dolphin ambiguously mediates between flesh (it is composed of "mire and blood") and spirit (it carries riders to Byzantium). Melville, *Moby-Dick*, ch. 133-35: in one characteristic passage he writes, "A gentle joyousness—a mighty mildness of repose in swiftness, invested the gliding whale. . . . Not Jove, not that great majesty Supreme! did surpass the glorified White Whale as he so divinely swam." Shakespeare, *A Midsummer's Night Dream*, II.1.150-54: the mermaid represents the mystical power of poetry. I feel obliged to add that Lowell, unlike Prufrock, finds that the mermaid will sing to him.

8 Step-daughters: He addresses only one explicitly in the poem, Ivana, who was "burned" (*D*, 64-65). Caroline Blackwood's moving depiction of the child's hospitalization in "Burns Unit" is in *For All That I Found There* (note 2).

9 Lawrence, "Why the Novel Matters," *Selected Literary Criticism* (New York: Viking, 1966), pp. 102-108:

> Nothing is important but life. . . . For this reason I am a novelist. And being a novelist, I consider myself superior to the saint, the scientist, the philosopher, and the poet, who are all great masters of different bits of man alive, but never get the whole hog. The novel is the one bright book of life. Books are not life. They are only tremulations on the ether. But the novel as a tremulation can make the whole man alive tremble. Which is more than poetry, philosophy, science, or any other book-tremulation can do. The novel is the book of life.

Lowell, of course, hopes to create in his verse-novel *The Dolphin* a tremulation that "can make the whole man alive tremble." Lawrence's essay in its entirety throws interesting lights on the poem.

The origin of Lawrence's and Lowell's phrase is of course Biblical.

In the Old Testament, the "book of life" means *natural life* (Psalms 69:28, Exodus 32:32, Isaiah 4:3), and in the New Testament it means *eternal life* (Revelations 3:5, 13:8, 20:12, 21:27). Lowell intends to echo both of these meanings, since he locates the "eternal" wholly within the natural.

10 Ricks (note 2), p. 831. *The Dolphin* and *Paterson*: In his early reviews of *Paterson*, Lowell praised the collage effect of the poem: "[Williams's] monologue is interrupted by chunks of prose: paragraphs from old newspapers, textbooks, and the letters of a lacerated and lacerating poetess. This material is merely selected by the author. That the poetry is able to digest it in the raw is a measure of power and daring—the daring of simplicity." Yet he also remarked that "it is a defect perhaps that human beings exist almost entirely in the prose passages" and that "no characters take on sufficient form to arrive at a crisis. The people melt into voices" ("Paterson II," *Nation*, June 19, 1948, pp. 692-94). In *The Dolphin* he sought to avoid these faults while pursuing what he took to be Williams's essential theme: "It is the divorce of modern life, of intellect and sensibility, spirit and matter, and of the other stock categories that come to mind. His 'quest for beauty' is a search for the whole man, whose faculties are harmonious, and whose language corresponds with the particulars and mystery of reality" ("Thomas, Bishop, and Williams," *Sewanee Review*, 55 [1947], 500-503).

11 Lowell to Axelrod, July 27, 1977. "Dry or vacation moment": in summer 1977 Lowell revised an unpublished essay on New England writers, and in the weeks before his death completed two poems, one about Caroline Blackwood and the other about Elizabeth Hardwick. These are, respectively, "Summer Tides" (*New Review*, Oct. 1977, p. 3) and "Loneliness" (unpublished).

12 William McPherson, "Lowell: A Final Chapter," *Washington Post*, Sept. 17, 1977, C, p. 1. Auden, "In Memory of W. B. Yeats."

13 Lowell to Rolando Anzilotti, quoted by Anzilotti in "Robert Lowell: *The Dolphin*," a paper delivered at the Modern Language Association Meeting, Dec. 28, 1977. Lowell to Axelrod, July 27, 1977. Alvarez, *Review*, 34. Vendler, "The Poetry of Autobiography," *New York Times Book Review*, Aug. 14, 1977, p. 1. Lowell's intention to focus on daily moments as they really are does not mean that every "fact" he presents must be taken literally. For example, he told a friend that, "Bright Day in Boston" to the contrary, he visited his dentist at the appointed time (*DBD*, 83). Fantasies occur in daily life, and they make their way into *Day by Day* just as surely as do memories.

14 "After Enjoying Six or Seven Essays On Me," *Salmagundi*, No. 37 (Spring 1977), 114.

15 Lowell to Axelrod, July 27, 1977.

Index

Index

Index

Index

Index

281

Index

Index

Index

Index

Index

Library of Congress Cataloging in Publication Data

Axelrod, Steven Gould, 1944-
  Robert Lowell : life and art.

  Includes bibliographical references and index.
    1. Lowell, Robert, 1917-1977.   2. Poets, American—
20th century—Biography.
PS3523.089Z56   811'.5'2   78-51155
ISBN 0-691-06363-X